3

The Art of
Charlie
Chaplin

The Art of
Charlie Chaplin

John Kimber

Sheffield
Academic Press

To

My Mother
Lilian Maude Kimber

And to the memory of my Father
Leonard Robert Kimber
(1907–1976)

Copyright © 2000 Sheffield Academic Press

Published by Sheffield Academic Press Ltd
Mansion House
19 Kingfield Road
Sheffield S11 9AS
England

Printed on acid-free paper in Great Britain
by Bookcraft Ltd
Midsomer Norton, Bath

British Library Cataloguing in Publication Data

A catalogue record for this book is available
from the British Library

ISBN 1-84127-077-6 cl
ISBN 1-84127-078-4 pb

Contents

List of Plates

Introduction

Charles Barr

The Art of Charlie Chaplin reads like the welcome reprint of a classic critical text, yet this is its first publication. It might well have come out in the mid-1980s, had not its author, John Kimber, died after a short illness in 1985, not long after completing the manuscript. His widow Janet and I subsequently showed it to a number of publishers, all of whom recognized its merits, but, in the absence of John himself to promote it, none of them made a final commitment and the impetus lapsed.

Another obstacle to publication was, I suspect, the then unfashionable status both of the book's subject matter and of its critical method. It may seem strange to use the word unfashionable of Chaplin, since he is the subject of more books than any other figure in film history, and the flow of writing on him has never shown any sign of drying up; but within the rapidly expanding specialist academic and critical film culture of the 1970s and 1980s, he became somewhat marginalized and sometimes even maligned figure.

This was partly a reaction against his long popularity, and against the extravagant critical claims that had been made on his behalf. Had not A.J.P Taylor, in *English History, 1914–45*, called him 'as timeless as Shakespeare and as great'? Those intellectuals who despised the commercial film industry had always had time for Chaplin, the man who found a way of working so successfully outside its pressures and compromises; he could be taken seriously as an artist because he was so clearly and flamboyantly the author of his own films, as star, writer, director and even composer. Then came a new generation of film theorists and academics who did not despise commercial cinema, but were fascinated by the richness, and eloquence of the texts that could emerge from within it, and by the achievements of a range of director-authors at the other extreme from Chaplin: those who struggled with some success to express a personal vision and personal thematic in conditions of multiple collaboration and studio pressures. To many, the authorship of a Chaplin seemed less heroic, shallower, less *interesting*, than that of a Howard Hawks or a Don Siegel. In terms of comedy, Buster Keaton began to attract more critical affection and exegesis; he had never been as celebrated as Chaplin, his shot-by-shot 'direction' was more obviously intelligent, and he lacked Chaplin's sentimentality. The release in 1968 of Chaplin's last film, the disastrous *Countess from Hong Kong*, did nothing to help his standing.

Books on Chaplin, critical and biographical, still came out and sold respectably, but they were aimed, legitimately enough, more at the general reader and the film fan than at the big new market of film theorists, academics and students. And John Kimber's book is unmistakably, in the best sense of the word, an academic book, a work of critical scholarship written by an academic and now published by an academic press. It seems to me that the film studies market is much readier for it than it would have been in the mid-1980s, now that it admits a greater and healthier plurality of approaches.

Among all the hundreds of writers on Chaplin, I would wager that no one else uses the word 'technologico-Benthamite' in relation to any of his films, as John Kimber does in discussing *Modern Times* in this characteristic passage:

> *Modern Times* is not only about the mechanisation of work, but about the plight of civilization. Our civilization has been characterized by F.R. Leavis as 'technologico-Benthamite', an expressive coinage that links the automatism of the machine habit with the facile idealism of social engineering. Machines are agents of standardization, and the target of Chaplin's indictment is the crippling naivety about the ends of life that makes standardization seem desirable.

It is very apt that the eventual publication of John's book can be traced back to a conversation I had with Ian McKillop, author of the recent critical biography of Leavis, the great Cambridge-based literary critic and teacher. We were discussing the influence of Leavis on film studies—always indirect, since he had no interest in the medium himself—and I mentioned John's work on Chaplin as a very pure instance of it. Ian was interested, asked to see the text and submitted it to Sheffield Academic Press, with the happy results that you see before you.

Born in 1936, John was a pupil of Leavis's at Cambridge in the 1950s, and formed a strong and enduring allegiance to Leavis's values and critical methods. His previous book, also published posthumously, was a massive bibliography of the works of Leavis and of his wife, *F.R. Leavis and Q.D. Leavis: An Annotated Bibliography* (New York: Garland Publishing, 1989), completed after his death by M.B. Kinch and William Baker. A number of other film scholars have been influenced by encountering Leavis personally as well as through his books, including Robin Wood, Peter Harcourt, James Leahy, and, in a more marginal way, myself. Wood has discussed his own debt to Leavis at length, notably in the revised version of his seminal work on Alfred Hitchcock, *Hitchcock's Films Revisited* (New York: Columbia University Press, 1989), but I think that *The Art of Charlie Chaplin* is as close as we will ever get to the way in which one could conceive of Leavis himself actually responding to, and writing of, a specific body of films. Chaplin was probably more his sort of artist than Hitchcock was. John Kimber's appeal to criteria of life and health and creativity, his distrust of abstract theorizing, his sensitive exposition of key passages and his insistence on discriminating firmly between the stronger and weaker elements in the films all seems authentically Leavisian, which is another way of saying that this is alert, rigorous, responsible criticism, of a quality that has not often been brought to bear on Chaplin's work.

John himself had none of Leavis's personal or professional combativeness. The main part of his career was spent as a senior librarian at the University of East Anglia in Norwich, specializing in literature. When film was introduced into the curriculum in the 1970s, he took responsibility for building up holdings in that area as well. As the first film specialist appointed there, I was deeply indebted to his sympathetic and expert help. Not only did he find the funds for all the basic texts, he trawled the second-hand market to establish some very special research collections, for instance, a set of virtually all the plays and novels, famous and obscure alike, on which Hitchcocks's films were based. And, over and above his official duties, he contributed generously to the teaching pro-

gramme, with a range of thoroughly researched and warmly received presentations on British cinema, on Hitchcock, and, of
course, on Chaplin.

John was struck down, in the New Year of 1985, by a brain tu-
mour, just when he seemed to be entering on a particularly happy
and creative period of his life. The Leavis bibliography was well
under way, the Chaplin text was complete and he was already
working on its successor, a book on René Clair. This was a characteristic enterprise: a study of a historically important figure whose
films, at least outside his native France, were no longer much studied or revived, but to whom John was passionately committed. His
book would assuredly have cleared the cobwebs away from the neglected figure of René Clair, just as this one cuts through the mass
of stale ideas and judgments that have accumulated around the
legendary figure of Charlie Chaplin.

This text of John Kimber's book has been prepared for publication by myself, Ian McKillop and Rebecca Cullen of Sheffield Academic Press. Sarah Easen helped to select illustrations for it.

Four pages of the typescript of John Kimber's book did not survive its long journey to the press. I have edited the sections in
which they occur to make continuous reading possible. Originally,
the book was to be called *Charlie's Art*. In our era of electronic data
recovery Sheffield Academic Press and I agreed that *The Art of
Charlie Chaplin* would be better and help to make the subject as
recognizable as it deserves to be.

Chapter 1

Charlie/Chaplin

Charlie and the Clown Tradition

I wish to demonstrate in this book that Charlie Chaplin is a great poet of the cinema. Although he is often awarded the title of 'poet', the use of this term usually turns out to be unhelpfully vague. My intention is to be as exact as possible in my use of the term—and sober: I want to enlist for Chaplin the serious attention deserved by one who is both original and who also draws strength from theatrical and social traditions older than the cinema. I dearly hope that in my use of the term 'poet' I can avoid that extravagance of film criticism by which workmanlike, craftsmen film makers have been transformed into cinematic Prousts and Tolstoys.

The greater part of the book is devoted to detailed analyses of individual films. These analyses are based on two assumptions: that the films have serious meanings (or we would not find them so moving and important); and that the meanings reside in the comedy and not in something outside it. And in this introductory chapter I attempt the task of setting down the general observations and contentions that the specific accounts serve to illustrate, which is hard, because Chaplin's remarkable multiplicity does not yield easily to the sequence and linearity that expository argument demands. The difficulty is to convey, in considering in turn, as I propose to, Charlie's relation to the clown tradition, the ingredients of his character, his patterns of behaviour and the deliberate or intuitive contribution of Chaplin the artist, how all these aspects are related. A useful way into the subject is provided by one of the very earliest films, whose representative quality offers some suggestive answers to the unavoidable question, Who *is* Charlie, to start with?

Kid Auto Races at Venice was possibly not, as has often been supposed, the first film in which Chaplin wore his famous costume. There is a conflict of testimony on this point between Chaplin and his biographers, but it was certainly the first such film to be released (in February 1914), so there is some justification for regarding it as particularly significant. The temptation to do so is anyway almost irresistible. *Kid Auto Races* would not merit much attention but for the value bestowed upon it by hindsight. It is one of Sennett's typical early location impromptus, shot quickly and off the cuff, an opportunity for the untried comedian to show his paces. What action there is takes place during a children's motor race at Venice, California. There is no story and only one character. A newsreel crew are filming the events, and Charlie's function is to get in their way, and in the way of the contestants, and to make a general nuisance of himself. His basic screen character seems to have sprung almost fully formed into life, and he uses numerous bits of comic business that he was later to elaborate. Most of the action is shot from the outside, by Sennett's unseen cameraman. However, we occasionally view the events through the lens of the dummy camera, and here an interesting use is made of the frame, into which Charlie strolls, sidles or peers, and from which he is shoved or yanked. The significance of this fragment resides not only in the portentous fact that our first view of Charlie is of him showing off in front of a camera, but in the fact of the showing off —the kind of relationship that is established between Charlie, the world he inhabits and his audience.

Actually, there are three audiences: the crowd at the racetrack, crammed behind ropes; the fictitious audience for whose benefit Charlie clowns before the dummy camera; and we, watching the actual film. Charlie exhibits a vain consciousness of all his audiences, particularly the one implied by the camera, which fascinates him. He parades before us with an air of strutting self-importance, or poses sternly with his hand on his hip. He demands that we admire him. To the exasperated protests of the camera crew he responds with gestures of dignified remonstrance, and promptly sidles back into our view. *Kid Auto Races* is, in effect, a piece of prolonged and multiple self-display. It demonstrates with special clarity two of Charlie's most prominent qualities, his abnormality (the eccentricities of appearance and action that distinguish him from the normal world he inhabits and from us, his audience) and his compulsion to performance (his consciousness of an audience and his apparent need for one). For brevity's sake, I will call these qualities oddity and display.

The qualities are obviously related: the first embraces the second, and the second implies the first. Charlie's oddity is first of all a matter of costume, that incongruous and ill-proportioned mixture of garments that looked sufficiently peculiar at the very beginning, when its constituent parts were still in fashion, and has looked more peculiar as the years have gone by. But more importantly, it is a matter of behaviour. Charlie's eccentricities of behaviour are legion, and are considered at greater length below. They mostly take the form of a consistent and deliberate flouting of legal, social and psychological norms, with effects ranging from the mildly bizarre to the almost insane. There is virtually no rule of conduct he doesn't disregard, and no legitimate expectation he doesn't confound. As for display, it is usually evinced by the deliberateness of the oddity and the implied consciousness of an audience on whom the outrage will tell. Occasionally it issues in overt gestures of audience awareness, when the pretence of fictional realism is momentarily abandoned, such as the little pirouette with which Charlie acknowledges our applause for his foiling of the jewel thief in *The Pawnshop*.

Charlie's oddity and display are the qualities that link him most unmistakably to a larger tradition. That Charlie's personality, behaviour and problems relate him to the great clown figures of the past, whether real, mythical or theatrical, has been recognized as long as he has received serious attention at all. It has also been recognized that in his case the relationship is more vital and direct than in that of his contemporaries and that it is a potent source of his appeal. An early instance is Pierre Duchartre's observation that 'though he may not be aware of it, Charlie Chaplin is undoubtedly one of the rare inheritors of the traditions of the *commedia dell'arte*'.[1] A later writer, Allardyce Nicoll, has explicitly denied that Chaplin's mimic art has much direct resemblance to the *commedia*,

1. *The Italian Comedy* (London: Harrap, 1929).

which depended upon spoken dialogue.[2] Both authorities are perhaps right. Duchartre had in mind a *commedia* scenario in which
Pulcinella, evading capture, impersonates a weathercock and other
objects. This certainly prompts the image of Charlie metamor-
phosed into a tree in *Shoulder Arms*, or assuming the form of a
standard-lamp in *The Adventurer* (in both cases for the same purpose). And Nicoll is right to warn against a too easy identification
of historically remote and dissimilar forms of comic drama, though
he goes on to describe a system of stock characters and relationships in the *commedia* that does not seem very different from that
of Chaplin's Keystone-to-Mutual period. However, it is not necessary to prove a direct historical link of influence between Charlie
and his illustrious predecessors. It is more profitable to see them
all as examples of a common type, exhibiting a remarkable consistency of characteristics throughout the ages. This is the procedure of an important book that was the first to treat the subject of
clowning wholly from a psychological and typological, rather than
a historical, point of view: William Willeford's *The Fool and his
Sceptre* (1969). Mr Willeford's complete argument is more elaborate than my purposes require (and in places, I admit, too obscure
for me to follow), but, in all my general observations in this chapter on clown figures and their significance, I have made grateful
use of some of his terminology, especially the indispensable terms
'boundary' and 'centre'.

    Willeford's basic contention is that the clown figure (which he
refers to throughout as the 'fool' comes from beyond the boundary of the secure and the known, and, arrived in our comfortable
reality or 'centre', puts on a recognizable performance (which he
calls 'the fool-show'). These ideas correspond to our sense of Charlie's oddity and display. It is the oddity that is the more important
for the moment. The fool transcends both cultural allegiance (the
costume and habits of a particular time and place) and all specific
rules of conduct. These propositions give a traditional sanction to
both Charlie's anachronistic get-up and his eccentricities of behaviour. From beyond the boundary, which is both social and psychological, the fool brings those disruptive modes of behaviour
and primitive habits of thought that the centre—of society and of

    2. *The World of the Harlequin* (Cambridge: Cambridge University Press,
1963).

the mind—chooses either to ignore or to conceal (is normally obliged to, in order to survive). He is profoundly unsettling in effect, introducing the irrationally unconcious into the rationally conscious centre, the possibility of chaos into order.

Such an account throws an interesting light on Charlie's compulsive rule-flouting, mentioned above, which is one of his most signal characteristics. And it is not just a matter of the obvious thou-shalt-not moral and legal rules, and those of social decorum. Charlie certainly flouts these. Morality–legality says that we should respect others' property, tell the truth and own up to our lapses: Charlie is a thief, a liar, and is not above sitting meekly by while innocent friends get manhandled for his misdeeds. Decorum demands seemly behaviour at social gatherings: Charlie is liable to assault the guests, try out unusual dance steps or practise his golf strokes on the side dishes. There are many other kinds of rule, for example, those less explicit ones governing intimate personal relationships, which uphold an ideal of respectful honesty: Charlie is capable of manufacturing pathetic dramas to win the sympathy of his girl. There are the rules that dictate our behaviour at moments of danger or crisis: Charlie's displays of heroic intention are apt to give way to a more prudent assessment of his chances. There are the simple rules of congruity, or reasonable expectation: Charlie negotiates the potholes of a slummy side street with the dandified air of a boulevardier. Most basic of all are what might be called cognitive rules, which determine what we perceive: Charlie continually interprets others' friendly nudges or slaps as evidence of hostile intention and responds with a hearty wallop (in *The Cure*, waiting for his turn with an arm-flailing masseur, he reaches prudently for a hefty back brush); menus are likely to make him think of hymn books, prompting a grudging display of piety, and baby-sized hymn books seem to him naturally designed for babies to read.

But it is clearly not enough to see Charlie as simply and solely alien and disruptive. To employ Willeford's terms: although our social-psychological centre cannot allow itself to be engulfed by the chaos that the fool brings from beyond the boundary, in order to prosper it needs to accommodate the possibility of chaos as an important fact of experience. And the fool, who straddles the worlds of darkness and light, is uniquely qualified to provide the recognition. So Charlie, although he is not *of* our world, is actively *in* it, an agent of release whose behaviour, as well as being negative and destructive, is potentially beneficent and transforming.

The way he gets in and stays in is largely by his talent of versatile role-playing. This is the most evident manifestation of Charlie's instinct for display. He is a natural actor, always on the look-out for a likely scenario: mostly offered bit parts, he usually manages to translate himself into the hero. If he tires of one role, he can switch to another while we are still adjusting to the first. Charlie's histrionic fertility is astonishing, and is one of the things that gives his films their peculiarly vigorous life. His role-playing can be emotional and immediate (vivid impressions of dignity, arrogance, aggression, gallantry and grief in bewildering succession), efficiently professional (boxer, sailor, janitor, fireman, waiter, dentist, cop), domestic and personal (father, husband, lover, friend), or calculated, in the form of deliberate imposture. Professional roles are the commonest, and amorous roles the most enjoyed, but imposture has a special attraction and force. It is as an imposter—whether Count Borko, the Reverend Parker or Henri Verdoux—that he acts out his most intimate dramas. For Charlie, imposture is the device by which he can most readily penetrate the defences of our stubborn and orderly centre, a conduit for the introduction of subversion and mayhem. To the audience it offers the pleasures of complicity and suspense. At the typological level it could be regarded as the function of display: the fool's chief means of mediation between oddity and normality.

Charlie's compulsive play-acting is not just a form of infiltration. His successful impostures, in particular, demonstrate not only the case with which he invades and occupies our world, but also his desire actively to transform it. Charlie's power of creatively transforming our stubborn, confusing reality is one of the most important single facts about him. And the ultimate beneficence of the enterprise seems to be testified to by another of the characteristics that Charlie shares with the real and imaginary clown figures of the past, his apparent immunity from the normal consequences of his actions. I am not just thinking of his endless capacity for outwitting cops and other authority figures, or of the success of his impostures (which are usually discovered in the end, in any case). These are active stratagems. I am thinking of the sort of immunity from punishment or blame that falls unbidden into his lap, so to speak, plucking him from danger and often transferring the direful consequences on to somebody else. A splendid example is the golfing scene in *The Idle Class*, when the blame for Charlie's numerous sporting solecisms and misdemeanours is visited, unknown to him, upon the hapless innocent he is tailing round the course. This immunity is a kind of magical luck. Its enjoyment by historical court jesters has been attributed to their talismanic virtue of themselves transmitting luck to those they abuse. In Charlie's case, it has the immediate dramatic effect of audacity and surprise, and, as I have suggested, the larger effect of confirming the justness of Charlie's creative role.

The power of creative transformation takes many forms. At its simplest, it is Charlie's means of making the world answer his own needs, by, for example, his casually insensitive use of other people: his habit of soliciting their attention by forcibly turning their heads towards him, of leaning his elbow on their backs or laps, or of striking matches on their rumps. Other people can be to Charlie either convenient objects or tiresome obstacles. There is little especially beneficent about this, it is true. A much more imaginative sort of transformation is his repeated employment of visual metaphor. This is the process by which objects are used, or actions performed, in terms of other objects or actions. Charlie, without betraying any sense of incongruity, will wipe his nose on a doormat, or his eyes on a beard; clean his boots with a toothbrush; search for fleas in a bearskin helmet; practise billiard strokes with a sword on a bunch of onions; fan a groggy dental patient with a towel, boxer-fashion; or feed a brood of children like chickens, by scattering cornflakes. The phrase 'poetry of cinema', which once had a place in the film critic's vocabulary seems never to have meant much more than a romantically charged visual prettiness. The pervasive metaphorical suggestiveness of Charlie's comic business is poetic in a more precise sense. Poetry is (among the many other things that it is) a pre-rational mode of thought, whose prevailing principle is the association of ideas. Its best images, like the gags I have listed above, provoke a feeling of simultaneous appropriateness and surprise. Fools are pre-rational thinkers, and hence to some extent inevitably poets as well. Enid Welsford has said that, in contrast with the energetic and rational hero, the fool 'by his mere presence dissolves events, evades issues, and throws doubt on the finality of fact'.[3] This goes further than what I have called transformation ('evades issues' suggests the interesting question of morality, which I shall consider below), but seems to include it. Charlie's metaphorical gags, as well as adding surprise and diversity to the comic business, could be described as his most regular method of throwing doubt on the finality of fact. They also constitute one of his most thorough invasions of our reality.

It is not fanciful to invoke the names of Shakespeare and Dickens in thinking of Chaplin's metaphorical audacities, even though it is obviously a comparison that cannot be pressed too far. Like them, he is a great English genius, and like them he seems to be compelled (rather than to have chosen) to register his experience abundantly in poetic terms. But there is a sense in which the instances I have cited are only the small change of Chaplin's 'poetry'. They strike us as the random and instinctive products of an ineradicable habit, with no meaning beyond their immediate occasion. Chaplin's mature films are poetic in a wider sense, in their fabric and dramatic organization: the extended passages of comic business are significant, and contribute to the expression of an often complex theme. The evolution of Chaplin's poetic effects, small-scale and large-scale, is considered at greater length in the next chapter: I want to return for the moment to the nature of Charlie the character's powers of creative transformation.

These powers can manifest themselves in individual bits of comic business or across the whole spectrum of a particular activity. To take the second kind first, there is the question of work. For it is Charlie's professional roles that provide him with his most frequent opportunities for creative violation of the rules. Although he is a natural aristocrat, he accepts the need to work: which is in any case a useful source of income, additional to the larger amounts he is apt to acquire by chance, or conquest. But he cannot help refashioning work according to his temperamental needs. He is not interested in it as a puritan discipline, a social duty or a contribution to the national economy. His attitude is more like D.H. Lawrence's: 'There is no point in work unless it absorbs

---

3.   Enid Welsford, *The Fool: His Social and Literary History* (London: Faber & Faber, 1935).

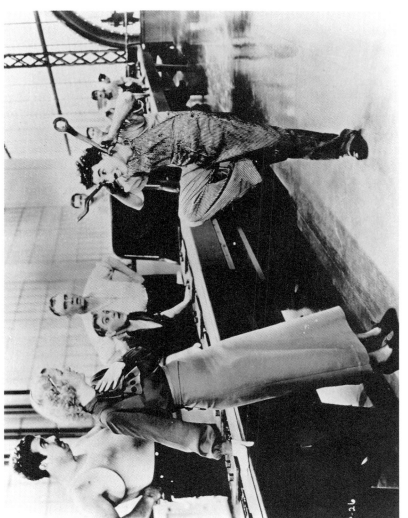

Plate 1. *Modern Times*

you like an absorbing game'.[4] Charlie's jobs being mostly menial, his work is hardly ever absorbing, but he does his best to turn it into a game. His common procedure is to turn it into dance. Examples are legion, but the most famous ones are probably his gleefully prancing disruption of the factory regime in *Modern Times*, and his shaving of Chester Conklin to the music of Brahms in *The Great Dictator*. Under Charlie's management, work is shorn of its merely functional ends and transformed into a self-justifying creative activity. This may be one of the things Welsford means in saying that the fool 'dissolves events'.

As well as manipulating people, objects and activities, Charlie manipulates situations. I have already mentioned his talent for imposture, and his unscrupulous manufacture of dramas for the enlistment of sympathy (in *The Pawnshop*, hearing Edna approach while he is throttling his rival, he throws himself to the floor in an attitude of piteous defeat). His powers of transformation also show themselves in innumerable active stratagems for the furtherance of whatever aim he has in hand. In the finest of the films, these scenes have, as well as a dramatic function, a poetic suggestiveness that contributes tellingly to the total effect, in the way I have mentioned above.

In *Shoulder Arms*, Charlie's contribution to the espionage department of the war effort is to disguise himself as a tree in order to spy on a group of Germans. He finds his disguise a mixed blessing (he can bash his enemies on the head without compunction, but finds himself vulnerable to wholesale conversion into firewood), and takes refuge in the anonymity of a nearby wood (an example of a clown's actively seeking the immunity that is his right). This escapade has the eventual effect, together with Charlie's other military exploits, of altering the whole course of the war. An even bolder stratagem (and surely one of Chaplin's most imaginative comic episodes) is the scene in *A Dog's Life* in which, in order to recover the stolen wallet, he revivifies, with appropriate bits of his own person, the thug in the café alcove whom he has rendered unconscious. It is hard to find words adequate to describe the spellbinding lifelikeness of this impersonation, in which Charlie conducts a complete conversation with his arms alone, effectively wrenching reality around to the fulfilment of his own ends.

4.   *Pansies* (Yorick Books, 1988 [1929]).

These last two instances have a special interest, and lead usefully to the next important point to be made about Charlie's art. They are examples of a particular type of imposture, one that provides a further significant link between Charlie and the traditional fool, a fondness for non-human, and especially animal, disguises. (The second example is of course actually a human disguise, but the peculiar circumstances—Charlie's, in effect, wearing another man's body—class it with this type of stratagem rather than with routine imposture. One would not have to look further for a bona fide animal disguise than the scene in the same film in which Charlie, to gain admission to the saloon, stuffs Scraps down his trousers and turns himself into a sort of man-dog). Non-human, semi-human and animal disguises are immemorial ingredients of the traditional fool's repertoire. Historically, they linger late in the hobby-horse and the wild man of the mummers' play. In the terms of Willeford's analysis, such disguises are first of all part of the fool's disruptive function: wildness and semi-wildness are unassimilated reminders of the pre-civilized chaos from which the fool emerges into the civilized centre. But they are also instances of another of the fool's enduring traits, which Charlie inherits and which is the most important single clue to his spirit: compulsive doubleness.

Doubleness, or duality, and its attendant qualities—contrariety, contradiction and confusion—are among the fool's most distinctive and determining features. It is easy to see that they are a necessary consequence of his condition. Moving from the boundary to the centre he can't help to some extent dragging the centre back to the boundary. By the fact of his irrational presence in our rational midst he inevitably has the effect of confusing the two. And to confuse the two is precisely his function. In Charlie's case, we have seen that his function is in a sense both of and not of our world. His effect upon our reality can be either destructive or creative, or both at the same time. And his oddity, the first quality he exhibits, is matched, especially in his later incarnations, by familiarity—a sympathetic humanness with which we can identify (a point to be developed later). He is a very contradictory case—could be said, indeed, to embody the principle of contradiction.

Duality operates in both the personal and the social spheres, and at every level of expression. It evinces every degree of refinement and elaboration. At one level, it means actually being two people

or two things. In a few films, Charlie plays two distinct characters—in *A Night in the Show*, for instance, he is both Mr Rowdy
and Mr Pest; in *The Idle Class*, both the husband and the tramp; in
The Great Dictator, both Hynkel and the barber. More often, as in
his various impostures and disguises, he only pretends to be double. At another level, it means occupying two social positions. It is
his impostures that usually enable Charlie to do this, but in at
least one film, *City Lights*, he contrives, thanks to the alternate attention and neglect of the fickle millionaire, to be genuinely rich
and poor at the same time. At another level, it means expressing
two attitudes or qualities. This is the commonest kind of all, and
could be described as Charlie's permanent condition. Some of the
attitudes are those which, elsewhere, are split between two characters: Charlie combines the qualities of Pest and Rowdy in being
both fastidious and vulgar, for example. He is also both good and
bad, considerate and selfish, wise and stupid, shrewd and naive, industrious and idle, brave and cowardly—the catalogue is almost
endless. It is the continual switching back and forth between these
attributes that gives his films the remarkable tension and vivacity
of their surface life, and his character the inexhaustible capacity
for surprise that serves to distinguish him more than anything else,
perhaps, from his rival comedians, contemporary and later. At yet
another level, duality means embodying two needs. Here there is
some overlap with the previous category, but Charlie's needs are
distinct from his attitudes, and more profound. A simple list cannot serve the same purpose, but it will be some indication of what
is meant by saying that Charlie needs, for example, both morality
and amorality, the material and the spiritual, control and licence,
nature and artifice. It is in his greatest films that his needs are defined and their conflicts resolved, in the form of comic-poetic
dramas that are the ultimate evolution of his art (*The Gold Rush*
explores the relation between the material and the non-material,
for example, and *The Circus* that between artifice and life), and
they will be considered most fully in the analyses of specific films.
At this level, the needs are more than Charlie's and are generalized into themes.

   The large and looming presence in Charlie's nature of duality
and opposition finds visual expression in the numberless images
of balance, deadlock and containment of forces that constitute

the most prevalent and significant type of image in the films. As
with the metaphorical gags, they are so common that to cite examples is to pick stones off the ground. Balancing acts are second
nature to Charlie, and the threatened loss of equilibrium an everyday hazard. In addition to the tug of opposites, the feelings they
always express are the imminence of danger and the demonstrated possession of skill. They are partly a function of Charlie's
instinct for display. They figure both his battle for a footing (literal and metaphorical) in our inhospitable world and the contradictory demands of his own nature. In the earliest films they are
usually casual and instinctive, with no significance beyond the pro-
vision of immediate excitement: the drunken or desperate teetering on the edge of a park lake for example, or the heroic grasp on
an unspilled tray of food on a bucketing boat. In other instances,
the display element is to the fore: in *Shanghaied,* it is devilment that
makes Charlie start juggling with the ship's dinner-time ham bone,
and in *The Pawnshop* sheer high spirits that prompt him to pick his
way precariously across a 'tightrope' that is stretched safely along
the floor. In the later films, the balancing acts are often extended
scenes, and correspondingly more significant. The most celebrated example is the cabin that clings hazardously to the edge of the
crevasse in *The Gold Rush*, while others are the rope-walking climax of *The Circus*, the roller-skating episode in *Modern Times*, and
the boxing match in *City Lights*, with its strange, dancing sense of
deadlock and staved-off threat. In these instances, as well as the
constant condition of Charlie's nature and the conflict of his
needs, the balancing acts are figurative expressions of the particular opposition of forces in the context from which they arise.
They are reminders that contradiction is not the same as complexity and evidence—in their demonstration of poise and skill—that
it is an inclusive complexity of effect at which the major films aim.
But whether casual or calculated, trivial or momentous, Charlie's
art is everywhere the art of the equilibrist.

Charlie's Needs

It is time to look more closely at the actual stuff that Chaplin's films
are made of. What are Charlie's everyday needs (as distinguished
from the profounder ones above)—his activities, preoccupations,
the motives that compel him into action? Although basic and mun-

dane, they are certainly not trivial, and are complicated by the contradictions rooted in Charlie's nature. They can be roughly divided into the personal and the social, though in Charlie's realms of action this is a difficult distinction to maintain. His personal needs all come under the general head of appetite. Listed baldly, they are money, food and women.

Oddly enough, considering the avidity with which he pursues it, money in itself is of little importance to Charlie. Having no desire to accumulate possessions, he doesn't even seek it for its obvious benefits. He is not particularly concerned about where it comes from. He presumably receives some for working, though, as we have seen, his attitude to work is disinterestedly non-functional, and there are few occasions on which we actually see him being paid. The kind of income he finds most attractive, and is most regularly in receipt of, or most tenaciously pursues, is the money that appears from nowhere, or from all manner of unofficial sources, or is just lying around to be picked up—what throughout I will call 'found money'. This can take the form of a vagrant coin (*The Immigrant*), a stolen wallet (*A Dog's Life*), Big Jim's mountain of gold (*The Gold Rush*) or the fortunes of gullible widowed ladies (*Monsieur Verdoux*). The needs that these particular windfalls satisfy are, respectively, relief from a pressing and potentially calamitous debt; retirement to a life of frugal industry and domestic bliss; entry to a world of luxury and ease; and sheer survival in a world of harsh competition. Charlie is capable of pursuing money from a purely altruistic motive, as in *City Lights*, but he values it most for its power of granting access to that world of luxury that he considers his native element, but from, which, without it, he is liable to be tiresomely excluded. Luckily for him, it is not always necessary actually to have money to belong to this world, but only to appear to have it: and he is a practised fabricator of appearances. Found money is a precarious source of income to rely upon, a fact that lends suspense to a number of the films. The café scene in *The Immigrant* is a prolonged and witty testimony to both the treachery and beneficence of found money: the picked-up coin, on which Charlie's hopes are pinned, whose loss produces so many anxious moments, is finally condemned as false, and Charlie's beans-and-coffee blow-out providentially paid for with his benefactor's tip. It is clear from all this that money for Charlie is a magical, talismanic and sometimes wholly imaginary substance, quite as much as a tangible one: disembodied, conjured from the air, an instrument of fantasy. (It is not until *Monsieur Verdoux* that we are given a more realistic view of money's origin and meaning.)

Food, whatever further value it acquires, cannot help being tangible. It is of the first importance in Charlie's world. He spends a lot of his time gaining access to it, having it served to him, serving it to others and eating it. Its prominence is witnessed by the abundance of café scenes in the films, and the frequency with which he himself turns up in the guise of waiter or diner. This is partly a matter of comic convention, as Chaplin explains in his account of his first days with the Essanay company: 'Now I was anxious to get to work. Although I hadn't a story, I ordered the crew to build an ornate café set. When I was lost for a gag or an idea, a café would always provide one'.[5] A café is a place of public resort, offering numberless opportunities for comic exploitation. But dramatic convenience can only ever have been a minor consideration. Food is a positive need to Charlie at a level deeper than convenience, as is figured perhaps in its having a balancing act of its own—the tray-carrying gags that seem to express the difficulties and hazards of its acquisition. Of course, hunger impels him to action, as it impels us all. And much of his food consumption operates at the simple level of satisfaction of appetite, such as the nicking of the bangers in *A Dog's Life* (the immediate result of which scene—Charlie's rolling under the fence to escape the cop—is interpreted very interestingly by Willeford in terms of 'boundary' and 'centre':[6] or Charlie's decimation of Syd's pies in the same film. In these episodes interest is centred upon the cunning and resource of Charlie's scavenging. But the element of eating that really appeals to Charlie, both in the café scenes and in the fashionable dinner parties at which he is usually present in his role of imposter, is the element of ritual. He responds feelingly to the idea of eating as an act of celebration. It is a ritual that he cannot help making peculiarly his own—hence his innumerable solecisms and violations of table etiquette. He is capable, in his early and cruder

5. Charles Chaplin, *My Autobiography* (London: Bodley Head, 1964).
6. See William Willeford, *The Fool and his Sceptre: A Study in Clowns and Jesters and their Audience* (Evanston, IL; Northwestern University Press; London: Arnold, 1969), pp. 134-35.

incarnations, of desecrating the ritual and employing food as ammunition. But his usual approach to food consumption is gentle
and considerate, almost loving. The emphasis is on the civilized
niceties, however much modified by his peculiar nature, and the
simple appeasement of appetite gives way to the conventions of
gourmet dining. For Charlie, food is a positive value, eating a creative act: a meal is a work of art. The boiling of the boot in *The
Gold Rush* is the most famous example of Charlie's way with food:
nearly as interesting in its different way is his unpaid-for restaurant banquet in *Modern Times*, designed to return him to the comfort of jail, whose multiple satisfactions spill over into his wonderful air, under arrest, of patrician ease and condescension. Food is
also an inducement to display. And in the films' recurrent actual
or imagined vignettes of domestic life, the act of eating is further
enriched by the associated feelings of affectionate rapport.

This last point is a reminder that food does not stand alone in
Charlie's pantheon of pleasures, but is associated with others,
such as drinking and dancing. Together they can be classed as festivity, the promotion of which is one of the clown's immemorial
functions. Drinking as such does not figure nearly so large in Charlie's activities as eating. This is possibly because it offers fewer
opportunities for comic business (the play with glasses and bottles
in *The Adventurer*, and the smashed hip flask in *The Pilgrim*, are ex-
ceptions that come to mind). Where the act of drinking is important, it usually has a special significance in the film (such as the
mix-up over Verdoux's poisons, or the beneficial draughts of water
that Hynkel administers down his trousers). But the effects of drink
are as prominent as the act of eating. Charlie's drunken sessions
are balancing acts in which sobriety and order are pitted against
insensibility and chaos. They are visible dramatizations of the struggle in his nature between darkness and light. Dancing has a similar function, being Charlie's attempt to establish a foothold in the
social civilities of our discouraging world: with always eccentric,
and often disastrous, results. He is likely on the dance floor to
find himself transfixed by chewing gum, pinioned to an enormous
dog, or simply incapable of remaining upright on the hyper-pol-
ished surface. In moving from food to festivity we have shifted
from personal to social needs, an indication of how difficult it is in
Charlie's case to distinguish the two. We have also led into his sec-

ond physical appetite. It takes two to dance, and it is on the dance floor that Charlie often meets or amuses his women.

Women, unlike money, are ends in themselves. Like food, they are tangible and desirable objects. Charlie's relations with them have three stages, which correspond to a threefold development of his character that will be elaborated below. The first stage takes the form of cynical dalliance. This basic Charlie has a sharp eye for a pretty face: presented with a middle-aged and a comely girl both in danger of drowning, he will after careful scrutiny rescue the pretty one first. He is a compulsive chatter-up, ready with whispered confidences, suggestive winks and playful back-kicks. Spotting Edna hiding, for her own good reasons, under his bed in her nightgown, his smile registers a pleased surprised that the world should be so agreeably arranged. He is most at home in the world of the earliest films, whose pervasive eroticism is symbolized by the recurrent nude statuettes that he is wont to examine with artistic severity. The Charlie in this stage shades off into another, high-spirited one, whose relations with women are more affectionate, and are usually shown, not in the making, but as already established. This stage of his love life is conducted on a level of pally equality, qualified by occasional mockery (he is capable of slyly playing the weight-lifter with Edna's doughnuts). His girls are liable to find themselves used as raw material for his mischievous transformations. He can be patronizing, even paternal, insisting on a high standard of table manners and personal cleanliness (*The Vagabond*). If Edna starts getting becomingly but unreasonably shy over being married, he will carry her bodily into the registrar's office (*The Immigrant*). It is this Charlie who is so fond of conjuring images of domestic bliss and material abundance, where fruits hang ready to hand and milk flows direct from cow to jug. The objects of his affection are either wholesome girl-next-door figures, tolerant of his eccentricities, or child-like waifs, dependent upon his protection.

The final stage in Charlie's amorous life is his assumption of the role of the romantic lover. In this he is susceptible to the whole range of feelings normally associated, in art and life, with love relations, from the delight of reciprocal passion to the misery of change, rejection or loss. It is the difficulties that are emphasized, his chosen women being often remote and inaccessible, because of wealth and class (*The Pilgrim*), temperament and background (*The Gold Rush*), alienated affection (*The Circus*) or the accident of circumstances (*City Lights*). Sometimes he gets his girl (in *The Gold Rush*, he gets a great deal more besides), but often he does not. In the first stage, rebuffs are a minor irritation—there is always another girl round the corner; in the second, Charlie's love life is usually happy and secure; but in the third he is vulnerable to the painful feelings attendant upon change or loss. In this case the pain may be countered by a fantasised denial (in *The Bank* he dreams a drama of heroic rescue and wakes up kissing a mop); or dissipated in a farcical denouement (the border-straddling conclusion to *The Pilgrim*); or the issue may be left tantalizingly open (*City Lights*). In *The Circus*, uniquely, he reconciles himself to his loss, and assumes the role of matchmaker to his girl and her chosen lover.

It is Charlie the romantic lover who most exposes his creator to the charge of sentimentality. There is no point in denying that the charge is often justified. Chaplin's treatment of romantic love can possess an inexcusable element of self-indulgence, especially when he offers uncritically to engineer situations in which his own pitifulness is emphasized. At such moments the effect is embarrassing, leaving us with unresolved feelings on our hands that we don't know what to do with. But I would maintain, first, that this is a much more minor nuisance than it is sometimes made out to be, and, second, that it is mitigated, even justified, by various circumstances. For one thing, the moments of romantic love are subject, like the rest of Chaplin, to the duality factor, and often, in the balancing interest of critical intelligence, the targets of a sudden process of deromanticization. Charlie's grave courtliness, studied gallantry and heroic attitudinizing are liable to moments of undignified collapse. In *The Gold Rush*, for example, where such gags are especially common, he opens the cabin door to greet his beloved with an air of tender expectancy, and gets a snowball in his face; repeating the scene on a later occasion, he is confronted by a hungry mule.

But Chaplin's sentimentality is not only qualified by these moments of farcical reversal. At a deeper level it is related to the whole of his attempt to introduce serious feelings into comedy, by grafting sophisticated literary and dramatic elements to the basic fool tradition, and allowing farce to be infected by reality. I don't wish to anticipate what I shall say below in defence of Chaplin's comedy of feeling. It is enough to suggest here that his sentimental excesses may be the price that is paid for the realism of his mature art. And it is not contradictory but complementary to this argument to maintain that, however serious and genuine the feelings that it issues from, Charlie's love behaviour has always a strongly theatrical element. Just as he is impelled to turn work into dance, so he is impelled to turn love into display. Whether at the cynical, affectionate or idealizing stage, it is the role of lover that fascinates him, and his energies are devoted, as in the case of his other needs, to converting feeling and appetite into performance.

As well as the personal needs that I have called appetite, Charlie evinces two compelling social purposes that provide him with an entry into our world's social life (though we have seen, in the spectrum of Charlie's needs, how finely the personal shades off into the social). These are work, and what for want of a better word I shall call rank. Work has been discussed above as being one of the prime targets of Charlie's powers of transformation: the effect of the transformations being usually to deprive the activity of its functional ends and replace them with creative ones. Charlie's professional roles are very important to him. He is not a shirker, and positively wants to work. (Our familiar idea of him as a homeless and jobless vagabond may seem strange in view of the amount of time he actually spends in paid employment.) He values work in the first instance for providing him with a footing in our world, and a sense of normality and belonging. It is clear that this is to a large extent a respectable front, and that his chief use for work is as material for his true purpose of creative disruption. Work offers an endless range of activities on which he can exercise his gifts. His professional roles are roles in the theatrical sense, like the lover's and the imposter's: work ministers to his unappeasable appetite for display. It also gives rise recurrently to one of his most remarkable pieces of oddity, an exhibition of his pre-rational mode of thought. This is his habit of work creation, the process whereby he actively manipulates the opportunities for work instead of, as custom dictates, waiting for them to come to him. Examples range from the employment of Jackie as a smasher of windows to stimulate the glazier's trade in *The Kid* to hastening his rich wives along

the road to our common lot in *Monsieur Verdoux*. Charlie's mind
cannot accept that the benefits of work must necessarily be accompanied by its tedium or hazards. His view of our view of work is
wittily caught in a moment in *Shanghaied*, when, in automatic response to the mate's aggressive arrival, he busily trundles an empty
trolley from one side of the hold to the other: the pure appearance of purposeful activity.

What I have dubbed rank, although intimately related to money,
is in itself one of the most important of Charlie's repertoire of
needs. The films exhibit a pervasive awareness of class distinctions,
and everything that they imply in the way of acquired luxury and
ease. The point of calling the quality rank is to stress that it is not
just the luxury and ease that Charlie values but the sense of social
superiority that goes with them. His original comic character,
whose appearance and mannerisms are preserved in his very first
film (*Making a Living*), was that of a drunken English aristocrat
who parades a fastidious consciousness of his superiority to everyone around him. This theatrical type turns into the earliest form of
Charlie's screen character, whose drunkenness and class-conscious-
ness are partly designed to lend some dramatic plausibility to his
remarkable callousness towards others. Fascination with rank issues
in Charlie's favourite imposture, that of a rich and titled celebrity.
The recurrence of this situation calls to mind the prince-and-
pauper fantasies of popular literature that involve an unexpected
inheritance, succession to a title or a sudden reversal of circumstances. Many of Chaplin's early stories operate at this fairy-tale
level. The whole obsession indicates how English a figure Chaplin
was, and remained: it took an Englishman to turn so frequently
for comic inspiration to a consciousness of class distinctions that
must have seemed outlandish to his original American audience.

The feelings associated with rank are ambiguous. They are partly feelings of ridicule. The pretentious denizens of rank are there
to be mocked: to fall on their backsides, have ice-cream dropped
down their necks or pies thrust in their faces. Chaplin has written
of 'the pleasure taken by the public in seeing richness and luxury
in distress'.[7] Our happy task is watch with relish as the class-bound
world of wealth and ease, with its stiff-backed formalities, is under-

7.   Quoted in Louis Delluc, *Charlie Chaplin* (trans. Hamish Miles; London:
Bodley Head, 1922).

mined and disrupted by Charlie the imposter. But another feeling
is present too: a feeling of the actual pleasure of participating in
the glamorous world from which we are normally excluded. Chaplin has also exclaimed, of a week spent in New York, 'How bounti-
ful and reassuring is luxury!'.[8] Like women and work, the possession and parading of rank minister both to Charlie's sense of security and to his love of display. He enjoys every minute of playing
the lord, and we enjoy it with him.

It is hard not to see this complex response, whereby we relish
and ridicule at the same time, as being at least partly derived from
Chaplin's own experience of poverty and deprivation. There is
evidence in what he has written of his own life that his attitude to
the world of the rich and powerful was a mixture of envy and defensive hostility. (An interesting comparison with Dickens suggests
itself here.) But the parallels with popular literary-dramatic fantasies mentioned above indicate that his fascination with rank is
more than personal. In contriving his typical situations, he dramatizes what most of us feel. The deepest origin of class fascination
comedy lies probably at the typological level, in the fool's ritual
relation to the king, to whom he was a scape-goat or stand-in to
ward off evil, or a sort of mock variation (being often historically
awarded imaginary or borderland kingdoms).[9] This relationship
could be regarded as the first, archetypal imposture. In *The Great
Dictator*, we recall, Charlie, by replacing Hynkel on the rostrum,
becomes, in effect, the king—achieving his most dramatic impersonation of all.

What the above consideration of Charlie's appetites and purposes reveals is that they are all, in one way or another, infected by
the feelings of duality and contradiction that have been described
as endemic to his condition. In each case the activity in question
becomes what might be called defunctionalized by getting translated into a form whose justification lies in the creative pleasure of
performance: food and money-seeking into the skill of acquisition; woman-seeking into gallantry; work into dance; rank into
display. The effect is drastically to qualify the view of Charlie we
might otherwise have as a money-grubbing, gourmandizing, womanizing, work-shy counter-jumper. It also changes our image of

8. Chaplin, *My Autobiography*.
9. See Willeford, *The Fool and his Sceptre*, Chapter 9.

ourselves. His apparent indifference to the obvious benefits of these common and often-despised concerns of life has the result of making them seem less burdensome and more enjoyable. To watch function turned into display is to feel the endless pressure of our purposes relieved, if only momentarily. Each appetite or purpose also exhibits its own kind of contradictions. The brute appeasement of hunger issues not only in Charlie's varied dexterity of food acquisition, but also in his grandly delicate manner of consumption. His womanizing ranges from the cynically lustful to the theatrically romantic, and is likely without warning to veer between these extremes, or settle on any point between. Work can be both sought and shunned, transformed into dance, and its incentives unscrupulously manufactured. The total impression is of a kaleidoscopic complexity, whose effect upon the audience is both bewildering and exhilarating.

Charlie's appetites and purposes are designed both to bring him personal satisfaction and to establish a base of operations, as it were, in our unaccommodating social reality. We have seen that it is impossible to distinguish absolutely the personal and the social spheres, but in neither, it is pertinent to mention at this point, is Charlie guaranteed to get his own way. His forays into our world result in both victories and defeats, and watching the films with attention is to some degree a matter, at pivotal moments, of chalking up one or the other on his behalf. Our world displays a remarkable power of resistance to Charlie's intentions, whether benign or mischievous. He may find himself winning or losing money food, woman, job, rank—sometimes winning and losing more than once in succession in the same film. These ups and downs, as well as providing surface drama and suspense, are clearly one of the conflicts that are dramatized in Charlie's numerous balancing acts. Indeed, they have a subcategory balancing act of their own, in the recurrent images of frustration and defeat, where the symbolized deadlock is signally to Charlie's disadvantage. An early example is his dough-kneading efforts in *Dough and Dynamite*, when the rubbery substance exhibits seemingly unlimited powers of elasticity; and, later, the labour exchange scene in *A Dog's Life*, when his frustrated attempts to gain the attention of one official or the other culminate in a display of useless and automatic slithering, which continues while they are packing up to go home; and even later, hearkening back to the first, Hynkel's pathetically ineffectual offer to demonstrate what he'd like to do to Napaloni by tearing apart the spaghetti. Charlie's transformations are vulnerable to abrupt losses of potency: at these moments our world takes its revenge.

The whole question of Charlie's personal and social aspirations is shot through with extensive and crucial ambiguities. Put briefly, the conundrum is this: both what he demands from life, and the satisfaction of these demands, are characterized by contradictory elements that he both desires and fears. More specifically, he seeks from life both the satisfaction of appetite and the security of a sense of belonging. But to seek the satisfaction of appetite is to expose himself to the danger of uncontrollable forces, while the security of belonging can involve an intolerable sense of constraint. He cannot have the appetite without the danger, or the security without the constraint: yet the constraint is a threat to the appetite, and the danger a threat to the security. It seems like an irresolvable puzzle. No wonder that Charlie's balancing acts, as much as by skill and poise, are characterized by danger and deadlock!

The conundrum is probably best understood at the social level, where it highlights the problems of morality and of random hostility, which are recurrent preoccupations in Chaplin's films. What I shall for present purposes lump together as Charlie's appetite (the desire for money, food, women, work and rank), together with his need to establish a stable social identity (*security*), draw him for their satisfaction into our world. But his appetite is characterized by amorality, compulsive rule-flouting and a cheerful indifference to conventional sanctions and supports (all conditions, we remember, of his fundamental oddity). These factors make him vulnerable both to the official hostility of policemen, clergymen and other authority figures (the guardians of legality–morality) and to the random hostility of criminals or of natural calamities (both rule flouters by definition—the conjunction of the two will not seem outlandish if we remember how, in *The Gold Rush*, the malevolence of Black Larsen becomes associated with that of both the blizzard and the bear). Our world seems to Charlie irredeemably infested with threat and *danger*. There is no defence against natural calamity, but the answer to the other hazards is apparently to accept the *constraint* of conventional morality, and of 'normal' habits of behaviour, a course against which Charlie's nature re-volts. I have italicized the key terms in the above account to bring out the schematic nature of the conundrum (in a way that I hope is useful), but must emphasize that it does not remain at the level of schema, but is dramatized with witty particularity and with in-creasing degrees of subtlety, in Chaplin's mature films, where vari-ous ways out of the impasse are suggested. The natural calamity problem is treated in *Shoulder Arms* and *The Gold Rush*, and the morality problem in *Easy Street*, *The Pilgrim* and *Monsieur Verdoux*. (Which should not be taken to imply that these are the only mat-ters with which these films are concerned.) At the personal level, exactly the same conundrum applies, though here the appetite in question is usually that for affectionate relationships, and the danger that of their rejection or loss: on this topic the key films are *The Vagabond*, *The Kid* and *City Lights* (where the whole prob-lem described in this paragraph is dramatized, at the psychologi-cal level and in symbolic terms, with unrivalled delicacy and imagi-native force).

Chaplin and the Three Charlies

There is Charlie, and there is Chaplin. In the last resort creature and creator cannot be firmly distinguished, but there comes a point when everyone who has written about Chaplin finds it nec-essary to try. So compelling, in its convincingness and power, is Charlie's personality, and so thoroughly does our sense of the life of the films depend upon *him*, that one tends to forget that there is a controlling intelligence behind him that with whatever degree of consciousness, is larger than he. The oblique stroke that divides his name in the chapter title is my attempt to register the ambi-guity of the phenomenon, the problem of two-in-one with which the critic is obliged to deal. In the preceding sections of this chap-ter I have tried to show that what impresses us as Charlie's power derives primarily from his peculiarly intimate relationship with the traditional clown figures of the past, manifesting itself, as he moves from his chaotic boundary to our orderly centre, in a compulsive oddity, a talent for display, and a pervasive contradictoriness of character and behaviour that issues in repeated images of balance and deadlock; and have proceeded to demonstrate how these qualities exhibit themselves in the practical concerns—Charlie's appetites and purposes, which compel him to action—of the films. In this section I wish to divert attention to Chaplin's contribution, defining that as everything that follows where the clown tradition leaves off. I am aware that this element is not everywhere easy to isolate, that it does not necessarily imply a conscious programme or prescription on Chaplin's part (I shall to a large extent argue the contrary), and that it is by no means all pure gain. But to describe and judge it is probably the critic's most necessary task, if any view of Chaplin as a great artist is to be sustained. In large part the describing and judging are attempted in the accounts of individual films that make up the bulk of this book, but a number of general observations are called for.

It is obvious that Charlie's art is not comprised in the assertion that he is a uniquely thorough modern embodiment of the traditional clown type, and in a description of what this type's qualities are as they show themselves in his films. Every modern comedian, in and out of films, exhibits some of these qualities, but not every comedian is a great poet of the cinema. The important point is that Charlie's unusually direct access to the sources of power of the traditional clown type gave him both a head start on his rivals and a rich accumulation of subject matter from which to fashion psychological and social themes. It enabled him to draw upon an ancient tradition in embodying an ambiguous attitude to good and bad, order and chaos, material and spiritual, life and artifice. His traditional stance on the border of our world obliged him to become both its victim and its master—both to suffer containment and degradation and to exhibit important possibilities of transcendence and release. But the translation of these potentialities into works of art needed the powers of contrivance, both intuitive and deliberate, of Chaplin the creator.

It must have been both intuitively and deliberately that Chaplin set about his first task of adapting his screen character. Had he remained for ever in his original incarnation he would have been an object of fascination but hardly one of sympathy. The arrogance, callousness and amorality of his earliest version, together with his powers of infiltration and transformation, would explain the attention he has received but not the affection in which he is held. It is obvious enough that in a short space of time, though

throughout a large number of films, Chaplin sophisticated and refined Charlie's character. In fact, there are at least three distin-
guishable Charlies (corresponding exactly to the three stages of
Charlie's love life described above). Although they evolved at different times, and have recognizable identities, it is often hard to
separate them with any accuracy. They do not always appear in an
unadulterated form. Often, and invariably in his best films, they
merge and mingle, offering themselves in a number of combinations. Charlie is capable of using his variety of selves to augment his
powers of surprise by switching deftly from one to another. Much
of the vivacity of the films derives from our uncertainty about which
Charlie we are to see next.

The first Charlie, the prototype, is the insolent aristocrat, who
contemplates his neighbours with lordly condescension. He is fastidious, irritable and vain. His dignity is constantly offended by the
vulgarity of the world he is forced to inhabit, which persists in ob-
structing his demands for attention and service. He is not above a
little vulgarity himself, especially when drunk, and will trade insults
and indignities with the basest. This is the Charlie that Chaplin
brought with him from his music hall repertoire. He has described
him as being based on an observed social type. 'I thought of all
those little Englishmen I had seen with their little black mous-
taches, their tight clothes and their bamboo canes, and I fixed on
these as my model'.[10] The comic potential of this character derives
from the extremity of his insolence, and from the assaults to
which his precarious dignity is subjected. This is the Charlie to
whom other people are either convenient objects or tiresome
obstacles.

The second Charlie is altogether more human and likeable. His
invasion of our reality is benign rather than hostile. He is the
light-hearted, high-spirited contriver of inventive comic business,
whose power of transformation takes the forms of mockery, facetiousness and practical jokes. He emphasizes Charlie's display
rather than his oddity (it is he who energetically sets about turning work into dance), though in his way he is no less odd than his
fellows. With the women in his life, who are tolerant of his eccentricities, he is flirtatious rather than predatory. His relationships in

10. Quoted in Delluc, *Charlie Chaplin*.

general are casual, and he is not averse to a friendly punch-up, but he has no dignity to stand on, and at his most aggressive is able to convey that it is really all a game. He is for many moods the most attractive Charlie: our reaction to him is one of pleasure at his resourceful mastery of events. He is found in his purest form in a film like *The Pawnshop* (which is a kind of compendium of second-Charlie behaviour and gags—all inconsequent flummery and display).

The third Charlie marks a move towards a much greater realism of presentment. He is a fully and recognizably human figure, characterized by his openness to a greatly enlarged range of feelings—especially to the vulnerable feelings of love, kindness, embarrassment, grief and fear. In particular he is Charlie the romantic lover, whose girl, often placed beyond his reach by circumstances, is the object of sincere and disinterested affection. It is clear that this new development has dangers. To start with, there is the danger that, in so totally occupying the centre, he will lose touch with the boundary—that by merging himself with the human he will forfeit the transcendent benefits of the disorderly and chaotic non-human periphery. This danger is alleviated by the facts: first, that the third Charlie only occasionally appears in an unadulterated form, and is most likely to exhibit, simultaneously or in rapid sequence, elements of the other two; and, second that he makes positive use of the new feelings to which he has found access. The development of the third Charlie made possible Chaplin's creation of the comedy of feeling—comedy made out of serious feelings, which employs them for comic ends. To a large extent, of course, all comedy does this, but not often with the feelings that characterize the third Charlie, and hardly ever with feelings so unmistakably genuine. For example, the fear of imminent violence is employed to sustain suspense to breaking point in *Easy Street*; and, in *The Immigrant*, the same fear produces the same end, complicated in this case by the social embarrassment of Charlie's solecisms. Also in *The Immigrant* is a subtler instance, and more to the point by reason of its relation to the love theme: the amusing mixture of solicitude and prudence that makes Charlie hesitate over how much money to slip into Edna's pocket. The prudence is a constant Charlie quality, but the solicitude, real and touching, is only made possible by his third incarnation.

These suggested alleviations of the danger of the comedy of feeling also apply to the commoner charge laid against it: that it issues in passages of embarrassing self-pity and pathos. As I said above, this charge cannot be evaded by Chaplin's admirers, and must sometimes be conceded to be true. The third Charlie is potentially—and on several occasions an actually—sentimental figure. There are moments when, by engineering the drama, he appears to be setting himself up for our pitying attention. But 'pathos' is too often used as a blanket term to cover both the moments of self-indulgence and those much more frequent moments when serious (and often admirable) feelings are employed to produce a complex comic effect. The pathos to which many indiscriminately object is the unfortunate residue of a humanizing intention that at its purest gives rise to the profoundest kind of comedy. It has in any case been exaggerated. The sentimental side of Charlie's nature has been coarsened by his commentators (not least, alas, by Chaplin himself on the soundtrack of the reissued *The Gold Rush*) to the exclusion of other qualities. 'The little fellow', 'the little tramp'—these patronizing sobriquets have tended to obscure the quite unsentimental feelings from which much of his comedy arises. (In fact, the evidence for Charlie's being a tramp at all is largely inferential. He spends more time actually working than any real tramp can ever have done. His permanent state of vagabondage is not the result of pity-inducing social conditions so much as of his traditional role of alien intruder in our familiar world.)

Chaplin's first large-scale assault upon the comedy of feeling was *The Kid*. This is often thought of as a sentimental film, but it is a good example of how unjust the charge of self-indulgence can be. There *is* sentimentality in *The Kid*, but it is confined to the novelettish unreality of the framing subplot or 'overplot'—Edna's seduction and desertion, her change in fortunes, the loss and recovery of her child. This is the part at which we wince. The main body of the film is devoted to something that is entirely different, and that is an excellent example of the benefits derived by Chaplin's developing art from the comedy of feeling: the establishment, in comic and realistic terms, of the affectionate relationship between Charlie and Jackie. Their growing sense of mutual need, the odd feeling of identity that is established between them, and the pride

and responsibility that Charlie's role of surrogate father gives him
(as well as his comically idiosyncratic notion of the nature of a father's duties) are all excellently done, and in a manner whose
emphasis is humorous and affectionate rather than sentimental.
So sure is our sense of the fineness of those passages that when
the time comes for an unabashed exhibition of feeling—Charlie's
ardent reunion with the tearful Jackie—we judge that he has
earned it. *The Kid* is also important in the development of Chaplin's dramaturgy. It shows that the need he felt to introduce a new
seriousness into his work was not confined to the realm of Charlie's character, but extended to the whole dramatic construction
of the film. It demonstrates a transitional stage in which the comic
bits and the serious bits are kept separate, in terms both of plot
and, to some extent, of feeling (for, as we have seen, serious feeling inspire the comedy), with unfortunate consequences when
eventually they have to come together. In later films Chaplin shows
a much greater adroitness in reconciling comedy and realism,
managing to weld disparate elements into a complex, seriocomic
unity. (In *The Gold Rush*, for instance, the inhabitants of the cabin
embody a spectrum of human types from seriousness to folly—
Larsen the serious villain, Jim half hero half fool, and Charlie the
fool—and so are able to coexist without incongruity).

So, as well as dangers, the new enlargement of scope brought
about by the creation of the third Charlie and of a dramatic framework suitable to contain him led to new possibilities: a larger range
of subjects for Chaplin to treat, a greater depth with which to treat
them. One important area that this greater realism affected profoundly was that of Charlie's relationship with his audience. The
development of the third Charlie gave the audience a vastly increased scope for sympathetic identification. The typical situation
of the third Charlie is a sort of mirror image of his appetites and
purposes: he is without all the things he wants. At his lowest ebb
he is impoverished, hungry, lonely, jobless and despised. He is
adrift in a threatening world to which he only half belongs, a prey
to the institutionalized hostility of authority figures and the random hostility of criminals and catastrophes. So his struggles to
achieve his ends and to overcome threats, which form the action
of his typical plots, contrive to dramatize widespread common fears
about the vulnerability of the individual life, its identity, and its

relations to society and to nature. Chaplin's cultivation of realism reinforced the bond with his audience that his original artistry had forged: by basing his comedy upon observed life, and the impulsion of common hopes and fears, he ensured the utmost of sympathetic audience involvement, and it is to these qualities that he owes his unprecedented popularity. Of course this is not the whole story. The sympathy-inducing realism is qualified, ranging in degrees from the minimal to the drastic, by those qualities that Charlie inherits from the fool tradition: his incorrigible oddity and his passion for display. At the same time as we register sympathy and resemblance, we recognize that we are watching something alien and that it is being deliberately paraded before us. It is the conflict between these feelings that gives the films, and our experience of watching them, so much of its tension, as our awareness of the action fluctuates and recoils. It is also one of the elements that lend their bafflement to Charlie's numerous balancing acts. William Willeford expresses the paradox of this conflict between identification and alienation by juxtaposing two ancient opinions about folly: that we are all fools, yet a fool is instantly recognizable. It could be said that Charlie's service to his audience is the traditional clown's function of mediating between their recognition of folly in others and their awareness of it in themselves. But to a much greater extent than any predecessors, Charlie makes us realize that not everything that is foolish is necessarily alien, nor everything alien necessarily foolish. His move towards full humanness complicates an already complex pattern of challenge and response.

This book is not a study in sources, but it would be misleading not to acknowledge that the new seriousness with which I have been crediting Chaplin did not come to him unbidden, but must have been suggested in part by elements in the various dramatic traditions to which his experience gave him access. It was not only ideas for plots and routine comic business, for instance, that he inherited from English music hall and pantomime: a large part of the repertoire of music hall songs was devoted to realistic incidents of domestic and social life, with emphasis on the poverty, deprivations and enjoyments of working people, and often registering niceties of class distinction and social pretension. His intimate acquaintance with this material has clearly left its mark. (He has often testified to his devotion to the sentimental songs current in his childhood, whose nostalgic cadences reappear, in his own music for his films.) It is important to remember, too, that part of his early professional experience was on the legitimate stage, where he acquired both skill in serious acting and a discriminating judgment of style and technique. It is to this experience that he probably owed his interest in dramatic construction, as well as the lifelong fascination with theatricality and the creative life of the actor that finds its final expression in *Limelight*.

Chaplin's ambition to graft straight dramatic elements on to his comic plots would seem to derive from his experience of other people's films. His arrival in Hollywood coincided with the emergence of the film from its fair booth stage into a recognized vehicle for the expression of realistic life and serious themes. The art film did not spring spontaneously into life but itself derived from the conventions of the nineteenth-century theatre, in which Chaplin had received his earliest training. So it was not unknown territory into which he was venturing. The earliest story films reflected the nineteenth-century stage's fondness for combinations of romantic plot, realistic settings and spectacular action. But the form was gradually being refined, and made capable of subtler expressions of feeling, by the innovative efforts of D.W. Griffith, soon to be Chaplin's friend.[11] It was this kind of serious film art to which Chaplin aspired. His earlier efforts (*The Vagabond* and *The Kid*) owe more to other films than to life, and are unsatisfactory partly on that account. But very shortly, in *A Woman of Paris*, he produced his own wholly serious and original achievement in the sensitive and realistic mode. The point to emphasize for present purposes is that his efforts to render his comedy more subtle and responsive have their place in the larger history of the film as an art.

When we speak of the clown as a type, as, following Willeford, I have repeatedly done, it is as well to remember that the type has historically assumed a great variety of forms. It follows that when we examine influences some particular forms will seem to tell strongly and others not at all. One aspect of the fool tradition that

---

11. The historical process is convincingly described in A. Nicholas Varda, *Stage to Screen: Theatrical Method from Garrick to Griffith* (Cambridge, MA: Harvard University Press, 1949).

so far as I can recall never manifests itself in Charlie is the long association of folly with learning and other expressions of mental
ability. (I am thinking of the fool type who assumes the authority
of a knowledge or capability he does not possess: a type whose
modern English incarnations are Will Hay, Tony Hancock and the
Arthur Lowe of *Dad's Army*). Charlie's impostures are professional
and social, never intellectual, and in any case he never allows inca-
pacity to embarrass him. But another historical development of
the type did, it has been suggested, have a real influence. This was
the transformation wrought upon the *commedia* character of Pedrolino by Jean Gaspard Deburau in his Théâtre Funambles performances in early nineteenth-century Paris. The change was so
drastic as to leave little in common with the original. Pedrolino was
an early servant type, apparently more personable than his fellows,
though his character exhibits over the years the same bewildering
variety as the other *commedia* types. Deburau's Pierrot retained the
character's traditional ruffed and trousered costume but introduced into his behaviour a new element of the pathetic and romantic, emphasizing his deprived and victimized condition. This Pierrot's direct descendant is Marcel Marceau's Bip, but he is also revived in the English pantomime and circus, and in this form would
seem to have made a decisive contribution to the third Charlie. (It
cannot be a coincidence that it was as a version of this type that
Chaplin chose to appear in the harlequinade ballet in *Limelight*).
If this is true it could be seen as lending a dramatic licence to
Charlie's much-maligned pathos by investing it with at least some
of the authority of a venerable theatrical tradition, and so making
it seem more a matter of stylization than of self-indulgence.

An influence that seems to me to have told decisively is that of
Dickens. I do not know what direct evidence there is for Chaplin's
having read Dickens, but it is a fact that Dickens's influence upon
English popular culture of all kinds was enormous and diverse. His
novels provided a significant element of the popular theatrical fare
of the late nineteenth century, in the form of both direct dramatizations and character monologues. It is impossible that Chaplin
should not have encountered him, perhaps frequently, in one or
other of these forms. Whatever the precise facts, it seems to me
that *The Kid* could not have been conceived, or taken the shape
that it did, without the presence in the background of *Oliver Twist*.

There are important differences, of course. The film could in one sense be described as the novel in reverse, for in the film the sense of insecurity that is common to both works centres upon the threat of Jackie's abduction by the forces of paternalistic authority rather than, as in the book, Oliver's abduction by those of a darkly criminal underworld. Chaplin does not, in this instance, represent safety as residing in middle-class social norms (or rather, he does at the end, but it is an ending unusually hard to believe). The main point is that both dramas derive their feeling from poignant stories of recovery and loss, and from the events we witness being derived obscurely from other events in the past (enacted at a different social level), with which they are finally reconciled. Quite apart from the question of direct influence, Chaplin has often been called the Dickens of the cinema, and the resemblances between the early experience of each, and the way it emerged in their work, are sufficiently striking. Both knew poverty and deprivation in childhood, and the unsettling effects of fluctuations in fortune (though in the popular accounts of the life of each this element is exaggerated, and it is overlooked that the normal character of each home was securely lower middle-class). Both were driven by unusual ambition, capable of exceptional energy, and earned rapid fame and success. Both were liable to visitations of misery and self-doubt. Both were raised in London, a city of abundant life and violent contrasts (and the London of Chaplin's youth was still that of Dickens in most respects). These experiences issued in the work of each in a preoccupation with feelings of vulnerability, with poverty, wealth and class, and with sudden changes in fortune; in evocations of the problems of living in modern industrial cities (it has often been remarked that the streets of *Easy Street* and *The Kid* resemble those of London rather than any American city); and in an occasional proneness to sentimental self-indulgence. I have already noted how Chaplin's metaphorical audacities are a sort of visual equivalent of Dickens's verbal ones, and are the product of similar habits of thought. But the most important resemblance for this stage in my argument is the way in which the art of each developed. Dickens's later novels are conscious and responsible works of art, in which the unassimilated feelings and fantasies that pervade the early work are employed, in a drastically modified form, on behalf of a serious critique of social life. My contention is

that what happens in Chaplin, while by no means identical either
in achievement or character (I deal with the question of the
degree of consciousness below), is remarkably similar. If *The Kid* is
his *Oliver Twist*, then *Monsieur Verdoux* could be called his *Great
Expectations.*

I have been speaking of elements of his art that Chaplin may be
deduced to have borrowed from theatrical and literary traditions.
I think it is not an exaggeration to say that what he *invented* is the
film as a form of comic-poetic drama. I said at the very beginning
that I based my interpretations of the films upon the premises that
they had serious meanings and that these meanings are to be
found in the comedy. We have seen that early on he set about so-
phisticating and refining the character of Charlie by giving him
access to a greater range of experience than was available to the
basic comic type he inherited from the clown tradition. (The form
this process took is traced in greater detail in the next chapter.)
One result of this was that the comedy began to owe a great deal
more to the clown's inner life—his attitudes and responses—than
to the conventional knockabout of external action. Further, by basing the action of his films upon widely held hopes and fears about
both our individual selves and our social relationships, Chaplin
ensured both an inexhaustible supply of material and the fullest
sense of sympathetic identification on the part of the audience.
But this is not the only kind of seriousness I mean. I am thinking
of the sort of serious meanings that make a work of art seem alive
and significant rather than inert and conventional—the unmistakable sense of a vital aspect of experience captured and conveyed. I
am assuming a general agreement that Chaplin's finest films do
give us this sense. If they were not serious in this way we would not
find them so important, or, in however obscure a way, so relevant
to our own lives. The admitted fact that the 'meanings' of comedy
are not usually so obvious or readily formulated as those of non-
comic art does not mean that they are not there. They await discovery by patience, directed attention and a cultivated receptiveness.

Chaplin's themes derive from, but are not identical to, what I
have called his appetites and purposes. They can be seen as the
translation of appetite and purpose into need by the generalizing
process that symbolism entails, and take the form of an enquiry, in
dramatic terms, into the psychological and social needs of human

nature. If this sounds arid, it is hard to find a form of words that does not: the living process is enacted, in its fullness, in the works of art themselves. At least the words may suggest both the urgency and the seriousness of the enacting. I have attempted to suggest something of the complexity of the result in describing above the 'conundrum' of Charlie's deeply ambiguous attitude to the demands and promptings of his private and social selves. The films are attempts to express and resolve the contradictions that attend virtually every aspect of Charlie's experience. The basic conflict is the pitting of need against fear. For example, there is the need and fear of moral constraints (*Easy Street*, *The Pilgrim*), heroic endeavour (*Shoulder Arms*, *The Gold Rush*), affectionate relationships (*The Vagabond*, *The Kid*, *City Lights*), material satisfactions (*A Dog's Life*, *The Gold Rush*) and professional activity (*Modern Times* and just about every other film). In addition, a significant number of films dramatize Chaplin's ambiguous feelings about his own role of performer (*The Circus*, *Limelight*). It is immediately apparent that each film is not limited to a single theme (though one invariably predominates): *The Gold Rush*, for instance, combines, cleverly but easily, the themes of predatory nature and of the tyranny of material satisfactions. And every film is concerned in some measure with the work theme and the love theme. In the culminating achievement of Chaplin's career, *Monsieur Verdoux*, all his themes converge in a single drama to whose impressive complexity it is difficult to do justice.

The method of the films is that of poetic significance. And the significance resides in the passages of comedy and not in anything that is tacked on them or sandwiched between them. This is even, indeed especially, true of the sound films, where part of the burden of expressing the theme is given to speech. In *The Great Dictator*, it is not to the barber's rhetorical trade that we go for the meaning of the film, but to the images of Hynkel dancing with the globe, and of the barber shaving his customer to the music of Brahms, for these express the conflict between active creativity and barren megalomania that is at the heart of the film. A sign of the poetic method is its generated sense of pressure of purpose. The significance bears upon all parts of the action: nearly everything contributes, very little is redundant. It follows that the meaning of the film may be contained in, or partly sustained by, passages of business that appear to have little to do with what one thinks of as the main theme: of no film is this truer than of *City Lights*, the pervasive (and relevant) suggestiveness of whose comedy has never been properly recognized. But in most of the films it does not take unusual powers to understand the significance of what is being offered: it is easy enough to see that the boiling and eating of the boot in *The Gold Rush*, to take the most famous example, expresses Charlie's ambiguous attitude to food consumption, and so relates naturally to the overall theme of physical survival (though the dance of the rolls in the same film presents the expositor with a more delicate problem). For detailed accounts both of the themes of the films and of their manner of presentation, the reader must turn to the chapters that follow. My purpose here is to contend that together they constitute a form of major art for which the credit is wholly Chaplin's.

Imputing to Chaplin artistry of this quality is to raise the question of how conscious the artistry is. It is not a simple question to answer. The degree of consciousness varies from film to film, and between one kind of creative activity and another. I take it as agreed that an artist can produce all manner of successful effects, and create significant patterns, of which he is not completely aware. There is one level of activity at which Chaplin's artistry is wholly conscious. This is the level of creation of specific comic business, the mechanics of film-making and manipulation of audience response. There is plenty of evidence in Chaplin's published writings that he had thought hard about the mechanics of his trade, and brought to bear upon his day-to-day work the fruits of past experience. Individual bits of comic business were meticulously rehearsed and carefully calculated in terms of camera position, succession of shots and effect upon the audience by way of such dramatic qualities as surprise, suspense and advancement of the story. There is no visible evidence, at least after the earliest crudest efforts, of Chaplin's much-impugned indifference to the mechanics of film-making. The evident skill and deliberation, at the purely cinematic level, of *A Woman of Paris*, give the lie to this charge. Similarly with Chaplin's powers of dramatic construction. I do not think he has ever been given sufficient credit for the skill with which his films are assembled, in terms of relation of episodes, distribution of effects, pace of action, parallelism and contrast, catastrophe and climax. His dramaturgy is very efficient, the only major criticism seeming to me to be that the pace of the later films is too slow, and some of their material repetitive or redundant. I hope to justify this claim in the analyses that follow.

It is at the level of theme and poetic method that it becomes hardest to say how conscious Chaplin was of what he was doing. His own writings are not very forthcoming on this point. The only evidence is provided by one's subjective judgment and general sense of likelihood. It seems to me clear that at this level the organizing was instinctive and unbidden rather than deliberate. I do not think that, in the line of mature films from *A Dog's Life* to *City Lights*, Chaplin was ever fully aware of the subtlety of what he achieved; nor, if he had been, that the films would have been any the better—rather the reverse, I shall argue shortly. In general, it seems to have been the immediate dramatic qualities and effects of the story that he consciously attended to—the establishment of relationships, the creation of appropriate feelings. The poetic suggestiveness was left, so to speak, to take care of itself, which it did with great efficiency. And this is all you *can* do with it, however finely tuned your consciousness: it either arises unbidden from the depths or it doesn't, except as lifeless contrivance, exist at all. The 'poetry' is testimony to the existence of depths, to the seriousness of the theme, and to the urgency with which the theme is forced into expression. As I have said, the degree of consciousness must differ from film to film. It is impossible to believe that, in making *The Gold Rush*, Chaplin did not realize that, in addition to telling an exciting story, he was dramatizing an important dilemma about the purposes of life. But I find it equally hard to credit that he *was* aware of the subtlety of effect and organization that he produced in *City Lights*, a film that is *about* the unacknowledged depths of feeling.

In the films from *Modern Times* onwards, the question takes a different form. For these films are the result of a clear and deliberate intention. They issue unmistakably from Chaplin's conscious desire to address himself to the modern world, to adapt his traditional character and methods to the expression of certain themes felt to be momentous and unavoidable. Here, in judging the results, one finds oneself totting up an account of profit and loss. On the profit side, one cannot but applaud the enterprise and the energetic courage with which it was tackled. Charlie's increasing irrelevance to a fast-changing world worried Chaplin, and, for all one's affection for Charlie, it is impossible to feel that he was wrong in being worried: and the themes that thrust themselves forward as demanding attention—the dehumanizing of work, the perversion of political power and the moral sickness of modern civilization—were such as should rightly have engrossed the creative instinct of a major artist, as they did the thoughts of intelligent ordinary people. And the burden of the themes is, as before, borne by comic passages of poetic suggestiveness and power. Altogether I judge these later films to be successful major works of art, an accolade not always afforded them at the time or since. But there *is* a loss account, and in it one must record that consciousness was not to Chaplin an unmixed blessing. His conscious grasp of his themes was weak and superficial, and resulted in comic business that is banal or facetious, in miscalculations of tone, and in an urge towards embarrassing and redundant explicitness. The worst sufferer from these vices is *The Great Dictator*, with its facetious names, clownish storm troopers and platitudinous peroration, but none of the later films is entirely free of them. So one finds oneself postulating two Chaplins—one who trusts his instincts and allows his themes to clothe themselves, and one who thrusts them into ill-fitting garments of his own making—and imputing the virtues to the one and the vices to the other. It is an unavoidable conclusion, and one to which I shall be forced to have recourse in discussing the films in question.

The issue of Chaplin's self-consciousness relates interestingly to that of his relation to his contemporaries, and to later representatives of their common tradition. I have neither the space nor the stomach for an extended comparison, but the subject cannot be avoided altogether, and moreover it seems to me to provide an opportunity for leaving the emphasis on the right place. I am thinking in particular of Buster Keaton, whose critical fortunes have risen astronomically in recent years as those of Chaplin have declined. In part this has been a salutary redressing of balance. Keaton is most certainly a great genius, and his long spell of neglect was a misfortune. There is no doubt that for decades Chaplin did hog the limelight. Keaton's films are characterized by resourceful invention, wit, excitement and visual beauty. The best of them are better constructed than even the best of Chaplin's, and purged of all impurities: Chaplin perhaps never made a *perfect* film, as Keaton can be said to have done. However compared with Chaplin's, Keaton's films strike me as being characterized by a certain impoverishment of inner life. Their perfection is surface polish and dazzle, their excitement a matter of adroit acrobatics and physical action that assault the senses and leave the feelings unmoved. The difference is chiefly one of character: Buster's has none of Charlie's depth or complexity and hence none of his endless capacity for surprise. One could not find oneself describing Buster or his world in anything like, or equivalent to, the terms I have been using in this chapter. So to call him greater than Charlie, as has been done, strikes me as a serious misjudgment.

What goes for Keaton goes for the tradition he can be said to have inaugurated. (This is to leave out of account Harold Lloyd, another neglected genius ripe for wholesale rediscovery: but Lloyd, who remains always anchored firmly to the circumstances and habits of a specific time and place, is as much a comic actor as a clown, and so does not invite comparison here.) Jacques Tati, for instance, is very much a Keaton type of clown, and his character is even simpler and sparer: in his later films, indeed, he tends for long periods to vanish from view. (It is only fair to add that Tati's late films are highly original works of art that involve a radical revision—perhaps even a dissolution—of the tradition of clown comedy, and about the success of which, in common with many others, I find it onerously difficult to make up my mind.) Another modern artist, who seems to me to owe as much to Keaton as to the Stan Laurel he frequently cites, is Marcel Marceau, who has single-handedly revived the art of theatrical mime. There is a considerable Chaplin element in Marceau too, but the resemblance only serves to underline the contrast. Marceau is always a joy to watch, and is gifted with a wonderfully supple and athletic body: in the miming of physical action he has no equal. But it is when he needs most to be like Chaplin that he most falls short: in registering sudden changes of feeling, for instance, or any feeling at all—at these moments one is so often forced to judge him crude. And his repeated tendency towards stylization, rather than realism, of gesture makes part of his performance unnecessarily hard to understand.

I do not claim to have done more than rough justice to Chaplin's rivals and successors in this summary account, or to suggest that it comprises all that can be said about them: my aim is unashamedly to use them as a foil to his distinctiveness. Where he scores so decisively over them is in his comedy's unprecedented naturalness and closeness to life. It does not just issue from the common life we share and recognise, it seems itself to *be* life: to offer itself, even at its most bizarre, with all the ease, directness and vividness of an event actually witnessed, or an experience actually felt. It follows that it is in terms of our own experience that we ultimately justify our estimate of his art. And this is a truth about art in general, not Chaplin's alone. The point of dwelling upon such an emphasis in this context and at this time resides in the current state of film criticism as well as a desire to do justice to Chaplin. I began this chapter with a complaint about contemporary film criticism and will end it with another. For some time, its main characteristic has been a habit of submission to the glamour of a variety of dubiously authoritative intellectual systems, whose chief effect has been to isolate art from life and to treat it as a self-sufficient activity needing a species of wizardry to elucidate it. To those of us who looked forward to the creation of a responsible film criticism when there was none, such a development could hardly be more dismaying. My two complaints are related, of course: since you cannot justify taking seriously a mediocre product of the commercial cinema in terms of its human interest, you are forced to do so in terms of its significance as a system of signs, or as an illustration of some other arcane sophistry. To such fallacious 'approaches' Chaplin gives the lie. It is perhaps little wonder that for a time his reputation declined, to the advantage of figures more amenable to fashion, because less given to the embarrassment of appeals to actual experience. The approach to Chaplin can only be through life: Charlie's art is an art of life, and it is in our lives that we register his importance.

Chapter 2

Keystone to Mutual

When Chaplin joined the Keystone company in December 1913 he was a novice in the art of making comic films. When he left the Mutual company in July 1917 he was a veteran whose finest work was still to come. In between he made some 61 films, excluding a number of unauthorized compilations. These films comprise a key period in the evolution of his art, in which he discovered the nature of his talent and began to extend its limits. They are the films that established his unprecedented popularity, and must still be among the most fondly remembered: for a long period, when the later films were unavailable, they were the only Chaplins that anyone was likely actually to be able to see. They exhibit what seems, looking back on them, an extraordinary wealth of imaginative comic business, and an unequalled variety of incident, mood and drama. They can be said to constitute Chaplin's apprenticeship. Yet they are more than a testing ground: some of them are the work of an undoubted journeyman. In quality they range from trivial concoctions, which only an addict would want to see more than once, to some of the best things he ever achieved. If Chaplin had died, or stopped making films, in 1918, he would still be regarded as an important comedian. As it is, the voluminousness of this early output poses the critic whose sights are set on the later achievements something of a problem.

I cannot hope to do justice in the short chapter that follows to the range and quality of this material. The Keystone-to-Mutual films need a book to themselves (and more than one has in fact been devoted to them). But my concern is with the films of Chaplin's maturity, and the nature of their distinction, and I pay to the early period only the attention that serves this end. It is a reluctant economy, since this part of Chaplin's career is as attractive as it is prolific. However, strategy apart, it seems to me that the films of this period are in any case too often considered as an homogeneous group. Their sheer number calls for discrimination, and their difference in quality makes it inevitable. So discrimination is what attempt. In the next chapter I consider at length three films only from this period: *The Vagabond*, *Easy Street* and *The Immigrant*. The real distinction of these three has never been sufficiently recognized. They stand out, not only in prefiguring the themes of later films, but in possessing on their own account distinctive qualities of feeling, structure and significance. The salient factor is significance: the most important lesson learned by Chaplin from his apprenticeship was the discovery of how a film could be made to *mean*. The demonstration of this belief with regard to these three films has determined my treatment of the other 58, which consists of suggesting the overall kinds of development and refinement that took place. To this end, I propose to consider in turn Chaplin's comic performance (to which the greater part of this chapter is devoted), Charlie's character and the dramatic qualities of the films.

The Comic Business of the Basic Charlie

Among other things, the Keystone-to-Mutual films are a huge repository of comic business. It was as a comic performer that Chaplin first came to public attention, and in a way that distinguished him from the conventions of the films in which he appeared. There could be no doubt among the original audience that they were watching something different. Keystone today has become almost synonymous with slapstick comedy, but viewed from this distance, it is hard to avoid the conclusion that its products have acquired a reputation in excess of their merits. They are certainly original and lively, and performed with much panache: their fanciful chase scenes are particularly exhilarating. But they are also crude, implausible and lacking in dramatic and human interest. Their stock in trade is the comedy of childish aggression and physical indignity. They are more responsible than anything for the still-prevalent idea that silent film comedy is only suitable

for children. Keystone's real claim to attention, for any but the
least discriminating appetite, is that it provided a training ground
for the art of Chaplin.

Chaplin's relations with Keystone were mixed. Ever a creative
opportunist, he cannot but have appreciated the value of the
experience he would gain. And his own conscious ideas about
comedy were at this stage probably little more sophisticated than
Mack Sennett's. Yet there is plenty of evidence that the instinctive
subtle artist within him rebelled against the witless knockabout
and frenetic pace of the Keystone house style.[1] Before joining the
company, he had privately formed the opinion that its films were
'a crude mélange of rough and tumble'. He took particular exception to the director assigned to him, Henry Lehrman, who apparently 'had but one gag, which was to take the comedian by the
scruff of the neck and bounce him from one scene to another'.
Lehrman is said to have believed that 'comedy is an excuse for a
chase'. Chaplin knew that it was a great deal more, and tried to
put his conviction into practice by introducing his own relaxed
and intimate bits of comic business into the action. Finding that
his best effects were extracted in the cutting room, he reserved
them for the moments of entry and exit, which he knew were less
easily removed. Finally he rebelled openly, and after an argument
with Sennett won the right to direct his own pictures. This did not
enable him to transform Keystone overnight. He had to feel his
way slowly to a full realization of the character he had so casually
created. The films made under his own direction gave him scope
to experiment and to develop his powers of mimicry and movement. Most of them still conformed, inevitably, to the Keystone
style: there was no other pattern to follow. He had to work out
every improvement for himself. What is surprising is not that he
took so long to find his own manner, but that he did it so soon.

Chaplin was hired by Sennett to replace Ford Sterling, up to
then his leading comedian, who was departing to form his own
company. The two films they made together while Sterling was
working out his contract afford an instructive contrast between
the Keystone style and Chaplin's intuitive artistry, In an era that
appreciated 'ethnic' comedy, Sterling was a Dutch (equals immi-

1.   All the quotations in this paragraph are from Chaplin, *My Autobiography.*

grant German) comedian with pork-pie hat, goatee beard and a manner of irritable frustration. In *Between Showers* (which concerns a struggle between Charlie and Sterling for the privilege of escorting a buxom girl across a flooded street, and for the possession of a stolen umbrella), Sterling's emphatic pantomime of frustrated gallantry and larceny serves mainly to highlight Chaplin's telling economy of technique. Charlie's chatting up of the girl is confidential and casual: he taps his hands behind his back in a nice display of intimate relaxation. Landed with the umbrella he struts about experimenting with ways of carrying it, and starts to polish it with his sleeve. Sterling's contribution is his standard routine of jumping on the spot to express impotent rage. In a later film, *Tango Tangles*, the characters appear, unusually, out of character and without make-up, but the effect is the same. It is a dance hall impromptu, in which Sterling and Arbuckle play musicians, and Chaplin a drunken patron, such story as there is concerning a quarrel among the three over the possession of a girl. Once again the instructive contrast is between Sterling's crude, grimacing mimicry and Charlie's delicate clowning and surprising eccentricities. Charlie's drunk is limply ingratiating in a scene with the hat-check girl, languidly jerking his head by way of lecherous invitation, and following up with a playful back-kick; in stripping for combat with Sterling he abstractedly, and under the influence of a habit of association that we recognize as characteristic, starts to remove his trousers as well as his coat. The qualities that most impress us in Charlie's comic performance at this period are its spontaneity and its inventiveness. Spontaneity includes the ease and naturalness of his manner and the rapid immediacy of his comic effects; inventiveness includes his decided eccentricities of behaviour and continual power of surprise. We should not find it an insuperable paradox that behaviour that comes so naturally to Charlie seems so surprising to us. It is a spellbinding combination, and must have seemed so to the original audiences. From the first and all the more from appearing in uncongenial contexts, Charlie is projected as a powerful and individual presence.

It is as a presence that we are first aware of Charlie, not as a participant or a fabricator of effects. There are times when he does not appear to be part of the ostensible context at all, but to be operating in a world of his own, according to rules of his own devising: this is what makes his behaviour seem so disconcerting. In this respect he differs from his contemporaries. Keaton and Lloyd, for example, were both expert practitioners of large-scale comic effects that demanded a plausible context, and depended for their success upon an amplitude of apparatus, or the carefully timed management of people and objects. Keaton's deployment of trains and boats, and Lloyd's building–scaling routines, are cases in point. They also went in for gags involving build-up and variation, in which the audience's expectations are aroused by the repetition of a particular event and are either frustrated or satisfied in an unexpected way. Charlie's comedy, on the other hand, rarely needs an elaborate context, but is fashioned from the simplest details of common experience. René Clair has written,

> I bet that if you lock him up in a shop, an empty room, or a coal-cellar, he will find in his prison sufficient comic material to raise the same roars of laughter with which his films are always greeted the world over.[2]

His clowning is spontaneous, self-sufficient and intimate. However much careful preparation preceded it (and we know that a great deal did), it seems to have been improvised from the materials at hand. While other clowns' gags, however brilliant, bear the stamp of lengthy calculation, Charlie's simply happen, presenting themselves to us with all the immediacy of life. There are no real equivalents in Charlie's art to his contemporaries' large-scale effects: nothing either as calculated or as realistic as Lloyd clinging to a clock face, or Keaton swinging across a waterfall. He does, it is true, quite often employ 'variation' gags, especially in relation to potentially dangerous objects: examples are the trap door entrusted to his operation in *Behind the Screen*, or the medicinal spring in *The Cure*, into which he is in constant danger of falling. But even these gags issue naturally from the action, with no sense of excessive contrivance. Their elements are simple and their impact direct.

When you look at it, the self-sufficiency of Charlie's comedy derives partly from the fact that so much of it involves only the use of his own person, or of articles of his costume. His face is obviously one of his most valuable instruments. The real-life Chaplin was a very handsome young man, as numerous photographs tes-

2. René Clair, *Reflections on the Cinema* (London: Kimber, 1952).

tify, and even his ridiculous clownish incarnation is far from un-
handsome. D.H. Lawrence compared Charlie favourably with the
conventional and vacuous good looks of Valentino, detecting in
his face 'a gleam of something pure': he was probably thinking of
Charlie's basic expression of other-worldly abstraction, the one that
signals to us so unmistakably that he has wandered from a foreign
region, a trespasser from the border of the rational and conscious.
This look shades off easily into the stare of fastidious disdain that
is part of Charlie's immediate theatrical heritage, the manner of
the insolent gentleman whose response to the world is conditioned
by the degree to which it contributes to his comfort or appetite.
After this, the range of expression is almost endless: Charlie's face
is the chief servant of his astonishing histrionic versatility. But the
predominant expressions of these early films are the undisguisedly insolent and hostile; the affectedly gallant and ingratiating (as
when chatting up a girl); the calculatingly shrewd (that pursing of
the lips and wrinkling of the nose that presages some opportunity
for advantage, or for the infliction of revenge); and the smile of
coy propitiation that always follows Charlie's discovery in the performance of some disreputable act he can't brazen his way out of.
This last is a special favourite, employed throughout his career,
and making probably its last appearance in the scene where Henri
Verdoux is attempting to drown Martha Raye. It is also the most
obvious example of Charlie's commonest method of using his face
for comic effect, switching rapidly from one expression to another. It is the swift alternation of facial expressions that gives such
unexpectedness and interest to the often otherwise unremarkable
play of events, and as much pleasurable surprise to us today as it
must have to the original audiences—who had certainly never experienced in films a comic versatility so abundant and realistic.

   It is not just Charlie's face that is put to comic use, of course,
but his whole body, and the costume with which it is—I was going
to say, lumbered, but this word doesn't do justice to the odd way
in which his various appurtenances strike us as at once ungainly
and appropriate. Chaplin early realized that it was necessary for
the whole of Charlie's body to be seen for the full effect of him to
be taken, and that this necessity involved camera positions he had
at first an occasional struggle to establish. Obviously, the total incongruity of his appearance could only be appreciated in full-

length shots, but these were also needed for the successful record-
ing of physical comic business. This often takes the form of routine knockabout—the comedy of chases, fights and physical indignity—that Charlie is as adept at as anyone. But more important
are first the constant surprisingness of his general manner of movement—its mixture of clumsiness and agility—and, second, the specific impersonations of attitudes, conditions and activities that he
attempts. Charlie's manner of movement displays the same volatil-
ity as his facial expression. His famous clod-hopping shuffle is
ungainliness personified, giving him almost the appearance of a
cripple, but it doesn't prevent him from sudden and unexpected
demonstrations of poise, dexterity and speed, especially when
remedial or punitive action (or a hasty retreat) is called for. And
his disconcerting changes of expression are paralleled by equally
abrupt and disorientating variations in physical manner. At one
end of the spectrum these are habitual and ungoverned by context. At the other they take the form of a particular joke, his role-
switching tactic, in which an innocent action is substituted for a
guilty one: a good example being the moment in *The Pawnshop*
when, at the entry of the boss, his punch-up with his rival is
converted into a pretence of washing the floor. No less important
are his specific impersonations. In the comparison with Ford Sterling, I have mentioned his drunk act and his gallantry bit, both
needing all the resources of his body to convey their effect. Equally realistic is his habitual air of aristocratic insolence, which is so
much more than a disdainful expression: it is a strutting way of
walking, and a haughtily condescending carriage of the head and
arms (an effect regularly disrupted by his feet's clumsy attraction
to obstacles).

A large number of Charlie's routine gags involve his costume.
Willeford has described the symbolic function of the clown's costume as occupying, in its disproportion and incongruity, a sort of
halfway house between order and chaos. Charlie's certainly fits
this description, and is an important element in the powerful presence he projects. Various accounts have been given of how the
costume was acquired, all of them emphasizing the fortuitous and
improvisatory aspect. But the fact, to which Chaplin has testified,
that the Charlie character was based on an observed social type
suggests a greater measure of calculation, since the costume di-

rectly contributes to our sense of the type. The point to be made
for the moment is that the constituent parts of Charlie's costume
—his hat and cane, in particular—are not passive items of adorn-
ment but active instruments of comedy. His hat is always politely
raised—an instance of the importance of English social customs to
Charlie's art—even to inanimate objects ('I entered and stumbled
over the foot of a lady. I turned and raised my hat apologetically,
then turned and stumbled over the cuspidor, then turned and
raised my hat to the cuspidor')[3]; it seems to spring of its own voli-
tion into the air; or it is rolled down his arm and caught by his
hand in a demonstration of casual expertise. His cane has an even
more varied existence. It is twirled with the careless ease of a
boulevardier (usually dislodging its owner's hat in the process, or
clumping the back of his head), or is employed for tapping,
poking and hooking. It is useful for holding up trousers, and on
one occasion steals a handbag all by itself. Indeed, it increasingly
takes on a life of its own, displaying a particular fondness for tapping people's behinds without provocation. In one film (*His Night
Out*) it gets spoken to very seriously, apparently about its short-
comings, and lovingly put to bed. Charlie's boots, the other item
in his identikit image, are not of equal prominence, except as
instruments of aggression. Their moment of glory has to wait until
The Gold Rush, when they are so surprisingly employed as a stalk-
ing-horse to lull Big Jim's suspicions. But the feet that they so for-
midably encase are the object of a subcategory of foot-hurting gags,
being, despite the boots' protection, vulnerable to dropped bricks
and other malicious obstacles, and with each injury having to be
mollified by some mildly agonized hopping about.

The final class of comic business in Charlie's standard repertoire is that involving objects and other people. Of these it can be
said that the Charlie of the early stage makes little distinction between the two. His solipsistic-insolent self regards inanimate and
animate nature equally as either tools to be used or obstacles to be
endured. Objects are valued as means of creating havoc. The two
chief kinds are the long horizontal (ladders, planks, mops, dumb-
bells and anything of similar shape that can be employed to knock
innocent bystanders off their feet) and the hazardous stationary
(buckets, doors, movie cameras, spiked helmets and anything else

3.   Chaplin, *My Autobiography*.

that can be tripped over, walked into or sat upon). When not sub-
mitting to being used, objects generally play a meanly unaccommodating role in Charlie's world, seeing it as their duty to frustrate his powers of transformation: a whole film (*One a.m.*) is given
over to his battle with their stubborn recalcitrance. (However, they
are liable, by way of retaliation, to find themselves put to all sorts
of unconventional uses: subjected, for example, to Charlie's cleanliness compulsion—an umbrella, a hotdog and a loaf being among
the objects that get carefully wiped with his sleeve). And people
are the objects at which havoc is directed. Charlie's callous and
aggressive use of others is one of the most prominent characteristics of his behaviour at this period. He is likely to turn people's
heads towards him to solicit their attention; tug them along by the
beard; sling his leg over their laps or bent backs (sometimes with
an overtly sexual intention); wipe his hands on their coat-tails or
beards; strike matches on their chins, bald heads or backsides;
and tap cigarette ash into their hats, hands or open mouths. These
are all of course elements of his incorrigible oddity, all the more
startling for usually lacking either plausible context or provocation. The irruption of such compulsive and irrational clowning
into the Keystone stereotype must have caused not a little consternation (after a beard-wiping gag, a fellow-actor told Chaplin admir-
ingly, 'They've never seen that kind of stuff around there'). But
Charlie was also prepared—or obliged—to muck in with the comedy of physical hostility or indignity that was part of the Keystone
stock in trade. A number of the earliest films consist of little
besides fighting and missile-throwing (in which the chief joke is
that an innocent party must be clobbered or struck). Charlie's
contribution to this mayhem was his proficiency in the art of
the kick, whether delivered (in *Mabel's Busy Day*, having floored
Chester Conklin, he proceeds to put the boot in, in a thoroughly
scientific manner) or only intended (detected in the act of raising
his foot, he will gaze at it with innocent curiosity and readjust it
with his cane, or start briskly dusting his trousers). It is hardly
necessary to add that Charlie is a recipient as well as a dispenser,
of physical indignity: both he and his enemies are equally liable to
ordeal by water, fire or custard pie.

I have been trying to describe the comic business of the basic
Charlie, the one to whom the earliest audiences responded so

unreservedly, but have been unable to avoid suggesting at the same time some lines of development. For some of the business (for instance, that connected with his costume) hardly changed at all throughout his career, and some of the developments started early. The surprising oddity, the random eccentricities that contributed so powerfully to his presence, were there from the beginning: in his very first film, *Making a Living*, the only one in which he wears a different costume (a moustached and top-hatted milord) he licks his lips appreciatively after kissing a lady's hand; turns the newspaper editor's head forcibly towards him; pounds the same gentleman's knee for emphasis, and replaces it when it is withdrawn; and allows his shirt-cuff to slide down his cane before deftly retrieving it. This now looks like standard behaviour, but they certainly can't have 'seen that kind of stuff around there'. But there is decided change. It takes the form of increasing refinement, range, complexity, poetic suggestiveness and dramatic relevance; and it operates in virtually all the areas I have described. Charlie's face, for example, becomes susceptible to a greater range of expressions: the vacant, insolent and shrewd give way to the look of calm absorption in the eccentric activities that to Charlie are work (usually including an element of the knowledgeably off-hand) to expressions of genuine interest in the predicaments of others, and finally to delicate registrations of his own feelings of hurt, rejection and loss. In *The Bank*, the restrained mortification with which he witnesses Edna's casual disposal of the bouquet he has left her has always been recognized as a milestone in the evolution of the comedy of feeling. And in a similar fashion, his whole body is put to increasingly subtler uses. I find it hard to believe, as Theodore Huff has claimed, that Chaplin actually taught his fellow comedians at Keystone how to fall without hurting themselves: such knowledge must surely have been part of every comic's stock in trade. What is certain is that an almighty amount of falling about goes on in the early films, and that Charlie contributes more than his share. But the scene of his tumble from the ladder in *The Pawnshop* is of a different order. It is part of a work operation: he is polishing the all-important golden balls and rocking the ladder back and forth in order to reach them. And it is a balancing act that builds up a fine momentum of suspense as we wonder whether he is going to maintain his equilibrium or not. At the climax he turns setback into mastery, retrieving himself with a smart backward somersault as he lands in the road. Charlie's bodily movements take on inexorably the qualities of the acrobatic and balletic. A good example of the latter is his use of the shoe department's sliding ladder in *The Floorwalker*: it suggests irresistibly the action of the skater, and he shoves it along with an appropriately elegant swing of the leg.

Charlie's use of people and objects—his relation to the world he inhabits—undergoes, at least in part, a similar change. Where people are concerned, although his attitude to women moves from the undisguisedly lecherous to the gallant and solicitous, his attitude to men remains conditioned by their usefulness to him rather than their intrinsic interest. Though he does develop a nice line in comradely rivalry, characterized by practical jokes and high-spirited larking about. His relations with Syd, his co-worker in *The Pawnshop*, are of this kind: the fights with which they beguile their working hours are not the vindictive booting and walloping of the early films but cleverly choreographed performances that enable Charlie to try out his classy prize-fighter impersonation. A vein of sly mockery attends even his treatment of the adored Edna in the same film: he pretends to have broken his toe with one of her doughnuts, then surreptitiously hoists it, weight-lifter fashion, into the air. While even the tetchy pawnshop owner, persuaded by Charlie's pathetic mime of non-existent dependants to rescind his dismissal, is rewarded by a loving hug for which the legs are enlisted as well as the arms. The last of the Mutuals, *The Adventurer*, seems at first like a reversion to an earlier type. Being concerned with chasing, fighting, the disruption of decorum and a running feud with Eric at his most Mephistotophelean, but it also contains a prolonged and stylish variation on the comedy of physical indignity, in a gag which is for Chaplin unusually calculated and elaborate. This is when the blob of ice-cream he drops down his trousers, and which we can sense from the play of his expression is working its way down his leg, lands upon the amply exposed back of a lady on the terrace beneath and disappears down her dress: Eric's misguided attempt to retrieve it being rewarded by a clout from her husband, and Charlie above being able to indicate to the alarmed Edna his detached disapproval of the unseemly imbroglio. As well as a refined elaboration of the physical discomfiture joke, this is a good example of Charlie's magical immunity from blame for the consequences of his actions. Where objects are concerned, the chief change is that his use of them tends to become ever more creative and fantastic. *Behind the Screen*, for example, is a movie-making film in which the chief element is the comedy of drama-confusion, or Charlie's largely innocent playing of havoc with someone else's deliberate performance: the presence of movie cameras provides plenty of opportunities for hazardous stationary object gags, and that of the trap door (administered by Charlie) contributes its predictable complications. But Charlie is the property man, to and his treatment of the props is a good demonstration of how he had discovered other uses for objects than the merely aggressive. Ordered to collect up chairs, he contrives to sling so many round his arms and across his back that he ends up looking like a human porcupine, and the bear–skin rug he is detailed to brush is subjected to a hilariously elaborate session of *haute coiffure*, as Charlie, attending with diligent engrossment to hair partings and shampooing procedures, launches into his barber shop act.

The porcupine chairs and the laundered rug are examples of metaphorical gags, which I have already mentioned, as Chaplin's chief contribution to the repertoire of silent comedy business, and as being the ingredient that provides his films with their pervasive air of poetic suggestiveness. These gags are the ultimate refinement of Charlie's art. It is of their nature, however calculated they may have been, to seem inspired and improvised. Their effect is to provoke in the audience a simultaneous impression of absurdity and fitness, and they are the reason why to watch a Chaplin film is to experience a series of pleasurable shocks. They make their appearance from the very beginning of his career, but the general tendency is for Charlie to move increasingly from off-the-peg gags to this kind of creative improvization, which, being addressed to a specific situation, is not susceptible to classification. The metaphorical gags themselves change in the films of this period—are refined, elaborated, prolonged—and reach their ultimate perfection in the great comic sequences of the mature films. The best idea of their evolution will perhaps be obtained from a brief examination of a series of increasingly complex instances.

At its simplest, the comic metaphor is a product of Charlie the traditional fool's child-like, pre-rational habit of thought, which prompts his putting a given object to a use that though incongruous, is related to it by a leap of imaginative association. This is what is happening when he casually wipes his nose on the doormat in *His Trysting Place*. The same sort of thing, but rather more disturbing, is the moment in *A Film Johnnie* when the film crew that Charlie has gate-crashed dash out to take advantage of the dramatic possibilities of a real-life fire: their opportunism strikes us as a bit callous, but Charlie's contribution, which is to warm his hands at the blaze, seems even more so. The contrast between the action that his habit of association has so naturally prompted and the distressing circumstances serves to emphasize his unamenable oddity. Charlie's professional roles, when he embarked upon them, provided him with activities that intensified his responsiveness to the metaphorical habit. In *Laughing Gas* an anaesthetized patient suggests the need for boxing ring revival procedures, and is ministered to with a flapping towel; in the same film the extraction pincers are employed to secure a pretty girl-patient by the nose so that Charlie can kiss her—it is their grasping properties that inspire him here, and the gag is also a good example of Charlie's shrewd eye for any kind of erotic advantage. In the later films of the period, the metaphorical habit runs to extended episodes. *Behind the Screen* is an interesting example because it is concerned, in a self-conscious way, with aspects of comic filmmaking that were already considered historical. The film culminates in a prolonged custard pie fight ('this highbrow stuff', one actor calls it) between rival members of the crew—Charlie's gang and Eric's gang—and the idea of a battle gives rise, on Charlie's part, to the practices and rituals of real-life warfare—he sternly surveys the field through binoculars improvised from a pair of bottles, and waves his handkerchief for a truce before getting in a sneaky extra shot. The old-fashioned knockabout is cleverly stylized and dignified by the association.

There is probably no need to dwell upon what is perhaps the best-known example of Charlie's metaphorical habit, his dissection of the clock in *The Pawnshop*. It has been extensively described and analysed and it is certainly one of his most brilliant passages of virtuoso comedy. Apart from its sustained ingenuity, and its self-conscious prominence in the film as an example of Charlie's professional skill, the point I want to emphasize for the moment is that it is a multiple metaphor. The skills that Charlie devotes to his clock-repairing efforts include the surgical, the disinterestedly scientific (like a demonstration in biology), and what at moments appears to be the culinary. The object keeps shifting its function as his stern and confident fiddling proceeds, until the whole mess, in its final disintegrated state, is given up as a bad job. Finally, an example of a metaphorical gag that includes a variety of other comic elements turns up in the sanatorium scene in *The Cure*. Charlie, stripped for massage and the cold plunge, takes refuge from Henry Bergman's beefy masseur (whose arm-flailing energy bears for his taste all too aggressive a stamp) inside one of a series of curtained cubicles. A number of times in rapid succession, the curtain is pulled back for his capture, and is promptly restored by him. This action, together with his state of undress, unavoidably suggests to him the *tableau vivant*, so that at each disclosure he is found striking a different theatrical pose, including his attitude of coy propitiation, and sterner ones that could be by Rodin. He finishes the proceedings with a neat pirouette by way of acknowledging applause. This high-spirited episode stands out from the rest of the film in which one of Charlie's sourer selves prevails, and its interest is that to metaphorical wit it adds an imaginative use of Charlie's face and figure, and a strong sense of his compulsion to display and of his power to reduce function to dance: demonstrating in a short space many aspects of his art that I have been considering.

The Threefold Charlies

The solipsism and arrogance of the Charlie discussed above are qualities of what I have earlier called the first Charlie, his primary incarnation. And another profitable way of examining the Keystone-to-Mutual films is in terms of the threefold classification I proposed in the previous chapter, that is, of Charlie's aristocratically insolent, creatively high-spirited and fully human selves. It would be tempting to posit a neat identification between these three versions of Charlie and the three companies—Keystone, Essanay, Mutual—for which he worked during this period. But when we try to see the process as pure progression, we find that there is actually a great deal of overlap, anticipation and anachronism. Just as his three selves can hardly ever be completely distinguished in a given film, so each cannot be exclusively assigned to a particular period. For example, the final appearance of the first Charlie in his purest form is in a Mutual film. This is *One a.m.*, which is also celebrated as his only solo performance. Considered as the valedictory appearance of the first Charlie, it *has* to be solo, since the Charlie of this period has formed a capacity for sympathetic relations with others that could not be abandoned. The film is basically an elaborate version of Charlie's drunk act, its vindictiveness mitigated by two novel circumstances—that only material objects are involved, and that Charlie is thoroughly worsted. In *One a.m.* the first Charlie's lordly disregard of vulgar realities barks its shins against hard facts: it is he who finds himself subject to the transforming powers of maliciously animate matter. The furnishings of the opulent mansion that he enters with such an air of proprietorship take on a life of their own: the decanter on the revolving table coyly eludes his grasp; he is hit with terrible persistence by the pendulum of the clock on the landing; the carpet wraps itself around him and delivers him neatly, like a parcel, to the foot of the stairs. The perseverance he displays in overcoming these obstacles is truly heroic: defeated by the stairs, he scales the hat stand mountaineer fashion; and learns to crawl underneath the pendulum to gain his bedroom door. The first Charlie, veteran of so many skirmishes, goes down fighting.

It is the second Charlie to whom many of the best films of this period give expression, and he is the one to whom I am most conscious of doing an injustice in this abbreviated account. Although he is a transitional figure in the progress of Charlie's relationships with others—representing the playful camaraderie that comes between insolent indifference and sympathetic concern—he is also a figure who is attractive in his own right and full of (one could say bursting with) comic potential. The hallmark of the second Charlie is that his eccentricity takes the form of an unpremeditated larky inventiveness, and a superfluity of high spirits giving rise to an abundance of high jinks. The lack of premeditation is important to our sense of him. One would say that the stories of the films in which he appears are merely excuses for the comic business, if it were not that one feels he would behave in the same way without any plausible context or occasion at all: it is a sign of these films that the ostensible action is frequently forgotten while Charlie *performs*.

This version of Charlie gives abundant expression to the aspect of display. I am thinking of such moments as the juggling with the ham bone in *Shanghaied* and the dissection of the clock in *The Pawnshop*: these are self-sufficient demonstrations of expertise. The second Charlie seems to me to appear in his purest form in the Essanay *Work* and *Shanghaied*, and the Mutual's *Behind the Scene* and *The Pawnshop*. The flow of high spirits in these films is dictated partly by the degree of menace to which Charlie is subjected, and this in turn is usually determined by the role of Eric Campbell. In *Work*, despite the ominous opening, in which Charlie in silhouette is seen pulling the wagon and Eric up the steepest of hills, their relationship is unusually friendly, and Charlie proceeds about his paper-hanging business with cheerful nonchalance (and with a predictable propensity for wreaking messy havoc); his chatting-up of Edna is accompanied by a nicely casual manicure act with his plasterer's trowel. In *Shanghaied*, the whip-cracking Eric is very much a threatening presence, and it is during his respite from the threat, as galley-hand, that Charlie's creative flights emerge: his acrobatic serving of unspilt soup, and, especially because so purposelessly, his juggling act and impromptu hornpipe. *Behind the Screen* finds Charlie and Eric again in a wary alliance, in which the threat that Eric represents is sufficiently reduced for Charlie to be able to take imaginative liberties, by measuring Eric's girth and checking it against the huge collection of lunch time pies he proposes to consume, and then, from a typical instinct of metaphorical association, beating a tattoo upon the empty pie tins. In this film, his affectionate interest in Edna is given a new piquancy by his penetration of her disguise as a boy: their resulting kiss gives Eric an excuse for a surprisingly coy display of misunderstanding. Finally, in *The Pawnshop*, the threat of Eric is relegated to the unimportant plot element, and to the end of the film, leaving Charlie —his relations with his fellow-workers almost entirely benevolent—free to weight-lift Edna's doughnuts, put the dishes through the wringer, do his championship fight act with Syd, polish the golden balls, and, in a variety of distinctive and resourceful ways, alienate the customers. The strong current of creative display is recognized at the end of the film, and offered for endorsement, in the pirouette with which he invites applause for thwarting the evil Eric. *The Pawnshop* is a treasure-house of second Charlie gags, and the purest expression of his spirit.

The third Charlie, the sympathetic and sensitive one, makes his first appearance surprisingly early. *The New Janitor*, made towards the end of his year with Keystone, is one of the most successful films of its period: a neat little drama of robbery and rescue, standing out by virtue of its relaxed tempo and unostentatious comedy. The early scenes establish the eccentricities of Charlie's professional role of janitor, as he knocks on the office door after entering, juggles the waste bin with his foot, spills its contents on the floor, and gathers up rubbish and important documents indiscriminately—all done with a nice and telling casualness. His later intervention in the attempted robbery include the well-known moment when he covers the criminals with a gun extended be-tween his legs (a gag repeated in *The Immigrant*, but perhaps more striking in this context). The third-Charlie elements are his roman-tic attachment to the stenographer (whom, this being a period in which fantasy predominates over realism, he is allowed to keep), and the moment of his threatened dismissal by the boss, when he is saved from the chop by his pathetic mime of the number and height of his dependent children: I had mentally marked this as the third Charlie's debut before finding confirmation in *My Auto-biography* that it was the moment when Chaplin himself first became conscious of the new capacity for feeling of the character he had created.

The New Janitor leads naturally to a consideration of *The Bank* and *The Tramp,* to the first of which its story clearly served as a model. These best-known Essanays are the ones which exhibit the third Charlie in his earliest substantial shape. Both films exploit the pa-thetic possibilities of Charlie's disappointment in love. In *The Tramp* he is usurped by a handsome rival (it will not be for the last time), and left to make his familiar exit down the deserted road; while *The Bank* contains the famous close-up of his doleful expres-sion as he watches the stenographer curtly discard the flowers he has left her. Both films also contain a lot of unsentimental comedy issuing from Charlie's professional roles of, respectively, farm hand (he extracts milk from the cow by pumping her tail) and janitor (he wreaks havoc among the customers with mop and bucket, in a nice series of long horizontal object gags). The trouble with both films is that the pathetic element is divorced from the other elements, and thrust a little too obviously upon our attention. The looming close-up of Charlie witnessing the collapse of his hopes is genuinely touching, but also a bit of an embarrassment, insisting as it does upon feelings that are too strong for the rest of the film to assimilate. The problem of the successful integration of comedy and feeling (or, in different terms, fantasy and realism) was one that Chaplin was never completely to solve. *The Bank* offers a characteristic solution, by means of which Charlie is allowed to enjoy his triumph in fantasy: dreaming of an attack by thieves, a heroic rescue, and a final embrace in which, on his awakening, the girl turns into a mop. Here the collapse into reality is a comic one, which mitigates the intensity of the earlier scene. But we are still left feeling uncomfortable, registering both that the problem has been evaded and that it could not easily have been overcome. The full emergence of the third Charlie was to involve niceties of tone and balance that Chaplin had not yet mastered.

It is to the three films considered later in this chapter that we must look for Chaplin's most successful expression, in the short film form, of serious feelings in comedy. The third Charlie is never wholly absent from the films of the Mutual period (except perhaps from *One a.m.*, but rather than discuss the nature of his appearance in this or that film I want to draw attention to a generally neglected film in which he plays an important and unexpected part. This is *Police*, to my mind the best of the Essanays, and a film that narrowly fails being classed among the best short films of all. The story begins with Charlie's release from jail, and goes on to show his enlistment by an old cell-mate in the task of burgling the mansion inhabited by a flimsily clad Edna and her sick mother. The comedy of what follows is excellent second Charlie stuff, deriving from Charlie's typically eccentric notion of the burglar's role and accentuated by the contrast between his companion's conventional loutish furtiveness and his own breezy nonchalance of manner. Charlie's burglarizing is both pedantic and indiscriminate: the two laws of burglary to which he subscribes being that anything that is locked must be opened, and that burglars take everything. Accordingly, he gets to work on the piano with a brace and bit, and submits the oven to the subtle manipulations of the safecracker; and, ordered to make a final round-up of loot, he gathers up promiscuously a pedestal, a stove, a lamp and vase-fulls of flowers, and tries to lift the piano for good measure.

The third-Charlie elements in this episode are partly a matter of the realism with which the clandestine nature of the enterprise is conveyed (Charlie has a panic attack when his flexed cane first fetches him an alarming wallop on the back of the head and then twines itself around a heavy vase and brings it crashing to the floor); but then revolves mostly, as one might expect, around the personal interest that Charlie takes in the frightened and fetching Edna. He defends Edna against the violent attentions of his friend, and is rewarded, on the unexpected arrival of the police, by being introduced as her husband. This enables him promptly to assume a wonderful attitude of proprietorial familiarity, lighting a lordly cigar and tapping the ash into the sergeant's outstretched hand. Edna's softening influence induces him to renounce his criminal career (though he is not too romantically stricken to indulge a sly glance as she extracts a coin from her stocking, or to bite it experimentally before giving way to an expression of rapture), but his disguise is penetrated and the film ends with a routine rumpus. An even more striking incarnation of the third Charlie comes earlier, in a surprisingly realistic doss-house scene, when Charlie tries to gain free admission by feigning the symptoms of consumption (imitating the genuine consumptive who precedes him in the queue). This grisly sequence is reputed to have formed part of a feature-length film, planned and abandoned at about this time, which was to be called *Life*. The surviving fragments of this enterprise are described by Robert Payne ('the greater part would take place in a doss-house among thugs and ruffians') and John McCabe.[4] *Life* seems to have been an interesting early attempt of Chaplin's to incorporate the more sombre aspects of his experience into his art: but the apparent portentousness of the enterprise prevent one from regretting that it never materialized. Chaplin probably realized that he was not yet ready for anything so ambitious. But the impulse to treat the seri-

4.   *The Great Charlie* (London: Deutsch, 1952); John McCabe, *Charlie Chaplin* (New York: Doubleday; London: Robson, 1978).

ous and grotesque aspects of life was obviously strong in him, and
finds its expression in this attractive little drama.

The Films' Dramatic Qualities

The gradual process of refinement and elaboration that I have
been tracing in Charlie's comic business, and in the range of feelings available to him, is also discernible in the dramatic qualities
of the films. By these I mean both their subject-matter and their
structure. The two elements cannot help going hand-in-hand, as,
indeed, do all the other aspects of Charlie's art treated in this chapter. For it is obvious that extensions in the quality of Charlie's comedy and feelings would be impossible without an extended range
of experience for them to feed upon—that is, an enlargement of
the subject-matter of the films. And new subject-matter suggests
the need for new methods of dramatic arrangement. The process is
the same as that described by Harold Lloyd as the transition from
'gag pictures' to 'story pictures':[5] that is, from films that were contrived occasions for standard jokes to films with a consistent narrative, plausible motivation and behaviour, and a reasonably natural atmosphere. The change is very evident in Chaplin's films of
this period. His simplest Keystones, in conformity to the Keystone
mould, were either location impromptus, films in which the action
was spontaneously, but mechanically, generated by a real-life setting, such as a race track (*Kid Auto Races, Mabel's Busy Day*), a ball-
room (*Tango Tangles*), a street (*Between Showers*) or a park (especially a park: *Twenty Minutes of Love, The Fatal Mallet, Recreation*),
comedies of crude intrigue, usually involving sexual rivalry or extra-
marital hanky-panky (*Mabel's Married Life, Those Love Pangs*) or both
at once (*Getting Acquainted*). The comic action consisted largely of
fighting, chasing, the infliction and the suffering of physical indignity and the general disruption of order. Chaplin was not able to
break the mould until he left Keystone altogether and gained independence for his ideas, and a stock company of character types, at
Essanay: even then it did not shatter all at once. But even at Keystone, in a few of the best films, he was learning how to escape
from the stereotyped house-style. And what made escape possible
was his discovery of Charlie's capacity for professional roles.

5.   *An American Comedy* (London: Longman, 1928).

At one time, if asked which activity provided the impetus for the majority of Chaplin's short films, I would have replied 'imposture', so central to our sense of Charlie does the imposter's role seem. But curiosity prompted me to embark on a rough classification of the films (aided by Theodore Huff's filmography for those I had not seen), and the surprising result was that the answer should be 'professional activity'. It turned out that Charlie's professional roles constituted by far the largest category in the tabulation: imposture coming well down the list, after such headings as drunkenness and love rivalry. Even allowing for the rough-and-readiness of the enterprise, and the large degree of overlap between categories, it was a thought-provoking conclusion. And it received decided, if surprising, confirmation in an article I subsequently turned up. This is one of the most unlikely sounding items in the Chaplin bibliography: Harry A. Grace's, 'Charlie Chaplin's Films and American Culture Patterns'.[6] He assigns each of Chaplin's 76 films a number and offers, with commendable thoroughness (if with daunting solemnity), a statistical analysis of their attitudes and preoccupations, with the aim of relating these to those of American society at large. His conclusions are genuinely interesting, if not always very remarkable ('Chaplin's films cast suspicion upon authority figures in business and public affairs'). But it would be too easy to make Grace seem ridiculous, and in view of my confession above I had better not accuse him of unnecessary labour ('What need'st thou run so many miles about/When thou mayest tell thy tale the nearest way?'). I am grateful, at any rate, for the conclusion which adds his professional certainty to my tentative reckoning: 'Of the 76 films made by Chaplin, fifty-seven per cent concern job situations or economic behaviour.' I can only conclude that I was misled in my earlier estimate by the probable fact that the eccentricity with which Charlie is want to tackle his professional tasks, and his uncertain tenure of them, make them *seem* like impostures.

So if we look at the Keystones again in the light of this fact, we see that the very best of them—those that survive today in their own right, and not as curiosities of Charlie's art—are professional role comedies: *Dough and Dynamite, Laughing Gas, The New Janitor.*

6.   Harry Grace, 'Charlie Chaplin's Films and American Culture Patterns', *Journal of Aesthetics and Art Criticism* 10 (1952), pp. 353-63.

And the same is true of the best Essanays (*Work, Shanghaied* [a melodrama, but one in which Charlie is *put* to work], *Police*), and of the second-best Mutuals (*Behind the Screen, The Pawnshop*). Of course Chaplin continued to make many excellent examples of other types of film: location comedies (*The Rink, The Cure*) and imposture dramas (*The Count, The Adventurer*). But the attraction of his professional roles is not hard to understand. They provided him with endless material for his imagination to work upon, with new and varied opportunities for his impudent transformations. And the benefits are apparent at every level of dramatic creation: for instance those of comic business, relationships and mood. The activity itself inevitably suggested kinds of comic business (rather obviously in the case of the paste and paper of *Work*, and the confectionery of *Dough and Dynamite*, but much less so in the case of *The Pawnshop*, where professional activity spills over into domestic); gave Charlie natural opportunities to relate to others (especially to girls—whether workmates, like the shop girls on whose bottoms he leaves the impress of his floury hand in *Dough and Dynamite*, or clients, like the pretty patient in *Laughing Gas*—and to bosses); and also, by its nature and the surroundings in which it took place, established an atmosphere that could be assimilated (like the raffish and disorderly kitchens of *Dough and Dynamite* and *Shanghaied*) or, more usually, played *against* (like the stuffily formal bank in *The New Janitor*, and the professional dignity of the dentist's surgery in *Laughing Gas*). At a further dramatic level, that of plot, the picture is more ambiguous. For, although a professional role could itself establish a plausible plot—the professions of banking and pawnbroking readily enough suggest the idea of a robbery, and the profession of robbery the idea of detection and capture—the chief attraction of Charlie's professional roles to Chaplin must have been that they freed him from the necessity of plot. The activity itself—the comedy it suggested, the relationships it involved, and the mood it either sustained or contradicted— were enough to carry the film along. The chief preoccupation of the best 'professional' comedies of the period was still, as with the other types, the disruption of order, but it was more like the creation of a new sort of order than the vindictive and destructive type of disruption so prominent in the weaker Keystones and Essanay. So *The Pawnshop* is almost wholly concerned with the imaginativeness of Charlie's pawnbroking, and his lively relations with his workmates; and the plot element, involving Eric as a sly and plausible client-crook, is relegated to the end, and used to give the film a sense of finishing neatly.

The Chaplin of this period, whether he was aware of it or not, must have been much concerned with questions of structure and shape. He realized that Charlie's professional activities freed him from the stereotype of plot and released his creative energy—the panache and audacity of his clowning is evidence of that. Yet he knew at the same time that a film must have some organizing principle if it is not to seem amorphous and miscellaneous. So nearly all the Mutuals, for instance, 'professional' and other, have at least a residual plot element in order to round them off (without it, one feels that *The Pawnshop*, at least, could well go on for ever). The problem was this: if stories of melodrama and intrigue, while providing shape, were limited and inhibiting; and if stories of spontaneous activity, while giving rein to Charlie's creative energy, lacked shape; what was the element that could give cohesion and unity to a film without damping its liveliness? The answer gradually arrived at after experiment, regression and interludes of apparent indifference (and not necessarily the subject of conscious formulation on Chaplin's part) was significance—the significance provided by a theme. In other words he discovered, as I suggested at the beginning of this chapter, what it means for a film to mean. His first venture into this territory is *The Vagabond*, in which his serious love feelings, up to then peripheral and slightly embarrassing are pushed into the centre of the stage and insisted on, in a story that dramatizes Charlie's proneness to amorous rejection and loss. The other two films are not dramatizations of his appetites or purposes, but of some of the consequences of their pursuit of which earlier films have made us well aware, though not invited us to contemplate so directly. In *Easy Street*, by the simple process of becoming a policeman, Charlie is forced to recognize, and act out the consequences of, his own moral ambiguity; in *The Immigrant* he classes himself with the lowest in order to highlight his station, both desired and achieved, in our inhospitable society. These films are very different in setting, pace and mood. And also in their use, or rejection, of plot: *The Vagabond* is framed by an 'overplot' that sounds unreal but is one in which the details have a more than mechanical significance (as I suggest below in respect of the artist's portrait of Edna); the melodramatic plot element of *Easy Street* is subordinate to a simple conflict of individuals that is also a conflict of moral forces; while *The Immigrant* dispenses with plot entirely—it can hardly be said to have a story, let alone a plot, the burden of its main scene being a powerful but complex current of suspense issuing from the fear of social embarrassment. And I am not offering these three films as being the only ones of the period worth seeing, or without fault. In fact, *Easy Street* seems to me about as perfect as it is possible for a film to be, but I am aware of what can be argued against the comparative thinness of interest in *The Vagabond*, and the awkward construction of *The Immigrant*. However, they are importantly alike both in anticipating the interests and achievements of the later films and in being in their own right decided successes of an original kind.

Chapter 3

Three Mutual Shorts

The Vagabond

This is Charlie's version of pastoral. Everybody who has written or thought about the film recognizes that it has a special atmosphere that sets it apart from the other films of the period, and that this distinction has to do both with its unusual rural setting and with the feelings of love and the loss of love with which the action deals. It is Chaplin's first thoroughgoing essay in the comedy of feeling, in which the feelings in question predominate and ask to be taken seriously. This fact, together with its apparent poverty of comic business—it has little of the hectic pace and unflagging inventiveness of the other Mutual films—has led to its being probably as much disliked as liked. Even its admirers seem a trifle embarrassed about their advocacy, and puzzled to explain exactly what it is they find so striking. It is clear, from the prominence which I assign the film in this chapter, that I count myself among its admirers. It seems to me to be the first of the three unquestionable masterpieces of Chaplin's Mutual period, and what follows is an attempt to justify this claim. One way of countering the charges of sentimentality and poverty of interest is to invoke, as I have, the concept of pastoral, and to suggest both that the conflicts of feeling—between different kinds of love, and between the qualities of rural and urban life—always associated with this mode are present in the film as operative forces and that the mode itself, once the film is placed within it, lends its formal and traditional sanction to the feelings exhibited. Another defence is to point to the fact, which nobody disputes, that elements of the drama—its relationships and feelings—anticipate those of some important later films: in particular *The Kid*, *The Circus* and, to a lesser degree, *City Lights.* And these anticipations strike me not merely as incidental but as interesting qualities in their own right that make one think afresh about the nature of their subsequent resurrections. Quite apart from its importance in the developing pattern of Chaplin's *oeuvre*, *The Vagabond* seems to me of outstanding interest in itself, as a dramatization of essential Chaplin themes, which are treated with a subtlety that has not often been recognized. Among other things, it has a fine dramatic structure and flow, and I want to start by considering these.

The opening scene must seem to everyone at first a sort of irrelevance, a piece of warming up, so discordant with what follows does it appear. The action is so devoted to chase and knockabout, and the set so cramped and confined—a long narrow bar, a long blank wall, a truncated street corner, a pair of swinging doors—that the passage seems to have strayed from an early Keystone. But first appearances are deceptive. This beer-hall scene has the obvious dramatic function of establishing Charlie's roles for this piece: the familiar ones of city-dweller and scavenger, and the rather more unusual one of professional performer. The comedy of the episode arises from the innocence of Charlie's scavenging: he is unaware that he is competing with the German band and creaming their profits, and the irony of his innocence culminates in his politely soliciting a contribution from the band-leader whose takings he has just purloined. The rest of the action concerns his nimble and resourceful efforts to escape their justified wrath while still, with typical Charlie prudence, hanging on to the cash. Two points can be made about this scene. The first is that, whether intentionally or not, the claustrophobic confinement of the beer-hall set provides an appropriate contrast to the alfresco sunniness of the scenes that follow. The second is that Charlie is subjected to disorientation and danger (abused and attacked in the course of his lawful business), and so seized with a pressing need to escape. Both he and we are ready for a change of scene.

We are hardly prepared for the extent of the change. Charlie next appears at the edge of a sunny field where, across a fence, Edna is busy scrubbing clothes in front of a gypsy caravan. The incongruity of Charlie's appearance in such a spot is aggravated

by the fact that he appears, in so unlikely a context, still to propose to practise his vocation. His eccentricity is emphasized by his
politely knocking on the fence before clambering over. This could
be seen as an importation of urban habits into country life: at a
deeper level it is more likely an expression of Charlie's child-like
habits of association—you always knock before you enter (just as,
in *Shoulder Arms*, you always close a door behind you, even when
its surrounding wall is missing). Once admitted, he proceeds to
serenade the fascinated Edna, first relating to her in his role of
performer. His performance is characterized by an energetic bravu-
ra that would not have disgraced Paganini. His furious bowing
generates an automatic physical momentum, like a piece of over-
enthusiastic gymnastics, or a machine out of control: ending up
with his toppling backward into the wash-tub (from which, before
his later reprise, he is careful to keep his distance). This (literal)
overspill of energy is both delightful and alarming, and highly
characteristic of Charlie when possessed. The theatricality of the
enterprise is emphasized by his applause acknowledgment act, as
if the whole thing were being enacted at the local Alhambra, complete with exits and entrances from behind the caravan (as well as
a nose wiping gag with his bow that is a nice lightning 'metaphor',
suggested unavoidably by the abrasive properties of the instrument). Edna is clearly enthralled by the performance, but she
equally clearly doesn't know what a performance is: there is a gaze
of mutual incomprehension when he holds out his hat for her
offering.

Charlie's canoodling with Edna, including his favourite trick,
from his repertoire of sexual invitations, of dangling his leg over
her lap, is interrupted by the arrival of the bullying gypsy chief
(Eric Campbell) and the wizened crone (Leo White in heavy disguise). We have already seen them at work tyrannizing the hapless
Edna. They make an amusing double act. Eric does his usual scowling and swaggering act, aided in this case by a huge whip whose
ministrations are doled out indiscriminately to friend and foe. His
ferocity is, as usual, compelling enough, but the rest of the gypsies
are on the whole a farcical and ineffectual bunch. After Eric,
Leo's hag is much the most successful in her function of combining a pressure of nagging vindictiveness with a proneness to farcical indignity: two of the funniest moments in the film are when

she accidentally gets on the wrong end of one of Eric's whip-cracking fits, and when, in pursuit of the purloined van, she trips flat on her face, bringing her fellow pursuers down on top of her. It soon becomes clear to Charlie that remedial action is necessary, and he initiates his drama of rescue and escape, starting by exchanging his cane for a hefty club. The suspense of what follows derives from Charlie's pitting himself, thus armed, against the gang of gypsy desperadoes. His first victim is lured by the sight of Charlie apparently fishing (with his club) from a rustic bridge, and duly clobbered for his curiosity. The others, including the formidable Eric, are picked off one by one from the bough of a convenient tree along which Charlie has insinuated himself. He has to stretch himself perilously further for each go, and at the last wallop, with an effect probably unintended but wholly appropriate, the club breaks in two, and the momentum of the swing brings Charlie to the ground. There follows the frantic escape in the stolen van, though not before hat, cane, violin and bow have been carefully retrieved.

We are now finished with melodrama and derring-do. What follows, the beautiful central section of the film is Charlie's *idylle aux champs*: his brief period of contentment and peace with Edna. This scene anticipates those vignettes of ideal domestic life that crop up in later films—the shack by the swamp and the dream of suburban bliss in *Modern Times*, and, more relevantly, the modest rural independence that concludes Charlie's fortunes in *A Dog's Life*. As in these other episodes, the sense of security so lovingly and idiosyncratically created can't help being qualified by a consciousness of the insecurity that has been left behind, or that is waiting to re-emerge. Domestic security has to do with boundaries and exclusions: and the marking of the boundary involves a knowledge of what is being excluded. But the emphasis is upon enjoying the idyll while it lasts; upon the creative act of establishing the domestic base. In *The Vagabond*, the idyll is saturated with a sunny sense of rural contentment and peace, and characterized by the knowledge of mutual need and a devotion to the practical arts of self- sufficient living. Any hint of idealization is mitigated by the highly characteristic eccentricity of Charlie's accommodations to rural life. These are, as one might expect, remarkable for their casual poetic suggestiveness and their creative ingenuity. After a prickly night in the hay, a rake suggests itself to Charlie as the natural instrument for scratching his back; and the breakfast eggs are transferred to the pan by a sharp crack from the tool-box hammer (what else are hammers for?). Most ingenious of all, and central to the episode, is the chequered shirt, which, spread neatly over an upturned barrel, and with its sleeves converted into undetachable napkins, gives the alfresco dining arrangements the right touch of *haute cuisine* elegance. This inspired improvization calls to mind Charlie's conversion of his bedspread into a splendid house robe in *The Kid*, and communicates, for all its oddity, a similar feeling of fitness and congruity. Also reminiscent of *The Kid* is the way in which his affectionate relations with Edna are established. It is done in terms of his favourite washing ritual (which, I suggest later, must surely be based upon personal experience—it is certainly common experience to which it appeals). Edna wakes up in a disgracefully dirty and dishevelled condition, bleary-eyed and scratching. Declining Charlie's offer of the rake, she proceeds, before his astonished gaze, to indulge in the skimpiest toilet in the annals of cleanliness—dipping a tentative finger in the water and running it around each eyeball. Stern measures are called for. Edna finds herself forcibly dunked in the bucket and energetically scoured, with that particular attention to the facial orifices that is Charlie's trade-mark. The episode—funny, satisfying, and not a little alarming (it is our own mothers we think of)—beautifully establishes both Charlie's solicitude and Edna's dependence: qualities the significance of which I enlarge upon below.

The idyll is not destined to last. But the threat, when it comes, is to its inner stability, not its outer. The rural peace is invaded not by the disreputable underworld of gypsy desperadoes but by the respectable world of civility, elegance and accomplishment. The well-bred, well-dressed artist, hungry for inspiration, whom Edna encounters on her expedition to the stream, is captivated by her beauty, and she by his charm. Attention turns to the effect of this development upon Charlie. It is at this point that the film begins to incur the charge of sentimentality. Opinions will always differ about this point, but my own conviction is that, when the events depicted are studied without prejudice, the charge cannot be justified; that, on the contrary, the potentially maudlin situation is handled with delicacy and tact. A feeling of jealousy at the threatened loss of love is not uncommon, nor in itself sentimental, but it can be self-indulgent. What saves Charlie from self-indulgence is a mixture of unaffected 'straight' acting, farcical interruptions and the habitual eccentricity of his accommodations to new experience. The straight reaction comes over with fine under-emphasis at his introduction to the well-meaning and likeable intruder, when Charlie's instinctive disquiet, and a dislike that he knows to be unreasonable, are tempered by a consciousness of the forms of politeness: his troubled expression conveys his knowledge that a threat that is private cannot be acknowledged. The embarrassment is all in the situation itself. The moments of farce, which always serve to mitigate the seriousness, arise from Charlie's inability totally to suppress his frustrated dislike. While Edna and the artist are engrossed in conversation, agitation forces him to get up and wander moodily around, covertly flick dead flies at his rival as the only available alternative to kicking the cat, and finally plant himself unwittingly on top of the burning hot stove. But the chief form his jealousy takes is, as often happens with his serious feelings, that of comic-poetic suggestiveness. His instinctive reaction to rivalry is imitation. The artist embarks upon a portrait of Edna, and Charlie has a stab at his own. The result is something like a child's portrait of Mummy. It is the sheer clownish crudity of the artefact, its total but unwitting remoteness from representational fidelity, together with the hopeful seriousness with which it is offered that saves the episode from sentimentality. We register that the moment is painful and embarrassing for Edna, but for us it is largely ludicrous. Charlie's portrait is associated with an earlier, and even more bizarre, imitation routine, when, in his fit of sulks, he begins a doodle on the side of the van that turns into a game of noughts and crosses. The irresistible reminder here is of *The Face on the Bar-room Floor*, where the same routine is enacted for much the same reason, but on a vastly larger scale. It is an example of Charlie's instinctive habits of thought, which in turn are conditioned by the incorrigibly low-class nature of his experience (it being one of the clown's prime functions to bring us down to earth). High art is just a sort of doodling, and doodling inevitably suggests that common occupation of a child's idle hour. Noughts and crosses is the only kind of visual art that Charlie knows.

At the end of the film, Edna's wealthy and elegant mother, of whom we have earlier had sporadic glimpses, recognizes her child from her portrait and comes to reclaim her. The high society world of the framing 'overplot' is brought into contact, as it inevitably must be, with the decidedly low-class world of Charlie the vagabond. The embarrassment of the subsequent collision of cultures cannot be so easily disposed of. The feelings of the actual moment of encounter are enlivened by some characteristic touches of farce: in his stupefaction, Charlie drops an egg on the shoes of one of the top-hatted socialites, and finds the gloved hand he is called upon to shake extended at an apparently impossible elevation. But the basic incongruity won't go away. And the difficulty of the problem is reflected in the trouble Chaplin evidently had in selecting a suitable ending. He apparently experimented with but never included, one in which Charlie, left alone, chooses suicide by drowning, and finding himself rescued by the formidable Phyllis Allen (the Peggy Mount of the Keystone era), plunges back into the drink. He must have realized that such a farcical conclusion, while dissipating the sentiment, would not have solved the problem of the relation between the disparate worlds. The ending he chose does not solve it either. It is probably true, as others have suggested, that the best ending would be for Charlie to be left alone, philosophically bearing his loss—or perhaps returning to the role of beer-hall serenader—and that the problem (which is to recur at the end of *The Kid* and *City Lights*) is in the last resort insoluble. There are no means by which we can be persuaded to accept Charlie as a permanent inhabitant of the world of fashion and wealth.

Yet for all this, the mother, the artist, and their posh friends are essential to the meaning of the film. The story to which they belong is of course in many respects ludicrously unreal, a stereotyped fantasy of popular literature and drama. Jean Mitry lists some melodramatic films of the period, dealing with abduction and recovery, that may have influenced Chaplin's choice of plot.[1] Yet it is essential to Chaplin's theme that he make a genuine attempt to bring Charlie into relation with the larger world of 'serious' affairs (however inadequately conceived). What the theme is, is

1.   Jean Mitry, *Tout Chaplin: tous les films, par le text, par le gag, et par l'image* (Paris: Seghers, 1972).

suggested by my calling the film at the beginning a version of pastoral. That is, the world of sunny rural tranquillity and seclusion, with its virtues of simplicity and self-sufficient industry, is set against the complex urban world of wealth, elegance and leisure. If this were one of Chaplin's feature length films, the duality would probably be complicated by all sorts of factors: as we have seen, it is customary for Charlie both to desire and fear each half of the equation in his metaphorical balancing acts. Here the emphasis is upon the insecurity of the isolated rural idyll and its vulnerability to the disintegrating and complicating effect of outside forces. Yet a feeling grows and persists, as Edna's friendship with the artist blossoms, that there is a world of sophistication and ease to which it is *proper* that she should belong: Charlie's unease registers this much, as well as his jealousy. And the theme of two ways of life is closely paralleled by that of two kinds of love. Edna's relation with Charlie is basically one of child-like dependence. The child-likeness of her relations with others is established from the beginning, when we see her as the cowed and compliant drudge of the bullying gypsies. And this impression is reinforced by Charlie's stern instruction in cleanliness and table manners, which so closely resembles the schooling of Jackie in *The Kid*. Charlie offers Edna a parent-like refuge, different from the gypsies' in being benign. Her love for Charlie is love as dependence upon the known and secure: but her love for the artist is love as fascination with the unknown and glamorous. The artist offers her the excitement of adulthood. And again, we can't but feel it proper that Edna should be allowed to grow up. (This is an idea that adds its own incongruity to Edna's insistence, in the ending decided on, upon returning to reclaim the abandoned Charlie: it does credit to her compassion and loyalty, but is at the same time a bit like wanting to sleep with one's teddybear).

That the conflicts of feeling that I have called the 'meaning' of the film are present in it may seem obvious enough. They did not have to be consciously intended to be expressed, and do not have to be consciously registered to be felt. But they, or something like them, are elements of the response of everyone who pays the film a more than superficial attention. What can easily be missed, and has not so far as I know been remarked on, is that in addition to the pastoral theme and the love theme, the film has an art theme.

It dramatizes two conflicting conceptions of art in a way that relates it to *The Circus* quite as strongly as the Charlie–Edna–Artist triangle (so clear an anticipation of Charlie–Merna–Rex). One of the French titles of *The Vagabond* is *Charlot Violiniste,* and this should prompt us to wonder why Charlie is made a violinist in the film. It cannot only be because of the importance, to which Chaplin has testified, of mood music in his conception of his films; or because of the instrument's associations of melancholy and seriousness of purpose. It is in order to establish him in the role of performing artist. Put simply, Charlie embodies art as performance, and the artist embodies art as representation. Performance suggests improvization flux, continuity with life: representation suggests deliberation, fixity, separateness from life. Charlie's practice of art as a function continuous with life is beautifully expressed in the scene of his serenading of Edna. His impetuous tumble into the bucket is a metaphorical leap from art into life: he can't, and doesn't want to, distinguish the energies appropriate to each. Edna's reaction is significant, and introduces the interesting way in which the art theme relates to the love theme. She is delighted by his performance, but alarmed by its tendency to spill over into life (which Charlie takes in his stride): she is too inexperienced to appreciate his concept of life as continuous creativity (which includes the creativity of his parental ministrations). Performance, momentarily enjoyed, is then forgotten. The artist, on the other hand, offers her something she can appreciate: his portrait, determinate, and detached from the flux of time and life, gives her a permanent image of herself as individual and desirable. This is his value, and the value of his picture (whose function as the agent of Edna's reclamation is a mere dramatic device). This conflict, like the others in the film (and all Chaplin's films) cannot be said to be simply resolved. Charlie recognizes both the necessity and the usefulness of representational art (it is the cause of his losing his girl), but he is hopeless at it, just as, later, he is to be hopeless at performing standardized circus tricks. Yet his own art, which can call upon the energies of the uncivilized boundary, displays an abundant liveliness that the tamed art of the civilized centre lacks. In this film, as in general, Charlie's art is an art of life: his performance never stops (and the eccentricities of his musicianship are indistinguishable from those of the rest of his behaviour). The balance of gain and loss is nicely judged. But enough has been said to show how this little comedy, apparently so simple and pure, embodies some of its creator's deepest concerns.

Easy Street

This film has never lacked admirers. It is the ninth of the 12 films that Chaplin made for the Mutual company, but it has for us something of the effect of a culmination. Its inventiveness, energy and rhythmic vitality mark it out as something special, the consolidation of a working period short in time but rich in profitable experience and cultivated instinct. It could have been called *Police*, and bears a clear relation to the earlier film. In it Chaplin succeeds in doing what he had failed to do in *Police*, tackling head-on the problem, endemic in his films, of order and chaos as they show themselves in social behaviour by dramatizing his uneasy allegiance to each. The result is a film of remarkable purity, centring upon a single conflict of forces whose simplicity and emphasis hardly seem to call for an elucidating commentary. It is also the film that appeared to herald a period of greater deliberation, a checking of the hectic speed of Chaplin's production: 8 of the 12 Mutuals were issued between May and December 1916, but only 4 between January and October 1917. Of those still to come, only *The Immigrant* approaches *Easy Street* in significance and intensity.

The intensity is striking and memorable (people remember bits of *Easy Street*, and can identify them, when the rest of Chaplin has become a blur), and it serves the significance. It resolves itself, when pondered, into two images: the ludicrous image of Charlie as a policeman, and the terrifying image of Eric Campbell as the implacable bully. And the significance resides in the interaction of the qualities that these images express: Charlie's diffident, uncomfortable relation to his policeman's role, and his predictably unconventional notion of its duties; and the brutal and anarchic disorder of *Easy Street* that Eric represents. These are the images and ideas that go to make *Easy Street* the best-remembered, as well as one of the best, of Chaplin's early shorts.

A policeman's uniform is perhaps the least likely that we expect Charlie, in the course of his professional life, to assume (unless it

be a clergyman's, which duly follows in *The Pilgrim*). Law enforce-
ment agencies are a prominent feature of that established order
with which he usually finds himself at odds: policemen are wont to
rank with thugs in his catalogue of menaces. So *Easy Street*, registering as it does the realization that one of a policeman's functions is to protect people from thugs, can be said to mark an advance in Charlie's habits of thought. But it would be too much to
expect Charlie to plunge directly into so incongruous a role, with
the careless ease with which he turns waiter or handyman. Some
mediating experience must intervene. The agency of mediation,
with which the film begins, is the Hope Mission.

The Hope Mission, in the film's polarity of value, stands at the
opposite end to *Easy Street*. It serves to dispense the refinement,
civilization and charitable amelioration that the Street, until Charlie's advent, has found little trouble in resisting. There is a long-
suffering look about the Mission's officers, together with the high-
mindedness, which suggests the intractability of the material they
have chosen to reform. Their function in the drama is to make
possible Charlie's assumption of a new role, by redirecting his way-
ward energies into morally orthodox channels. One of the officers
is Edna, doing her saintly lady bit in an anticipation of *The Kid*,
and it is hardly a surprise if her beauty contributes as much as the
minister's eloquence to Charlie's 'conversion'. Charlie is already
susceptible: the wondering expression on his awakened face, with
which the film begins, may be his reaction to the promise of shelter and a meal, but it may also register his pleasure at the music
he hears issuing from the Mission. And he ends by being 'born
again' with a theatrical show of conviction.

What the opening episode concentrates on, however, is his wari-
ness. Charlie judges the Mission, as he judges everything, in his
own peculiar fashion, which means bringing to bear upon this
new experience a mind at once alert to suggestions of his own
advantage and singularly free from preconceptions. It follows that
the item of furniture that most attracts his attention is the collect-
ing box, which he weighs judicially in his hand as it passes down
the line. His grasp of the proceedings is incomplete, to say the
least. Just as later, in *City Lights*, the night-club menu will suggest a
hymn-book, so here the extraordinarily diminutive hymn-book suggests something to be idly thrust into the pocket, like a bus-ticket:

later to be proffered helpfully to the neighbouring baby, to assist it in following the service. By Charlie's pre-rational code of reasoning, baby-sized books are for babies to read. As so often in the films, his innocence, while risible, is felt as a strength: issuing as it seems to from obscure modes of thought which modern man has discarded. His culminating solecism is to spoil the effect of his emotional conversion by producing the appropriated collecting-box from his trousers.

Charlie's enlistment in the force does not come easily, despite his softening up at the Mission. Between spotting the appeal for recruits and actually entering the station he undergoes a period of painful indecision. His little comedy of hesitation, as he parades irresolutely in front of the station, the action of entering converted at the last moment into a brave show of unconcern, is a beautiful example at the way the maturing Chaplin enlarged the authenticity of his clowning, and its range of sympathetic reference, by appealing directly to the audience's experience of similar embarrassments. Once inside, and suitably kitted out, he still finds the need for puzzling adjustments. The duty sergeant's back-slapping bonhomie is interpreted, inevitably, as evidence of aggressive intentions, and is answered by a reproving rap on the knuckles, and an indicated willingness to take off his jacket and step outside. Charlie's instinctive defensiveness is sharpened, but hopelessly misled, by the polite usages of civilization. His assumption of policehood, however, cannot be long delayed: eventually, fired by zeal, he issues from the door. It is wholly characteristic that his first arrest should happen at once, and that the victim be a passer-by convulsed by his incongruous appearance. The offender is summarily felled and despatched: Charlie believes in getting maximum credit for the smaller jobs before proceeding to the larger ones. And it doesn't strike him as wrong to use his newly acquired powers to punish threats to his personal dignity.

The larger job is Eric. He must be in more than one sense among the largest problems that Charlie, or anyone, has ever had to face. In no other film is Eric Campbell's huge bulk employed to greater advantage. It is impossible to over-estimate the contribution this dependable actor makes to the drama, in what is probably his best, as it is certainly his most memorable, performance. Eric is formidable enough, in all conscience, in the other films of the period. But in those he is usually given a social role—guest, waiter, boss—that puts at least some constraint upon his power to terrorize. In *Easy Street*, to terrorize is his profession—he hasn't any other. There is nothing to hold him back, and everything to spur him on. His crowd of admiring hangers-on are both an audience for his theatrical acts of terrorism and a reminder that his reputation and local standing are staked upon his keeping his position as top neighbourhood bully. So to Charlie's image of dubious and vulnerable authority he opposes a sensation of implacable vindictiveness that is truly frightening in its violence. Swarthy, cocksure and cruel, he exudes an air of physical menace from which his incongruously tiny hat can only partly detract. He immediately rivets our attention, agreeably chilling the spine with the promise of mayhem and massacre.

Eric eats policemen for breakfast. Our first glimpse of him is as he towers Colossus-like from the midst of a melée of incredible liveliness and extent, briskly sorting bodies and cracking heads. Evidence of his handiwork, in the form of dazed and damaged policemen, is carted into the station in an unending stream while Charlie is undergoing his induction. This riot is an unnerving sight, as well as a funny one, but the air of business-like efficiency in this glimpse of Eric at work suggests that it is an average everyday occurrence to him—his equivalent of opening the morning post. We are offered a brief but memorably vivid picture of a world in which unbridled aggression is the stuff of life. So the tension of an inevitable collision of opposites—Charlie's half-hearted legality, Eric's self-confident anarchy—has already built up to a fine pitch before the principals eventually meet in the deserted street.

The suspense of the scene that follows is tantalizingly prolonged. Its comic ingredients are Charlie's subdued but increasingly nervous awareness of menace, and Eric's baffled but patient containment of aggression. Charlie soon forms the opinion that reinforcements are needed, and reaches gingerly for the sidewalk telephone. Together they act out a little comedy. Eric, heavily suspicious but content to await positive proof of a hostile intention, contrives to miss noticing each of Charlie's desperate lunges for the earpiece. Charlie, finally securing the instrument, is obliged to convert his calls for help into a guilty pretence of inspecting or cleaning it. The suspense seems to be broken when Charlie, taking advantage of Eric's preoccupation with the telephone, fetches him an almighty wallop on the back of the head. But Eric still puts off the moment of reckoning. In other films the Eric figure is as much a buffoon as a menace (and hence so much less of a menace). Here he is certainly not a buffoon. But he is given a nice line in gallows humour as he obligingly offers Charlie alternative areas of his impenetrable cranium to bludgeon. Charlie dutifully complies, but with diminishing conviction. Bells ring and dams burst as Eric, tired of playing, grimly rolls up his sleeves and prepares to demonstrate his knot-tying on the lamp-post. It is what leader-writers call the moment of truth. Charlie, his native cowardice released, kisses his enemy's huge fist in an idiotic act of appeasement.

In the battles with Eric and his ruffians that follow, Charlie is able to survive because of his ambiguous position in our world. In *Easy Street*, which is a film about morality, public order and the containment of passions, this is specifically a moral ambiguity. Charlie is able to beat the denizens of *Easy Street* because he is even more alien to respectable society than they are. Indeed, despite their intimidating show of anarchic disorder, they are part of respectable society, and not only in having houses, wives and children: their code of conduct is simply an obstinate reaction to that of the Mission, and to that extent they subscribe to its rules. Charlie, who comes from beyond the boundaries of civilization, can afford to subscribe to neither, or to both. He is not just another villain: he is cleverer than the other villains, and moreover has no exclusive devotion to villainy, being equally accommodating to virtue and vice. So he is free to enlist unrighteous tactics in the cause of righteousness, as well as to take creative advantage of circumstance and accident.

Charlie's using, to render Eric insensible, the gas lamp that Eric himself has obligingly yanked within reaching distance, is the first crisis of the film, and provides its best-remembered moment. And Charlie's triumph over Eric is not simply the triumph of brains over brawn, but of freedom over habit; or more significantly, of poetry over prose. For Charlie's brisk seizure of opportunities is made possible, as always, by a poetical habit of mind; his calculations are based upon the association of ideas. The gas lamp suggests medical anaesthesia, which in turn prompts the image of a tranquillized Eric. Translating the image into reality is the work of a moment. The metaphor established, Charlie follows it through: his doctorly role dictates a consultation of the patient's pulse, and the diagnosed need for an extra infusion.

This brief moment is a beautiful instance of Charlie's creative powers. And it establishes him immediately as a person of consequence in the Street: the balance of conflict swings into his favour, and he is able to move over to the offensive. There is more than half the film to go, but from this point on his mastery is not in dispute. Not even Eric's return from captivity (rousing from his stupor and, Samson-like, casting off his bonds), though it causes Charlie some awkward moments, is a serious threat to the outcome. There is some very smart chasing up and down stairs and around the houses, and at one nasty point Eric locks them both in his living room and theatrically swallows the key. But Eric is eventually silenced by an almighty whack on the head from a cast-iron stove that Charlie has manhandled to the window: an act of extravagance that is another example of Charlie's pre-rational logic—his adversary's strength and bulk suggesting a missile to match. The final mopping up of riff-raff, whose kidnapping of Edna prolongs the threat to order, is accomplished with the help of a doped hypodermic, on which Charlie, during the tussle with the addict, unwittingly plants his rear end. While not normally resorting to stimulants, he doesn't object to turning them to advantage. He is galvanized into a beautifully balletic display of energy and vigour, a choreographed succession of wallops and kicks, culminating in a clinch with the swooning Edna.

'Love backed by force, forgiveness sweet/Bring hope and peace to *Easy Street*': the film's coda offers an image of order in its absurd extremity, echoes the extremity of anarchy that it replaces. It is scarcely believable, but it is satisfying to see Eric in his Sunday best escorting his missus to the Hope Mission under Charlie's cordial gaze, remembering politely to manoeuvre himself to the outside of the pavement. Like so many of Chaplin's films and many comedies in general, this one ends with an agreeable fiction that we are invited to enjoy without taking it too literally. But its status as fantasy does not alter its necessity. *Easy Street*'s achievement is to dramatize, with power, imagination and wit, its audience's deep-seated fear of irrational violence: and to organize the feelings it arouses it needs images of peace as well as havoc. The film's complexity issues from the recognition, focused in Charlie himself, that its polarity of values is not absolute. Charlie belongs as much to the Street as to the Mission, and the conflict of allegiance we witness is inside him as well as outside: the perplexity he exhibits is partly about which role he should be playing. *Easy Street* emphasizes an aspect of Charlie's character that later films both exploit and explore: his moral ambiguity.

A related issue that this remarkable film touches upon, and that Charlie's spirit illuminates, is the question of active benevolence. The Hope Mission is a hive of do-goodery, dispatching innocents like Edna to aid and relieve the local unfortunates. Charlie is far from callous, and fully capable of disinterested acts of compassion: arresting a woman pilfering from the grocer's stall, he proceeds, after hearing her pathetic history, to help her fill her bag himself (his earliest deviation, this, from his newly-acquired policeman's role). But his attitude to poverty and deprivation is not quite the same as the Mission's. Helping Edna dispense alms to the proliferative family of a weedy denizen, he doesn't set them in a frame of sentimental patronage, but responds to what he sees. The swarming kids suggest to him farmyard fowls, fit to be fed by the scattering of grain, and the dispirited father's reproductive efforts are rewarded with an improvised medal and a congratulatory handshake. This nice vignette demonstrates, again, Charlie's unusually large freedom from preconceptions, and the imaginative directness of his reaction to experience. It also emphasizes the margin of independence he invariably preserves between his usages and ours: however far he strays into our centre, he is never ours to keep, but is only on loan.

As well as looking back to *Police*, *Easy Street* looks forward to *The Pilgrim*. And the later film sheds an interesting light on both of the earlier ones. The purity of *Easy Street*, remarked upon earlier, derives from its being a struggle between extremes—high-minded goodness on the one hand, unbridled aggression on the other— symbolized by the two 'before and after' image, of Street in action, What is missing is any representative of 'normal' life—'good' without embodying an impossibly lofty virtue. Its omission intensifies the effect (so we don't really regret it) but simplifies the issue. *The Pilgrim* complicates the issue by playing out Charlie's moral drama against the background of Edna's and her mother's comfortable and secure middle-class home; and adding to the contest of good and evil the factors of an innocence that must be respected and a social etiquette that must not be breached. In doing this it takes up the challenge of *Police*, which is also about—or starts to be about —Charlie's attempt to prevent a villainous pal disrupting Edna's 'normality' and innocence. Both films even feature a sanctimonious clergyman, whose hypocrisy is a disorientating factor in Charlie's moral education. *The Pilgrim* takes over where *Police* leaves off. But one can guess that *Easy Street* had to come in between, if only because, unlike *Police*, it forces itself to face the powers of chaos, and gives them a solid and frightening shape.

The Immigrant

As well as one of the most successful, this is one of the most realistic of the Mutual comedies, but its realism is not what one might at first imagine. It appears to offer itself as a realistic rendering of the experience of the impoverished European immigrant to the United States at the time of the greatest influx. It has relevance, even authority, as a social document, and may well have been based upon Chaplin's personal observation. But its realistic status is qualified in a variety of ways; and its centre of interest, as often with Chaplin, is quite as much a generalized human predicament, which it does not take special knowledge to sympathize with. The representative quality of the action is emphasized by the similarity between the immigrant's deprived condition and Charlie's habitual vagrancy. Charlie is a professional displaced person, and the indignities suffered by the historical immigrants are very like those that he encounters everywhere.

Yet the differences are important too. Charlie is set signally apart from his companions by virtue of his dress, behaviour and reactions to events. His dress is his standard incongruous costume, his behaviour eccentric, and his reactions inspired by his own peculiar blend of self-interest and altruism. The film falls into two obvious sections—the scene on the boat and the scene in the restaurant. And in both of them the emphasis is upon Charlie's relation to the types of realism presented. Putting it schematically, one could say that on the boat the 'immigrant' realism is qualified by Charlie's oddity, while in the restaurant the 'social' realism is qualified by his display. The boat brings out his familiar mastery; the restaurant, his narrow avoidance of defeat.

The scene on the boat opens with an inspired joke: viewed from behind leaning over the side, straining and writhing in the throes of a fearful convulsion, Charlie appears to be being miserably sick, but turns out, as he swivels round with a triumphant grin, to have been bagging a particularly uncooperative fish. (This 'false pretences' gag turns up later in *The Idle Class*, with weeping substituted for vomiting.) As well as providing a rousing start, the joke could be taken as emblematic, in that it wittily dramatizes Charlie's relation to the immigrant experience—that of someone who is in important respects immune to its privations. This point is developed below.

The opening joke is one of a series based upon sea-sickness—a phenomenon to which Chaplin's imagination returns, in this sequence, with a sort of fascinated persistence. The others mostly involve a Russian-hatted fellow voyager (the reliable Albert Austin), whose miserable heavings at one point induce in Charlie a progressively sympathetic nausea, until they are retching in unison; and who at another point is only narrowly prevented from evacuating his dinner into Charlie's hat. A neat variation is the adoring smile, bestowed by Charlie upon the newly encountered Edna, which a message from his stomach converts into the unmistakable signal of a desire to spew.

These sickness gags could be said to be inspired as much by the idea of the boat as by the conditions of immigrant travel. They are Chaplin's poetic imagination at work, abstracting and elaborating the concepts conventionally associated with the situation in hand. Boats irresistibly suggesting sickness, the idea is pressed into service, with ingenious variations, in the creation of comedy. A similar suggestiveness dictates Charlie's luxury cruise manner, when we first see him, inhaling lungfuls of air as he negotiates the huddled bodies on the heaving deck: boats are for promenading and healthy exercise. The ease with which he maintains his balance in this episode is also a demonstration of a familiar Charlie skill. For boats mean loss of equilibrium, and equilibrium is the central Chaplin symbol—in this case, of the relation between the conditions of immigrant life and Charlie's resistance to their depressing coercion's. His promenading manner is a typical piece of display.

So it is linked symbolically with the scene in the galley, where he utilizes the rolling of the boat to sample his neighbour's victuals as they slide across the table towards him. Found food is as welcome to Charlie as found money: and his innocent purloining of provender gives a fresh face to the phrase 'balance of advantage'. Both his instinct for advantage and his lordly disregard for unpleasant conditions call for the skills of the equilibrist.

There is quite a lot of action in this sequence, which clearly does reflect the typical experience of the immigrant. This includes the dicing and card-sharping scene (gambling must have been a popular means of passing the time); the theft of Edna's mother's money (presumably a hazard of the crowded conditions and motley human cargo); and the moment of arrival in New York (when the rough sorting and herding of the passengers induces Charlie to turn a disbelieving gaze upon the Statue of Liberty).

This last moment is always remembered as a satirical comment upon heartless officialdom, who see the arriving hordes as an indiscriminate aggregation, distinguished only by identity discs and fit to be roped in like cattle. The scene certainly has this moralizing force: but what is interesting is that it is the only piece of comedy in the film that does (which is why it sticks in the mind). Most of the comic action, rather than emphasizing Charlie's identification with the immigrant's lot, seems devoted to exhibiting his irreducible difference.

Charlie differs most obviously from his fellow travellers in his dress. It doesn't occur to us to ask where he's come from, but wherever it is his customary hat and cane seem to have been the only luggage considered necessary for a hazardous Atlantic voyage. (In this the film prefigures *The Gold Rush*, where his foray into the frozen waste demands only the addition of a pick and shovel to his standard outfit.) More interestingly, he appears to be to a large extent immune to the hardships endured by his companions, as his promenade deck manner testifies, as well as the fact that he only suffers nausea by suggestion. In this respect the opening joke is particularly suggestive, representing as it does Charlie's wilful insulation from the events around him. It is Charlie's demonstration of his freedom from circumstances, as well as one of the recurrent instances of the traditional clown's invulnerability. Allied to his independence is his instinct for survival, shown by his food-filching in the galley and his settling of Mack Swain's hash in the card-sharpers' quarrel. And at least two episodes inspired by immigrant experience exhibit the quality of contradiction, that is so basic to his nature: his card-playing is a ludicrous mixture of sophistication and naivety, his showy cutting and shuffling being followed by a fumbling incompetence in dealing; and equally typical is the blend of romanticism and shrewdness in his second thoughts about how much money he should slip into Edna's pocket—even his altruism being balanced against his advantage.

Charlie's apartness removes him from too direct an involvement in the feelings displayed. The opening joke sets the tone because it suggests the light-hearted way in which Charlie approaches the privations of immigrant life. His ultimate independence is what relieves him (and us) from feeling the full burden of his misfortunes. His experiences on the boat count as successes in his endless battle with discouraging circumstances. He finds there opportunities for creative display, personal advantage and an altruism inspired by gallantry and affection. His awakened interest in Edna, and impulsive intervention in her fortunes, gives rise to one of the most thoughtful comic incidents in this sequence. This is the neat multiple irony of Charlie's apprehension by the steward for what appears to be daylight robbery but is actually an act of selfless generosity (he is caught with his hand in Edna's pocket), followed by the putative victim's discovery, not of a loss, but of a providential gain. The bemused steward finds himself in the position of witnessing an evident crime and having the testimony of his eyes authoritatively discounted. (Such confusion of appearance and reality looks forward to the fairground scene in *The Circus*, where the complications are even more elaborate.) Apart from its obvious comedy, this episode is a dramatization of Charlie's moral ambiguity. According to your point of view, he is either thief or donor, and in a total perspective the two together. We know that he is capable of both thieving and giving: and in the idea of his being charged with perpetrating a wrong that he is actually redressing, innocence and guilt become wittily combined.

Full of interest as the boat scene is, it is really only a prelude to the scene in the restaurant that occupies the remainder of the film. This is one of the finest passages of comedy in the films of this period. Like the boat scene, it can be interpreted in terms of the experiences of historical immigrants, who, in their foreign environment, must often have incurred the feeling of social embarrassment on which the restaurant scene is based. But it is also a familiar Charlie situation, and capable of being viewed as another round in Charlie's battle with unaccommodating social conditions. In the pattern of the drama it marks his move from a context in which he exercises confident mastery to one where his chief feelings are of insecurity and fear.

Charlie in the restaurant is doubly at a disadvantage: he is both impoverished and eccentric, neither of them qualities calculated to go down well. He is further unfortunate in encountering, in the inevitable Eric Campbell, a monitor of behaviour whose vigilance in detecting improprieties is matched by his willingness to regulate them with boot and fist. Eric turns in one of his dependably boorish performances, lumbering about with a scowl of sour irritation, venting his impatience with eyebrow twitchings and flicks of his cloth. (He is always at his best when called upon to be thoroughly disagreeable rather than, as elsewhere, ingratiating: here there is little call for charm and absolutely no sign of it.) The duel between Charlie and Eric, as usual teasing and prolonged (but, unlike in *Easy Street*, restrained up to a point by the compunction of social decorum), provides the action of the scene. Also as usual, it is the threat of violence suggested by the very sight of Eric's intimidating presence that gives the action its suspense.

Our attention is first of all focused upon Charlie's ignorance of the rules governing behaviour in restaurants (this is another trait common to immigrants and clowns). It takes a forcible demonstration from Eric before he can be prevailed upon to remove his hat, and then his compliance is rebellious and partial, giving him an opportunity for his familiar hat-springing gag. The meal that next begins starts out as a double act, with the dependable Albert Austin playing the part of straight man and foil. Charlie's fastidiousness is offended by Albert's soup-slurping, and Albert's sense of propriety disturbed by Charlie's method of bean consumption —first singly with his fork, then in shovelfuls with his knife. Together, after their preliminary mouthfuls, they enact a comically aggravated case of Burnt Mouth—a nice appeal to common experience. Charlie's later eccentricities include dusting his loaf with his sleeve (a gag from his standard repertoire), and, in a piece

of clownish logic, covering his coffee cup with his saucer to avoid
dunking his elbow in it. None of this endears him to Eric. The
basic comedy of tension between oppressive social custom and
Charlie's pre-social habits is soon enriched by complicating elements.

The first of these is the discovery of Edna, despondent and in
mourning, at a nearby table. This rearouses all of Charlie's amorous gallantry, the invariable spur to his display, but tempered in
this case, after he registers her condition, by a feeling of tender
solicitude. Display takes the form of a supercilious second order of
beans and coffee, by way of demonstrating to his beloved that he
knows his way around, and is not intimidated by types like Eric,
and then of a show of devoted attention, as Edna relates the
chronicle of her misfortunes. But Edna's chief function is to be a
mute but agitated witness of the accumulating embarrassments
that are now visited upon Charlie. She is both embarrassed on his
behalf and herself a cause of his embarrassment: since one of his
preoccupations, in stemming the tide of violence that threatens to
engulf him, is to maintain, where she is concerned, the pretence
that all is as it should be. He alternates frantically between placat-
ing or postponing the savage importunity of Eric and exhibiting
towards Edna the required mixture of composure and courteous
concern. Edna, of course, is not fooled, which adds to the burden
upon her: and in a film in which the role of Edna the actress
is necessarily limited to restrained expressions of sympathy and
alarm, it is a pleasure to record how well she does it.

What precipitates the sudden danger to Charlie's tranquillity
and physical integrity is the episode of the drunken client. This
feckless unfortunate, having phlegmatically demonstrated his inability to pay, is treated to a viciously elaborate version of the
bum's rush. After serving successively as punch-bag and football to
Eric and his mates (a melée in the course of which, predictably,
the manager gets clobbered out of turn) he is escorted without cer-
emony from the premises. The terse reply to Charlie's politely
anxious enquiry ('He was ten cents short') produces misgivings
that turn out to be only too justified when he discovers the hole in
his pocket through which the vagrant coin, on which his hopes
were pinned, has vanished. After the witnessed display of violent
retribution, its loss seems a threat as much to his life as his dignity,

and the film's sense of suspense is increased. Charlie's initial collapse is followed by a series of desperate expedients—hasty re-
hearsals of boxing skills, and a whole repertory of delaying tactics
—of which Edna is the compassionate but agitated witness: his powers of improvization are tested to the full. Even the unexpected
recovery of the coin, fallen from another diner's pocket, provides
only an illusory relief: Eric's practised teeth, compressing it into
a right-angle, demonstrate its treacherous falsity, and the cycle of
menace and procrastination begins all over again.

The arrival of the plump and prosperous artist (or theatrical
manager, according to which print you see), who is so smitten by
Edna's appearance, seems at first to be only an additional complication. He is somebody else to whom Charlie must pay polite attention while staving off the threat of Eric and his unsettled account.
But the artist's offer to pick up the bill introduces a new dimension of hope. Charlie's troubles finally seem to be over. However,
it takes all his talent for social miscalculation to plunge him back
into the dog-house, by overdoing the convention of courteous refusal. A beautifully comical ballet of offer and refusal concludes
with his benefactor actually believing him, and Charlie's once
again being left to settle his bill with an insufficiency of funds. The
solution is one that is, characteristically, provided rather contrived,
in the form of a further instalment of found money, on whose a
appearance Charlie can nearly always rely when in extremity. A
quick calculation reveals that the artist's tip will pay Charlie's bill
by itself, leaving a second tip (ceded by Charlie with a gesture of
lordly condescension, as his instinct for display resurrects itself) to
whose inadequacy Eric's disgruntled expression bears witness.

This restaurant scene has a virtuoso brilliance and must rank as
one of the best comic episodes that Chaplin had created so far its
dramatic qualities are growth and complexity. A changing and fluc-
tuating sense of suspense is provided by Charlie's relation to the
threat of Eric: first his solecisms and clumsy accommodations to
the restaurant code, then the prolonged evasion of threat neces-
sitated by his evident lack of cash. And the vagrant coin that is
found, lost, regained, damned as false and finally supplanted by
a more providential 'find' provides a sense of surprising and complicating reversals. The scene's emotional qualities add their deeper resonance. Charlie's affectionate relations with Edna—his gal-

lantry and attentiveness—together with his celebration of food consumption as a social art, are pitted against the surly and brutal incarnation of social conformity that is Eric. It could be said that two
of Charlie's invariable appetites—food and women—are brought
together and affirmed as values against the insensitive rigidities of
the restaurant code. But as in *A Dog's Life* (of which *The Immigrant*
is a small-scale anticipation) it is the third appetite, money, on
which attention is focused. It bridges both worlds and means different things in each. The film dramatizes the treacherous function of money. Charlie needs it not just for simple sustenance but
for the politeness it buys from slobs like Eric, as well as to bolster
his histrionic assumption of luxury and ease but his possession of
it is invariably volatile—now he has it, now he doesn't—and he
relies for rescue from his accumulating embarrassments on its
being handed to him, literally in this case, on a plate. Money, although treacherous, usually turns up eventually: that is its talismanic function. The paradox of its relation to Charlie's experience
seems to be that *because* he doesn't have it and makes no attempt
to earn it, he can rely on getting it in the end.

The relation between the restaurant scene and the boat scene is
partly, as has been suggested, one of contrast. Charlie moves from
a transient world in which he is familiar and secure to a stable one
in which he is despised and outcast. But there are important con-
nections as well: the final feeling is not only of discontinuity but
also of relationship. At the level of the realistic immigrant theme,
Eric's sour indifference, which only money will soften, is representative of the social world to which the immigrants are bound. At
the level of Charlie's appetites and purposes, both scenes revolve
around the losing and finding of money, with the neat touch that
in the first Charlie is the giver and in the second the receiver (for
his gift to Edna is as providential to her as his discovery of the coin,
and then of his benefactor's tip, are to him). The restaurant scene's
purpose is to add and diversify. To the theme of found money it
adds that of found food, with its associations of ritual and celebration. And, one could say, a found woman. For the affectionate
relationship between Charlie and Edna, tentatively established on
the boat, is confirmed in the restaurant. It is a triumph of the third
Charlie's humanizing art, tender but unsentimental, and itself
contributing, in Edna's restrained alarm and Charlie's anxiety to

placate her, a humorous complication to the comedy of the scene. So it is appropriate that we should be left with just the two of them at the end of the film, vacillating in the rain outside the marriage licence bureau: Charlie sly and cajoling; Edna frightened and bashful, before allowing herself to be borne bodily through the door. It is a genuinely touching moment. Only the bureau official's face, impenetrably severe and bald, hints at the hardships the immigrants have still to meet.

Chapter 4

First National

Pay Day and The Idle Class

This chapter is devoted to the films that Chaplin made for the First National company between 1918 and 1923. It was a critical period in his evolution, as in the evolution of film comedy generally. Seen in the context of his whole career, the products of this period have a miscellaneous and betwixt-and-between look: there are films of all shapes and sizes, on a wide range of subjects and in a large variety of tones. It was clearly a period of consolidation as well as experiment. What seems to have happened is that his new independence (more complete than that he enjoyed under Mutual), together with the conviction that his art *must* evolve, released creative energies that resulted in a series of ambitious comic dramas of an original kind: but that in the intervals of these achievements, when the momentum could not be sustained, he turned to reliable formulas. One interesting thing is that even the relative failures— the formula films—have qualities that are distinctly new, The lessons of the Keystone-to-Mutual apprenticeship were not forgotten.

I do not offer to deal with all the First National films, and some explanation of the omissions is called for. Two films have had, perhaps unfairly, to be relegated by default. I have seen neither *A Day's Pleasure* nor *Sunnyside* (both of 1919) enough times to pronounce upon them with confidence. All I have seen of *A Day's Pleasure* at all is the steam-boat sequence that was so incongruously spliced into *Shoulder Arms* (ostensibly as a dream interlude) in a pirated print that circulated briefly in the late 1950s. It seems that these early pieces were unremarkable. Chaplin himself described his work on *Sunnyside* as 'like pulling out teeth'.

There is perhaps even less reason to apologize for the scant treatment of *Pay Day* (1922) and *The Idle Class* (1921). They have never been classed among the finest of the First Nationals. But they are very far from being without interest. *Pay Day* has Charlie working on a building site and married to the dragonish Phyllis Allen; solacing his evenings (which need it) with companionable boozing. The building site sequence, which includes Charlie's demonstration, under duress, of miraculously accelerated working methods, is clever but laboured, with little of the spontaneous zest we might have expected. The film's central episode is even less characteristic, but, in its odd way, more interesting. Charlie and his mates are dispersing after an evening's carouse, and take a prolonged farewell of each other on the rainy street. Their expressions are glazed, their movements ponderous; they have trouble with their impedimenta, so that Charlie mysteriously becomes possessed of an alien umbrella, and then finds himself sharing two coats with portly Henry Bergman—a handicap when they wish to go in opposite directions, and Charlie, as the weaker partner, is dragged in Henry's wake. All this seems unduly prolonged, even tedious, until one realizes that Chaplin is not attempting to reproduce his Keystone-to-Mutual manner but to create a gentler, more realistic, less showy kind of comedy. It doesn't quite come off, but was worth trying, and is worth watching. The action accelerates to a more familiar pace with Charlie's attempt to catch a street-car home, when the crush of competing passengers pushes him in at one door and out at the other: he takes refuge in a refreshment stall, which his befuddled consciousness mistakes for the required conveyance, and, in the film's most memorable image, strap-hangs, to the bemusement of the proprietor, upon a conveniently dangling sausage. This is a metaphorical gag as striking as Charlie's best. The final section shows Charlie's attempts to enter his house without waking Phyllis. When the morning alarm does wake her, revealing Charlie still fully dressed, he pretends, with blithe presence of mind, to be preparing to go to work: moving abruptly, in a neat role-switching gag, from stupor to activity. The film ends with Charlie's bluff being called and his taking refuge in a bathful of water. The main criticism of it is that it could have ended at any other point, or have gone on for ever: its lack of centre and direction betray what must be judged the weakness of Chaplin's interest in his subject.

For this reason, despite its greater thoughtfulness and realism, it is less worth discussing than the best Mutual shorts.

The Idle Class is altogether more successful, and nearly merits a longer section to itself. It is the best of the lesser First Nationals. Its title, and its forceful opening images, indicate that it offers to tackle direct one of Charlie's basic preoccupations: that of class. The action consists of the events of a day at a fashionable health and sporting resort. It opens with a neat bit of parallelism that enforces the contrast between the rich habitués of the resort and the lesser breeds who are normally excluded. A variety of posh types are seen arriving by train and being driven to their hotels. But Charlie representing the lower orders, arrives as well, and in as much style as they: while they alight from the compartments, he clambers from the rods; while they drive off in their cars, he cadges a lift on the back. He has his own tatty collection of golf clubs, and his familiar air of lordly condescension announces his determination to colonize this new piece of fashionable 'centre'. There is a sharp satirical edge to all this that promises an interesting confrontation.

Charlie's infiltration of the idle class begins on the golf course. It was apparently the simple idea of Charlie playing golf, coming to Chaplin in just such surroundings, that was the germ of the film. I refer a number of times elsewhere to the fine sequence in which Charlie's numerous golfing solecisms and blunders are blamed, and punitively visited, upon the innocent sportsman he is following round the course: it is the most sustained example in Charlie's experience of the traditional clown's immunity from the consequences of his misdeeds. His involvement takes a more intimate, but no less familiar, form when he is stricken by Edna's beauty as she canters by on horseback; leading him to fantasize a little drama in which he earns her grateful admiration by gallantly arresting her runaway horse. And he is not destined to remain simply an outsider. For Chaplin plays two parts in the film: he is Charlie, and he is a denizen of the idle class itself, Edna's estranged and absent—minded husband. They are two distinct characters, of course, but to every non-Charlie role he plays Chaplin cannot help bringing a substantial portion of Charlie, so the eventual effect is of a sort of multiple Charlie, containing within himself the social division that is the subject of the film. And Chaplin as the Husband has, as it turns out, some of the best jokes and a lot of the comic action. He lends an air of preoccupation and mania to the proceedings. He is the 'tragic' side of Charlie, the one burdened by serious life problems, a sort of farcical Verdoux or Calvero. It soon becomes apparent that the absence of mind with which the titles credit him is a form of psychological insulation from others, revealing itself both as indifference and as ineptitude. The first of these qualities seems indicated in the famous moment when, turning round from what appears to be a paroxysm of grief at reading Edna's farewell note, he is seen to be energetically juggling the cocktail shaker; and the second in his stalking out of his room dressed to the nines in everything but his trousers, and in his managing to get himself impenetrably encased in his fancy-dress suit of armour. The armour, in which he spends a good part of the film, as well as a device to enable the two Chaplins to appear in the same frame, is a good emblem of his mental condition. The Husband is also Charlie's double, and their resemblance the reason for Charlie's being admitted to the ball, encountering Edna, and getting further involved with the idle class.

There is a lot of good comedy in *The Idle Class*, and, although the satirical sharpness of the opening is not kept up, much of it can be seen to serve the theme. I have mentioned the golfing sequence, in which Charlie's immunity is given emphasis by his brisk sporting manner (an observant piece of display), and by his genuine unawareness of doing anything amiss; and the paroxysm gag, whose effect, just as we are persuading ourselves to feel some sympathetic concern, is almost shocking in its apparent cynicism. Another good moment is one that exhibits the automatism that is Charlie's reaction to our world's social conditioning: he is knocked to the floor so many times by Mack Swain in the course of their argument that at last he obligingly lies down before attempting to speak at all—an action instinctively repeated when the butler tries to address him. And the husband's final act of lunacy, when the rest of the cast are striving to extract him from the armour, is to cosset himself against the blows of Charlie's hammer by interposing a tasselled cushion—the manly and energetic associations of hammer on metal being cancelled out by an object that is both effete and useless. He is eventually prised out like a sardine.

Yet the film does not engage us very closely, and is not drawn together very satisfactorily at the end. One problem is that the idle-
classy types are presented with an unusual degree of realism: an
indication that here, as in *Pay Day*, Chaplin was not trying merely
to reproduce a successful formula. There is very little of the familiar farcical exaggeration. We are invited to take Edna's woes
seriously, for instance, so that she spends a lot of the film acting a
Tragedy Queen. This means that Charlie's oddity is more notice-
able than usual, and he is more thoroughly set apart from the
world of luxury and ease. This robs his fantasized rescue and marriage of Edna of some of the poignancy they might have had in a
different context, since here we can't pretend to admit them as
possibilities. Yet at the same time he is deprived of one of his usual
defences, being without the insulation of arrogant indifference
that carried him through many previous encounters. It seems that
Chaplin cannot after all escape the confines of formula, and that
Charlie can neither join the idle class nor beat it. So the problem
of their confrontation is evaded. When the mess is sorted out, and
Charlie takes his leave, we feel that the handshake he accepts from
Mack Swain is his tribute to the new realism of his adversaries; and
the boot on the backside with which he follows it is his last forlorn
attempt to behave according to type. In the past, would he have
shaken hands?

Pay Day and *The Idle Class* were the last two-reelers that Chaplin
was to make. I have suggested that their relative failure is due to
his attempt to do something different that the familiar dramatic
forms could not accommodate, so that they look now like uneasy
alliances between the old and the new. He must already have re-
alised that his future did not lie in films like these, nor even in the
successful three-reelers, of which perhaps the best (*The Pilgrim*)
was yet to come. The comedy short still had a long and robust life
ahead of it, but all ambitious comedians were looking to the feature length film as the new form to exploit. Chaplin had pio-
neered this development with *The Kid*, and he must have known
that his art was evolving towards the feature length treatment of
subjects, and that it was upon the achievement of *The Kid*, with all
its imperfections that he had to build. It is for this reason as explained below that this film is extracted from its chronological
sequence in this chapter and treated at the end.

A Dog's Life

An amplified version of the most characteristic Charlie situation evolved during the Keystone-to-Mutual period. The world of the film is a sombre one. It is Charlie's home ground. Its spirit is expressed in the drabness and dilapidation of its decor. It is a world of repressive and unaccommodating social attitudes. Its money-dominated essence is distilled in those institutions—employment exchange, beer-hall, pie-stall—where the penniless individual can expect short shrift. Charlie, who seems to be its meanest denizen, is impoverished, hungry, harried and subject to both the official hostility of cops and the random hostility of criminals. The comedy of the film issues from the feelings of insecurity, deprivation, vulnerability and frustration engendered by Charlie's situation, which every audience can readily recognize is and share.

As a tale of mean streets and mean lives, *A Dog's Life* is a natural development from the great Mutual shorts. Its opening image of Charlie huddled miserably in the corner of a vacant lot is familiar and central. But although Charlie is shown as unjustly oppressed by our world in its harshest form, his relation to this world is not a simple one. For one thing, he is not just paraded for our pity. Although his corner of the lot is visibly uncomfortable, he occupies it with an air of established proprietorship, and treats it with the gravity and respect due to a home. Feeling a draught, he traces it to a tiny knot-hole in the fence, which he bungs with a piece of paper—ignoring the yawning gaps through which a gale is actually blowing. This incident demonstrates not only Charlie's touching ability to observe the domestic proprieties in an extreme situation, but also his basic oddity and strangeness. His attempted accommodations with our world tend to be of a kind that leave him more alienated than before. He would like to be one of us—if only because we seem to be having a rather easier time of it—but his stubbornly alien mentality keeps getting in the way. His incurable apartness is wryly emphasized by the episode in the beer-hall, when, listening to Edna's plaintive song, he mistakes his neighbour's tearful grimace for a smile, and smiles back, only to find he has committed an unpardonable solecism. Charlie can't decode our messages, and makes a hash of it when he tries. His native idiosyncrasy is one thing that qualifies the pitifulness of his situation, and complicates our response.

Charlie's relation to our world is most precisely defined in the figure of Scraps. Scraps is the film's central image, and its most important addition to the typical situation. Charlie had had a dog once before, a bulldog in *The Champion*, who seemed intended for a similar purpose, but whose dour stolidity and minor contribution prevented it from fulfilling so decisive a role. Scraps is lively and expressive, and her contribution is a major one. Her function is very interesting. Partly it is the simple one of companionship—of mitigating Charlie's solitariness by providing him with an ally against the hostile world.

But they are rather odd companions. Neither of them seem to subscribe to the conventional notion of the man–dog relationship. For Charlie, Scraps is not a pet but a pal. They live together on terms of undemonstrative familiarity, practising a casual but effective kind of mutual aid. Scraps allows Charlie to use her rump as a pillow, and is rewarded by his brilliantly improvised solution to her problem of getting milk out of the bottle (he dips her tail in it). Temperamentally, they complement each other. Scraps is a very human kind of animal (it is her intelligent alertness that discovers the all-important wallet in the first place, and rescues it at the end): Charlie, with his difficulties of communication, and the desperate shifts to which he is reduced, is a rather animal kind of human. Dog and man tend to become identified—at one point, when Charlie smuggles Scraps into the Green Lantern stuffed inside his trousers, with her tail sticking out of a hole, they actually fuse into a single being, a sort of man-dog. The effect is to give poetic definition to Charlie's degradation. The conditions of his life are dog conditions, and the qualities it calls for are dog qualities. Like Scraps, he is an outcast and a scavenger, vulnerable to attack, and reliant for survival on nothing but his wits. Scraps, in fact, is a sort of *Ur*-Charlie. For practical purposes, there is no difference between them.

'It's a dogs life'—and a dog's world. It is the harsh economic regime of our world that forces Charlie to shift for himself. Hard experience teaches him that he is alone, and that such justice, prosperity and happiness as he is likely to enjoy he must create for

Plate 2. *A Dogs Life*

himself. He doesn't flinch from the task. It is not in Charlie's nature to take anything lying down, and the battles he provokes with our world's heartless indifference form the substance of the film. He sets about the fulfilment of his human needs with characteristic nonchalance. The downward, or depressant, trend of feeling induced by his degraded situation is countered by a strong upward drive of optimism released by the energy and ingenuity with which he struggles for his due. It is the tension between these two sets of feelings that gives the film its particular dramatic life. Charlie's running battles with our world involve the whole range of his basic concerns, and lead him into both defeats and victories.

Work, we have seen, is one of Charlie's major concerns. He wants to work. He knows it is the only respectable means of obtaining a share of our world's satisfactions, and he wants his share. But in *A Dog's Life*, work is the field in which he suffers his biggest defeat. The employment exchange sequence is justly one of the most celebrated in the film. Attracted by the announcement of brewery vacancies, Charlie smartly contrives to place himself at the head of the burgeoning queue. But when the clerk lifts his hatch and beckons, and Charlie strides confidently forward, he is pipped at the post by a niftier rival. The process is repeated with the second clerk, again with the first, and then in strict rotation. The sequence builds up to a fine crescendo of frustration. And Charlie, in his distraction, acquires a purely automatic momentum, and is still sliding desperately from one hatch to the other when the clerks are packing up to go home. The balletic nature of this sequence, its beautiful precision and timing, has often been remarked (and is agreeably emphasized by the musical soundtrack of the reissued Chaplin Revue). It offers a telling image of our world's smug intractability, and of the power of the conventional work process to reduce the usually quixotic Charlie to the status of an automaton. For once he is worsted, and thrown upon his own devices. Excluded from work, he must seek its benefits through other than the usual channels.

His other defeat is in the field of festivity. Charlie, as we know, has a highly developed sense of the festive. For him, eating, drinking and dancing are among the most serious occupations of life. But in the dog's world his festive inclinations encounter sour discouragement. The local centre of revelry is the Green Lantern, where Edna performs half-heartedly as singer and hostess. The boorish and mechanical mode of enjoyment available here is represented by Edna's jerky style of dancing (with every step her shoulder fetches Charlie a thwack on the chin). Dancing, that basic social rite, is further frustrated for Charlie by a piece of chewing gum that adheres obstinately to the sole of his boot and clamps him to the floor (an image that recalls his dough-stretching efforts in *Dough and Dynamite*, and anticipates his struggle with spaghetti in *The Great Dictator*). Charlie earnestly wants to get into the swing of things at the Green Lantern, but he isn't allowed to. When he attempts to partake of the general ambience by aggressively rolling a fag with one hand, it crumples into an unusable mess. Offering to share his beer with Edna as a polite but thrifty alternative to buying her one of her own, he is given the bum's rush by the impatient boss.

But Charlie's victories outnumber his defeats. Some of his most notable victories occur in the important realm of food consumption. He is forced to be a scavenger and, as might be expected, enters thoroughly into the spirit of the role. He can be said to convert a sordid necessity into a delicate art. His scavenging is marked by resourceful adaptability and professional thoroughness. He asserts his powers early in the film by nicking the hot dogs whose aroma so enticingly penetrates the fence. The inevitable cop is first eluded by a little adroit rolling, and then immobilized by having his bootlaces tied together. This stylish demonstration of expertise is topped by the later scene at the pie-stall, another of film's celebrated set pieces. This episode, in which Charlie decimates the huge plate of pies under the increasingly sceptical eye of its owner, is a masterpiece of suspenseful timing. It plays upon our recognition, at once agonized and delighted, of the feelings involved—of Charlie's hunger and fear of discovery, and the vendor's ponderous suspicion of something vaguely amiss. The focus of attention is Charlie's desperate ingenuity, epitomised by his pretending, at the moment of virtual discovery, to be chasing a fly from the stall. Syd Chaplin's walrus-whiskered pie vendor makes a positive contribution to the little drama, as he gazes in myopic disbelief at his empty plate. His misfortune is to be an innocent representative of commercial respectability, a pillar of that that Charlie is pledged to subvert. The filching of his pies is the least of his troubles. At the film's climax, when the skirmish with the thugs spills out into the street, Syd's stall becomes a battleground: his possessions are demolished and his person soundly beaten up. There is an element of vindictive relish in the extravagance and gratuitousness of the assault to which he is subjected.

Charlie's decisive victory is over the thugs whose loot he innocently acquires. The wallet of money grabbed from the drunken toff is buried on the vacant lot, and later unearthed by Scraps. It doesn't occur to Charlie to inquire about its provenance. For him, as for the thugs, it is providential, the means of realizing a dream (his dream, unlike theirs, being generous and altruistic). For the purposes of the film it is promptly invested with the status of a desirable property, destined to be shuttled from hand to greedy hand. Deprived of his ownership, Charlie resorts to his most imaginative stratagem, which constitutes the film's third set piece. This is the remarkable impersonation scene in the curtained bar alcove, in which Charlie regains the wallet by restoring the unconscious thug to a semblance of life with the use of his own arms. As he had earlier seemed to merge with Scraps into a single beast, so he now assumes the form and faculties of another person. There is no more audacious an example of his versatile powers of transformation. The scene has its suspenseful element (the thug decides to wake up in the middle of the game), but our chief feeling is simple delight in Charlie's mastery, as he creates a character and enacts a drama, wholly in terms of gesture. A particularly nice touch is the tie-straightening action that comes near to throttling the unfortunate thug.

'When dreams come true': the final title ushers in a conclusion that is for Charlie, unusually explicit. But it doesn't matter that this charming domestic vignette has for us the status of a fantasy, and fails to eradicate our more familiar sense of Charlie's deprived and wifeless condition. It forms a quietly satisfying coda to the alarms and excursions of the main piece. Charlie's dream is not grandiose: a modest rural independence is all he asks, and gets. His eccentricity asserts itself even here—in the strange straw hat he wears, the way he props his farm implements against the mantel, and his quixotic methods of husbandry (crouching in the vast field, he carefully deposits each seed in a hole prepared by his finger). His relations with Edna, hitherto gallant and protective, have mellowed into playful familiarity. And, as well as surprising, it is finely appropriate that it should be Scraps's offspring that the camera, following he couple's loving gaze, reveals in the cradle at the close. The film returns satisfyingly upon itself, in a shot that concentrates its varied feelings.

A Dog's Life follows naturally from the best Mutual two-reelers. It has closest affinities with *The Immigrant*, with which it shares a story hinging on found money, Charlie's protective attitude to the heroine, his consciousness of social ostracism, and the sense of fearfully maintaining a pretence that underlies the key comic moments of the earlier, and of some of the later, film. The addition of a third reel meant new artistic power and freedom. It enabled the typical situation, which came to full flower in the three short comedies discussed in the last chapter, to be extended in various directions. As I have already suggested, with the addition of Scraps the situation took on a new dimension. And the longer production time available, as well as the new length, meant that more care could be lavished on individual gags. Formally, *A Dog's Life* is a great step forward. It is much more skilfully organized than any of the earlier films—probably more than any comic film that had yet been made. Nothing is irrelevant; everything contributes. But what constitutes its essential originality is that its organization is poetic. That is, the real life of the film is contained in the evocative power of its images and their relation to each other rather than in the mechanics of narrative. These images resolve themselves into two camps: Charlie defeated, and Charlie victorious. As much as a fable of social deprivation, *A Dog's Life* is a film about balance and mastery—about Charlie's precarious possession of our world, and his efforts to maintain it. Despite its idyllic conclusion in this case, the struggle is one he was to have to repeat.

Shoulder Arms

This is Charlie's war game. To say this is to suggest that its relation to the actual historical event with which it purports to deal is not a simple one. It has been praised for its authenticity, even compared favourably with serious dramas made later with the benefit of hindsight. And it is true that a great deal of care seems to have been taken with costumes and settings: to the unpractised eye at least, no detail can be faulted on this score. In a film completed and released before the war was over, this suggests much painstaking preparation. However, in terms of feeling and attitude, *Shoulder Arms* is discordant with what we have come to think of as one aspect of the peculiar spirit of the First World War. This aspect, expressed in personal accounts, poems and soldiers' versions of popular songs, is composed of the anger, bitterness and cynicism generated by the perceived discrepancy between the war's public voice and its private face—between what politicians were saying and what soldiers were suffering. 'He did for them both with his plan of attack': this is not the note that is struck. Charlie's attitude to the war, in so far as he is conscious of it, is one of cheerful acceptance. He doesn't worry about causes or issues. There is nothing about the film on a conscious level that could offend the most fervent jingoist. He betrays no hatred, however: the enemy are not portrayed as demons. But they *are* farcical buffoons. Their troops are all ludicrous shapes and sizes—one soldier a flabby giant, his officer a strutting midget, fit only for Charlie to spank. Good-humoured contempt is the prevalent feeling. And the film's value as a realistic document is further qualified by the way its later stretches depart radically from probability and take wing into realms of fantasy.

But if it is not in any useful sense a film about the First World War, *Shoulder Arms* is very much about war. It confines itself to war situations, and feeds avidly upon war feelings. Danger, discomfort, death, fear, loneliness, bravado, courage, camaraderie—these are the serious facts and feelings that give the comic action its wary edge. In the first half at least, there is a certain nervous tension in the clowning, a sense of being braced against the facing of horrors, as if the whole film were, like Charlie, whistling to keep its courage up. The serious facts at one point intrude with unmistakable force: who can fail to be disturbed by the scene in the flooded dugout, when Charlie and his friends settle themselves to sleep, with every appearance of contentment, in two feet of muddy water? It is the discrepancy, at once comic and painful, between the uncomfortable facts and their comfortable acceptance that gives this scene its particular intensity. The image with which it closes has a general suggestiveness. Charlie learns to live with the water by detaching the horn of a gramophone and using it as a respirator. And *Shoulder Arms* can be said to be about how he learns to live with the fact of war. Its structure is very simple—Charlie and war. The two confront each other, hesitate, circle, skirmish, come to a watchful agreement. The pattern of defeats and victories discernible in *A Dog's Life* is to some extent repeated. But there are important differences. Charlie has rather more respect for war than he had for the representatives of the dog's world. Yet in spite —or perhaps because—of this, his victories over war are very much greater. They are indeed so great as to make the phrase 'learns to live with' seem decidedly inappropriate. Charlie, with characteristic audacity, doesn't resign himself to war: he picks it up by the scruff and shapes it to his own ends. The first half of the film is given over to mutual accommodations and concessions, the second half to Charlie's exhilarating fantasies of mastery and power.

Charlie's accommodations with war follow a natural sequence, as he encounters in turn each of its harsh conditions. His first reaction to its disciplines takes the form of well-meaning but helpless incompetence. Charlie, as always, is anxious to do the right thing. But the drilling session at the base camp is marred by his rifle's habit of plonking itself down onto the next man's foot, and by the refusal of his own splayed feet to perform the about-turn in anything approaching the regulation manner. At the end of the session he scampers back to his tent with the innocent pleasure of a child released from school. (Where the 'serious' affairs of the world are concerned, Charlie almost invariably *is* a child, albeit a shrewd one.) A sterner initiation follows, as the comedy of incompetence gives way to the comedy of discomfort. I have remarked upon the disturbing quality of the dugout scene, but the acute sense of discomfort it generates is alleviated by Charlie's incorrigible oddity. He doesn't simply accept the horrors of trench life: he takes advantage of them to indulge in a little crafty larking about —by directing a ripple of flood water into the sergeant's open mouth, for instance, or blowing a lighted candle towards his foot. This casual clowning is of a piece with his idiosyncratic improvisations—the horn employed as a respirator, the puzzling cheese grater dangling from his pack that turns out to be a sensible backscratching device. At this stage, Charlie treats war with wary respect, but doesn't allow it to intimidate him. He remains, amidst its hardships, his pliant but irrepressible self.

He comes nearest to defeat, or at least to discomfiture, in the letter delivery scene. This must be one of the best-remembered parts of the film. It is also the part that, by focusing upon the war realities of loneliness and rejection, comes closest to self-indulgence. However, by a miracle of tact, it contrives to be serious without being sentimental. That it does so is due largely to Chaplin's skilfully unemphatic playing of the crucial moments. From child-like expectant excitement at letter delivery time he lapses into a dismal consciousness of neglect when none of them turn out to be for him. As he leans disconsolately against the wall, his eye drops idly to the letter from home that a fellow soldier is reading. His attention caught, his face proceeds to register, in tune with the soldier's, a succession of appropriate feelings—interest, pleasure, alarm, reassurance. It is a beautiful example of Chaplin's mimic art: one could reproduce the letter's content from his subtle play of expression. The scene derives its seriocomic tension from the soldier's unawareness (and eventual offended discovery) of the touching sympathetic identity that Charlie establishes between them. The embarrassment of the inevitable rebuff is dissipated by the farcical device of the joke parcel that Charlie's mates foist on to him (it contains a chunk of Limburger that he has to don his gas mask to investigate). The abrupt change of tone deflects the scene from any drift towards indulgence.

Danger, and the fear it induces, are among the ever-present facts of the soldier's situation. Charlie's first experience of them takes the form of shell explosions that make his helmet jump when he is on guard duty. His reaction is a nervous whistling pretence of indifference. Later the real crunch comes, when he is faced with going over the top. Here, despite a whole almanac of unfavourable prognostics (including a broken mirror and a 'No. 13' identification tag), he responds with a stern display of heroic intention: thrusting himself first up the ladder (which promptly topples backwards), and only politely yielding precedence after a clearer view of what lies ahead. It is, understandably, the theatrical, or display, element of heroism that appeals to Charlie rather than the reality. But if the film makes every comic use of the feelings that attend the imminence of danger, it is oddly reticent, at this point anyway, about the danger itself. We are not allowed any glimpses of actual combat, but next see Charlie leading in the trench full of German troops he has so casually 'surrounded'. This evasiveness is certainly in part deliberate—Charlie's strenuous engagements are to come later—but it probably also reflects Chaplin's consciousness that there were aspects of war with which he did not feel equipped to deal. At any rate, we are to understand that Charlie has undergone his baptism by fire, and from this point his dealings with war take on a tone of contemptuous familiarity: epitomized by his cocky attitude as he ushers in his captives, toting a nonchalant cigarette. At the celebratory beer party he casually makes use of passing bullets to open the bottles (a good example, this, of the domestication of danger); and later, fancying a little target practice, keeps a confident tally of snipers felled.

Discipline, discomfort, loneliness, danger, familiarity—Charlie has run the whole gamut. He has taken the measure of trench warfare and is ready for bigger things. And everything that has happened so far in the film has had an establishing function, defining Charlie in relation to war conditions: if only from the point of view of the audience's expectations, some sort of elaboration, in the form of a decisive engagement with war itself, cannot much longer be avoided. We must, sooner or later, see Charlie the soldier actually at work. The artistic problem, as the evasive treatment of Charlie's first taste of combat indicates, is that, while the first, establishing part of the film is, if not realistic, at least founded upon realistic feelings, any comparable realism in the treatment of combat scenes is hard to imagine. There is a limit to the kind of serious matter that realistic comedy can assimilate and still remain comic. The simple solution is to abandon realism. Charlie volunteers for a dangerous mission, and at last we see him on the field of action, except that at first we don't see him. What we see is a patch of scrubby landscape with a thick, dead-looking tree in the middle. Then the tree seems to move in an oddly familiar way, and it reflectively scratches its bum. It is a hilariously decisive moment. Realism bows out, and fantasy takes command.

The tree impersonation sequence is one of the film's boldest strokes. It has a multiple function. Its obvious, if ludicrous purpose is to provide Charlie the infiltrator with adequate camouflage. But its very absurdity also, in the way I've suggested, provides Charlie the character with protection against too serious an involvement with the realities of war. It establishes the fantastic nature of

the involvement we are to expect, and serves as a suitable prologue to the even more fantastic events that follow. It conveys an
even deeper resonance when we recall the traditional clown figure's fondness for animal and vegetable disguises—Charlie could
be the Fool in the mummers' plays, or the sacrificial Green Man
of the ancient folk festivals. Our initial surprise gives way to delighted recognition. After all, if Charlie can turn himself into a
man-dog, why should he not also become a man-tree? It is another
example of his inexhaustible powers of transformation, and of his
magical invulnerability. In practice, this latter advantage turns out
to be a qualified one, and to provide much of the comedy of the
sequence. In so far as his enemies don't know he is a man, he is
invulnerable, and can bash them on the head with impunity; but
in so far as they believe he is a tree, he is very vulnerable indeed,
and has to expend much desperate energy in foiling attempts to
cut him down. The comic potential of his combined man-ness and
tree-ness is fully exploited. Prompted by resourceful instinct, he
takes refuge in a wood, among his kind, and manages literally to
lose himself: giving rise to the ridiculous spectacle of Henry Bergman's fat German exasperatedly bayoneting every suspicious-look-
ing tree, in the hope that it might be Charlie.

When Charlie eludes his pursuers by crawling through the
drainage pipe and sloughs off his skin, the film's final phase
begins. For the first time he is alone in the thick of things, in his
own person. But he is not alone for long. He proceeds to assemble
a fresh cast of allies and adversaries, and to enact an exhilarating
drama of capture, rescue, subterfuge and triumph. The drama's
first act concern's Charlie's discovery of Edna in the ruined house,
and his escape from the marauding Germans; its second, his rescue
of Edna from the enemy's headquarters; its third, their audacious
conspiracy with Syd, the captured sergeant, to hijack the Kaiser.
The action is fast and suspenseful. At the same time, there is a new
emphasis on Charlie's relationships: his difficulties of communication with the apprehensive Edna, resolved by an explanatory bit of
mime, and the affectionate rapport established between them;
their joshing camaraderie with Syd in the concoction and execution of their plan. The hijack enables Charlie to demonstrate one
of his favourite impostures: his strutting German officer, flinching
nervously as the guard of honour presents arms, and casually strik-

ing a match on the door of the Kaiser's car, is a momentary resurrection of his aristocratic, insolent self. It also gives rise to certain
well-milked comic ironies. Charlie the officer, meeting the captured Syd, alternately hugs him for reassurance and boots his backside for effect. Each of them finds himself in the position of having rank to pull—Syd resorting to his when Charlie's act gets too
realistic, and Charlie using his to discourage Syd's display of gallantry towards Edna. The episode culminates in an euphoric welcome home, with Charlie aiming a contemptuous kick at the
haughtily retreating Kaiser.

Charlie's bewildered awakening, back in his tent at the base
camp, and the relegation of his exploits to the world of dreams,
are a concession to our sense of probability. The idea of Charlie
single-handedly winning the war by capturing the Kaiser and his
entourage is, after all a bit too much to swallow. But, like the
similar endings to other films, it is a device that enables us to have
our cake and eat it—to participate in Charlie's fantastic transformations of experience without losing touch with reality. Its fault is
that it is too obviously a device, provoking more doubts than it
satisfies about the status of what we have perceived. Apparently
there was originally intended to have been a more elaborate finale,
in which Charlie was fêted by the leaders of the victorious nations.
This was to have been balanced by a prologue showing Charlie's
domestic life before his call-up. Both sections were, very wisely,
jettisoned. One effect of their removal is, by the exclusion of any
naturalistic context, to render more plausible the fantastic nature
of what we are eventually offered. Another, more important, one
is to focus attention steadily upon the film's central concern—the
confrontation between Charlie and war. The novelty of *Shoulder
Arms*, in the context of Chaplin's art, is that it shows us Charlie
devoting his peculiar resources to an engagement with an extreme
and unfamiliar form of experience. The conflict is a pure one, the
tensions it generates correspondingly keen. Any irrelevance would
ruin the effect. As it stands, *Shoulder Arms* is a triumph of artistic
tact.

The Pilgrim

This film takes up and elaborates one of the favourite dramatic situations of Chaplin's short films—the imposture drama. With the

exception of *Monsieur Verdoux*, it is the most complex and subtle version of that situation he was ever to devise. Its obvious precursors are such films as *The Jitney Elopement, The Count* and *The Adventurer* (with the last of which it has been known to be ingeniously spliced to form a pirated but plausible hybrid), but it goes far beyond these in sophistication, reality and dramatic power. It can be said to be about the *idea* of imposture—specifically, of imposture in its moral aspect. It explores, with all the resources of Chaplin's poetic art, the moral conditions, consequences and complications of the imposter's role. At the heart of this role is a conflict between the imposter's real, and his assumed, self. He is committed to a double life, the two halves of which may at any time find themselves in friction. And he must devote his energies both to fostering the ignorance of others and to concealing his own guilty knowledge. It is from the discrepancies between these pairs of opposites—reality and illusion, singleness and doubleness, ignorance and knowledge, innocence and guilt—that the comedy of *The Pilgrim* springs.

Charlie's previous impostures were mostly undertaken for financial gain, or the attainment of some short-term advantage. But in *The Pilgrim* (as in *The Adventurer*) he assumes his role in order to escape recapture by the police. His original role is one of fugitive from justice, and this gives a sharper edge to the feelings that inevitably attend the imposter's situation. Chief among these feelings is fear of exposure. This fear manifests itself in both conscious and unconscious forms. Its unconscious manifestation is a sort of schizophrenia—radical uncertainty on the imposter's part about his own status. Which of his selves is he supposed to be at any one moment? He isn't always sure, and has difficulty in maintaining the appropriate pretence. So he can be led, by doubts about the significance of what he perceives, into some comical misinterpretations of other people's behaviour. This is what gives rise to the comedy of the scene at the railway station, when Charlie unwittingly gets involved with the eloping couple and their little drama of escape and pursuit. The enraged father, galloping up the lane, he mistakenly imagines to be gunning for him, and is taken aback to find himself not just gained upon but strenuously overtaken by his supposed pursuer. His hither and thither dash for freedom turns itself, under the puzzled gaze of a station official, into a brisk exercise trot. Alighting at his destination, he sees the waiting sheriff as his inescapable nemesis, but finds his hands, outstretched for handcuffing, genially shaken in welcome. Another result of the imposter's schizophrenic condition is his unwitting solecisms, or betraying lapses into the habits of his actual self. Having respectably purchased his ticket, it still seems natural to Charlie to ride, hobo fashion, underneath the train. Later, in the church, he finds particular difficulty in adjusting to his new profession: he tries to treat the altar rail like a bar, applauds the hymn singing, and, during a lull in the proceedings, whistles nonchalantly and pulls out a packet of cigarettes. We can accurately deduce the conditions of his old life from his instinctive reactions to the new: the whole scene is a hilarious example of Charlie's bungling decoding of messages.

On a conscious level, fear of exposure leads to the devising of active stratagems to avert betrayal. The simplest of these, and one of Charlie's favourite devices, is the sudden role-switching tactic, whereby, at the point of imminent discovery, a guilty activity is promptly converted into an innocent one. Charlie's pretence, when discovered by the sheriff in the act of absconding through the chapel's rear window, to be sampling the roses on the trellis is a charming example. He is subsequently goaded to greater efforts. The arrival on the scene of the thug, his former jailbird pal, introduces an interesting set of complications. The thug, to further his felonious intentions, assumes a respectable persona of his own in order to insinuate himself into the household where Charlie's priestly status is safely established. There follows a complex masquerade in which varieties of knowledge are played off against varieties of innocence. 'You know I know you know I know you know': every possible irony is exploited for comic effect. To protect his own role Charlie is forced to connive at the thug's but he is also committed to thwarting the thug's criminal strategy. And both of them are interested in maintaining the illusions of Edna and her mother, their innocent hosts. All of which gives rise to the hilarious succession of role-switching gags, when Charlie's tussles with the thug are transformed, at the approach of Edna or her mother, into a smiling pretence of camaraderie.

When the thug makes off with the church takings, he poses the gravest threat so far to Charlie's cover. Charlie's bold solution, which gives rise to the most surprising scene in the film, is to assume a double imposture. With some ingenious adjustments to his dress, and trimmings borrowed from a puzzled passer-by, he reverts to a variant form of his original criminal status—a tough hombre (a sort of miniature Buffalo Bill) whose stern appearance enables him, without exciting protest, to recover the money by participating in a convenient hold-up at the local bar. This device, as well as a typical Charlie transformation, is an example of the positive aspect of the imposter's role. For him, fear of exposure is balanced, and often outweighed, by the power that his imposture confers. For Charlie, in the bar scene, it is the power of effective action. Earlier, it was the power of infiltrating a respectable household and paying court to Edna. In the church sequence, it is the liberating effect of imposture that strongly emerges—in the metaphorical audacity of Charlie's treating the sermon as if it were a music hall act. For an exhilarating moment it is the second, high-spirited, Charlie who holds the stage, recovering his sense of himself in the confident theatricality of his performance. More generally, the imposter's power consists simply in the gratifying advantage over others, shared by the audience, that his duplicity provides. It is a precarious advantage. His confident sense of power is always liable to be threatened by the fear of exposure. It is the conflict between these feelings that gives *The Pilgrim* its special intensity.

This account of *The Pilgrim* could suggest that it is only an assemblage of stock comic devices. It is of course a great deal more than that. Its use of those devices is so insistent and extensive because they serve an end—the expression of a significant theme. It is in relation to serious concerns that the idea of imposture is, with such skill, repeated and elaborated. For the film's comic drama of truth and pretence is acted out in moral and social terms. To start with, Charlie's basic dilemma has an unmistakable moral resonance. He is an escaped convict masquerading as a priest: each of his roles embodies a conventional notion of, respectively, badness and goodness. We know that Charlie is not really, malevolently, bad: he simply resides beyond the jurisdiction of conventional morality. His amoral innocence is a primary element of our established sense of him. We can readily explain to ourselves, without any prompting, the temporary embarrassment of his convict's garb. These complications get an extra twist from the entry of the thug. The thug really is bad. And Charlie, by this time, really is good, having been 'redeemed' by his love for Edna. His struggle with the thug is devoted to protecting as much Edna's *innocence* (of the ugly realities the thug represents) as her *ignorance* (of his own duplicity): the two terms can't readily be distinguished. The thug, of course, though really bad, is pretending to be good. We are committed, as the action unfolds, to a lively multiple consciousness of the characters and their moral roles.

A priest is not just a conventionally good man. He has a social role: he is the professional good man of the community. And Charlie's priestly imposture involves him directly in the world of an American small town, its citizens, functionaries, habits and places of resort. The ruling passion of this world is respectability. What Charlie quickly discovers is that this respectability is, for the most part, a sham: a show of virtue that conceals a disreputable actuality. Charlie's amorality, his indifference to conventional codes, is especially well-suited to exposing the sham. The portly minister's subscription to a teetotal sect does not prevent him from concealing a hip flask about his ample person: nicked by Charlie, and accidentally smashed upon the sidewalk, it induces in the minister an embarrassed, but ironically belated, consciousness of betrayal. The stuffily, stiffly correct bourgeois couple who visit Edna and her mother are accompanied by their son, an undisciplined brat, whose infliction on everyone present of various puerile indignities they don't feel it necessary to rebuke. Charlie's remedy for this child's excesses, one of the most memorable and satisfying moments of the film, is a calmly admonitory boot in the rear. More generally, our sense of the town's confused moral atmosphere is suggested by the proximity of the three places of resort that we are shown, which seem to have a representative significance: Edna's charming cottage household, whose respectability is real and unaffected; the austere chapel, whose profession of virtue is a sanctimonious sham; and the sleazy beer-hall, where lawlessness reigns unchecked. There is a disquieting cleavage between the town's principles and most of its practice. It is a frontier town in more than a literal sense.

This best point takes us beyond the more obvious ironies of the minister's hip flask and the visitors' brat. It suggests what closer investigation amply bears out, that *The Pilgrim* is one of the most thorough demonstrations of the poetic nature of Chaplin's art. Its images and episodes have, in addition to their narrative function, a direct and significant evocative power. And their significance resides in the way they define and elaborate the central theme of moral imposture. Three examples are especially relevant: the sermon, the episode of the hat and the border-straddling finale.

Charlie's sermon, the film's celebrated set piece, is not just a piece of virtuoso clowning. One of its functions is, as already suggested, to give Charlie the opportunity for a confident and unequivocal display of his role-playing powers. But it gains a special significance from its text—the story he chooses to tell. The general appropriateness of the David and Goliath story to Charlie's relations with our world has often been noted. And it prefigures in an obvious way Charlie's later tussle with the thug. Its specific appropriateness is even more striking. David is an imposter, a shepherd masquerading as a soldier. Unhampered by orthodox notions of combat, he is able to defeat Goliath by a stratagem that is Charlie-like in its idiosyncrasy. His supposed innocence, confronting Goliath's supposed knowledge, conceals a knowledge of its own that makes Goliath's look like innocence. One of the attractions of the biblical story is our delighted sense of the advantage over Goliath that David's imposture gives him. As well as sharpening the film's moral focus (the David–Goliath battle is an archetypal moral confrontation), and elaborating the general themes of duplicity and disparity, the sermon, in the liveliest fashion, both illustrates (in the story it tells) and demonstrates (in the confidence of Charlie's performance) the power-conferring aspect of imposture.

A different emphasis is provided by the episode of Syd Chaplin's hat. Syd, with his sternly parted hair and severity of expression, is the incarnation of stuffy formality. His hat is the outward symbol of his respectability: without it he is indecently exposed, and its retrieval is a matter of vital importance (as the retrieval of theirs is, in a not dissimilar way, to Laurel and Hardy). Its metamorphosis into a pudding is tantamount to sacrilege: a violation of good form he finds it impossible to forgive. From the film's, and the audience's point of view, the function of the incident is punitive (calling to mind the demolition of Syd's pie-stall in *A Dog's Life*): our reaction is one of impenitent relish. Syd's sense of outrage countered by a different set of feelings on Charlie's part: the loving care he bestows upon the preparation of the pudding hat (delicately lathering it with a dollop of cream), as well as his customary response to the spectacle of food, is an expression of he benevolent domesticity associated with his new role of Edna's suitor. The scene is a beautifully contrived maelstrom of incongruent feelings, in the centre of which, itself an unwitting cream-plastered imposter, sits Syd's hat. In its absurd image is concentrated the film's treatment of sham respectability.

The border-straddling finale has a more obvious function. Among other things, it has a rich typological significance, registering directly Charlie's typical condition: since he has come from the border to disrupt the centre it is only fitting that the centre's representative should cart him back to the border. But it also serves the theme of innocence and guilt. It is preceded by the comedy of mistaken intentions, in which Charlie now a true innocent, his two selves reunited, fails to understand the sheriff's invitations to fresh duplicity. Escorted bodily to the border, he experiences a brief moment of elation at the prospect of freedom, but, as the bandits open fire, he quickly discovers that there is no more safety on one side than on the other. Trapped between law and lawlessness, his brilliant solution is to steer a prudent course between the two, one foot in the territory of each. It is at once an obvious compromise —an acceptance of duality and confusion—and, in its resourcefulness, a sort of triumph. It is Charlie's finest balancing act, focusing in a single image the film's complex concern with the problem of moral ambiguity. It shares this concern, and the same solution, with a greater, and even more complex, drama in which varieties of imposture are employed to harmonize the conflicts between good and evil, innocence and knowledge, illusion and reality. 'Like doth quit like, and measure still for measure': *The Pilgrim* is in some respects a sort of comic *Measure for Measure*, in which Charlie doubles as the Duke and Angelo. In neither does the acceptance of moral ambiguity preclude the achievement of a satisfying conclusion.

The Pilgrim, its serious preoccupations notwithstanding, is rooted in a very real world. We can't fail to notice that its metaphysical drama is acted out in terms of Charlie's worldliest concerns: money, food and women. And the actuality of its images is one of its most striking features. There is a fine appropriateness in faces,

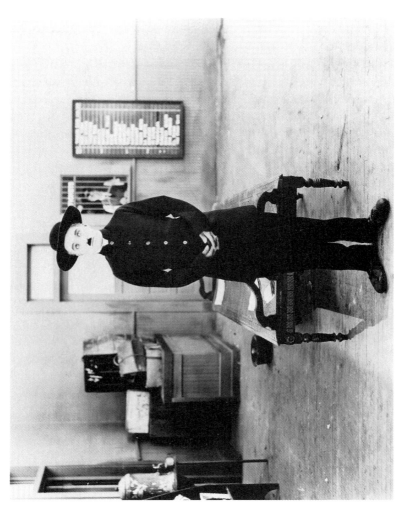

Plate 3. *The Pilgrim*

figures, dress, buildings and furnishings that gives substance to the film's definition of its themes. Mack Swain's plumply nervous minister, who bears so signal a resemblance to Dickens's sanctimonious Mr Chadband; Syd Chaplin's stiff and sour-faced citizen, and his fussily bonneted wife; the thug's flashy suit and battered physiognomy; Edna's white-haired mother and their antimacassared home; Charlie's own ministerial garb, with its quaint broad-rimmed hat—these don't just illustrate, but embody, the moral drama. They *are* what they represent, registering their significance with immediate visual force. The social context of the drama is rendered with a realism unusual for Chaplin (and, in the case of Edna's household, with real affection). Its blend of ironic comedy, moral complexity and visual reality makes *The Pilgrim* not only perhaps Chaplin's finest First National but one of the finest of all his films.

The Kid

Chronologically, *The Kid* falls between *Shoulder Arms* and *The Pilgrim*. But it invites special treatment by virtue of two qualities that set it apart from the other major films of the period: its length—discounting *Tillie*, it is Chaplin's first feature length film; and its ambition—it is his most sustained assault to date (and one of the most determined he was ever to make) upon the comedy of feeling. Thematically, it follows on from *A Dog's Life* and *The Vagabond*, from each of which it borrows elements. It marks a return to the dog's world of social and emotional squalor that charged with autobiographical resonance, features so obsessively large in Charlie's universe. And it involves itself in the associated feelings of this world with a new directness and completeness of surrender. But whereas *A Dog's Life* concerned Charlie's attempts to maintain a precarious foothold on our unaccommodating social structure, *The Kid* goes one step further in chronicling his heroic establishment of an actual domestic base in our world—and one significantly more real than the half-acknowledged fantasy with which the earlier film concluded. From *The Vagabond* is borrowed the high-life drama of passion and disappointment that precedes, and at points infiltrates, the main action. The elaboration and detail of this part of the film, compared with the earlier treatment, is almost certainly not just a response to the demands of the six-reel format (though it probably *is* that), but the result of deliberate choice. Structurally, for whatever reason, *The Kid* consists of a comic drama of Charlie's relations with Jackie set within a sentimental one of Edna's loss and recovery of her son.

To get the sentimental bit out of the way: its obvious function is a framing one. It is designed both to reinforce the main action by comparison and to set it off by contrast. It shares with the Charlie–Jackie story a situation that demonstrates the vulnerability of affectionate relationships: both parts of the film hinge upon the loss and recovery of a beloved object. It diverges from it in style and social tone. It operates at the other end of the social scale, and its feelings, and the manner in which it deals with them, are correspondingly elevated. It is the main action of an Elizabethan drama relegated to subplot status. Its contrasting function it fulfils very well, with an emphasis that certainly was not intended. For the trouble with the Edna story is that it is hopelessly unreal. It is solemn and rarefied to the point of absurdity. Some of its images have a simple evocative power. The sad-faced bride and her grimly ancient husband, whose sharp heel vindictively crushes the fallen blossoms, provide one of the better moments (which Chair contrived to put to casually telling use in the scene of Albert's arrest in *Sous les Toits de Paris*). And its stylization of manner goes some way towards alleviating its unfortunate impression. But its patently novelettish provenance, its heavy-handed symbolism, and the unrelieved seriousness with which it invites us to respond to its emotional simplicities, finally combine to defeat credibility. Edna herself remains a remote and pedestaled figure throughout, in whom it is difficult to arouse much sympathetic interest; while the ponderous volume of 'The Past', opening with ludicrous readiness at the page entitled 'Regrets', is probably the crowning unreality.

Fortunately, *The Kid*'s main focus is upon something very different. The relationship between Charlie and Jackie, which the body of the film is devoted to exploring, is rendered with the assurance and actuality of Chaplin's finest art. It is an extended version of the Charlie–Scraps relationship in *A Dog's Life*. In both films, each half of the partnership tends increasingly to take on the attributes of the other, and at a key moment actually to fuse: just as Charlie became a man-dog at the Green Lantern, to the consternation of the clientele, so in *The Kid*'s doss-house scene he becomes a man-

child, when Jackie dives under the bed clothes to escape detection
(presenting to the bemused proprietor the spectacle of Charlie's
knees elevated at an apparently inhuman angle). Scraps is a wonderfully human dog, but there is a limit to what a dog can do:
Jackie furnishes much more malleable material. *The Kid* soon outstrips its model both in resourcefulness of invention and in depth
of feeling. With the extension of feeling—in particular, with the
film's unashamedly direct dramatization of the sense of loss and
vulnerability—comes the danger of sentimentality. Everybody recognizes that *The Kid* is Chaplin at his most Dickensian. It could be
described as *Oliver Twist* rewritten from Mr Brownlow's point of
view—if one can imagine a Brownlow endowed with all the reality
and attractiveness of Fagin. Certainly the scene of Jackie's forcible
removal by the orphanage officials recalls, in its dramatic intensity, Oliver's recapture by Sikes and Nancy. But the film's pathetic
aspect has had more than enough attention. Its balance is a nice
one, to but if it never quite tips over into outright sentimentality it
is because of the scrupulous care with which, in the central part,
the Charlie–Jackie relationship is established.

This relationship is essentially educational in character. It could
be described as education in action. *The Kid* is, in an unaffectedly
direct way, *about* the idea of education and nurture. And not
Jackie's education only. The process is conceived as a mutual one.
Jackie is given a home and security, and instructed both in the
domestic proprieties and in the ways of the world: Charlie in turn
derives from his responsibility the satisfactions of a social role, a
domestic base and an awakened emotional need. A more interesting literary parallel is with *Silas Marner*, George Eliot's fable
about the regenerative powers of affection. Both heroes display an
innocent perplexity in the face of the fatherly role: both achieve a
new sense of identity in the enactment of their self-allotted task.
Charlie's improvised hammock and bottle even recall Silas's
equally rough-and-ready expedient of tying Eppie to his loom.

There is a beautiful intimacy and spontaneity in the scenes between Charlie and Jackie, a sense of established familiarity. Each,
as already noted, tends to take on the qualities of the other, Jackie's
prompt role-switching tactic, when discovered by the cop in the act
of stoning the windows, is worthy of Charlie himself. His education takes two forms: private and public. The private part involves

personal cleanliness (the face-washing rituals to which Charlie devotes such concentrated energy are directly reminiscent of *The
Vagabond*); table manners (Jackie is instructed in the correct way
of eating shovel fashion with a knife, and in the delicate use of the
finger bowl); and domestic economy (Jackie's offer to retrieve the
coin he has just inserted in the gas meter receives Charlie's
approving sanction). These scenes exhibit Charlie's quixotic
version of the fatherly role at its most absolute and secure.

The public part involves their common encounters with the
outside world. One problem that soon arises is how to deal with
the forces of random aggression. Jackie gets caught up in a scrap
with a neighbourhood child, which Charlie officiously formalizes
into a boxing match—working in between rounds some mimed
illustration of the vulnerable portions of the opposition's anatomy.
However, instruction in the public sector tends to come a cropper
from the insecurity of Charlie's own social role: his off-hand appro-
priation of credit for Jackie's pugilistic prowess transforms itself,
on the menacing entry of the thug, into an ingratiating desire for
his protégé's defeat.

A similar set back is met with in one of Charlie's favourite fields
of public operation, that of work. Nothing so clearly demonstrates
the creatively idiosyncratic nature of Charlie's dealings with the institutions of our world than the treatment of work in *The Kid*.
According to the rule book, a glazier's flow of business is determined by the number of broken windows that happen to need
replacing at any one time. Charlie sees no reason why something
so important to his own well being should be left to chance. He
finds nothing sacrosanct in the laws of supply and demand. So it is
with a clear conscience that he can create his own work opportunities by getting Jackie to break a few windows on the sly. Such a
solution to the work problem is the product not of criminal guile
but of a child-like innocence. It founders inevitably, upon our
world's hostility to Charlie's kind of creativeness—in the form of a
cop's baleful discovery of the stone-toting Jackie, whom Charlie
thereupon deems it prudent to try, unsuccessfully, to disown. Charlie's usual way with work is also demonstrated in his solo scenes,
when his glazing function is both turned to aesthetic account (he
moulds the putty with a sculptor's finesse) and made the occasion
for a bit of amorous dalliance (discovered by the cop in the act of

flirting with his wife, Charlie interprets the murderous grip on his throat as a piece of over-boisterous love play).

Charlie's principal benefit from his relationship with Jackie is the achievement of a secure domestic base, a bastion against the hostile forces of the outside world. It is something that he struggles to attain in all the films, rarely with such success. Its domesticity, enacted with loving detail, takes the form both of the instruction of Jackie in appropriate habits and usages and of an emphasis upon the lavish consumption of food—another of Charlie's major satisfactions. Its security is concentrated in a brief moment that, although only a few seconds long, it is not surprising to learn that Chaplin took several days to shoot. This is the moment when, arising for breakfast, after poking his foot interrogatively through a gap in the seam of the multi-coloured blanket, he shuffles down inside the bed and emerges with his head in the gap, promptly transforming the blanket into a splendid house robe. Our response to this scene is compounded of delight in the audacity of the transformation, and, paradoxically, a sense of its fitness and congruity—its casual deftness emphasizes Charlie's newly established domestic identity. For once we see him unhamperedly moulding the world to his own needs. He has clearly moved a long way from the more characteristic incongruity of his first appearance, jauntily negotiating the pitfalls and garbage of a slummy side street, when his elegant fastidiousness is played off against the squalor of his surroundings. The change is a measure of his emotional progress in the film, made possible by his developing relationship with Jackie: he moves from reluctant involvement (at one point contemplating dumping the baby down the nearest drain) through acceptance, inspired improvisation, conscious responsibility, to a final awakening of emotional need.

It is the reality of the feelings involved in the Charlie—Jackie relationship that lends urgency to the final drama of loss and recovery. Threatened with the removal of the kid, Charlie is galvanized into heroic activity, bringing to bear upon the forces of the hostile world a new-found spirit of courageous resistance. The white-whiskered orphanage official, a beautiful incarnation of stuffy formality, finds himself soundly walloped, plastered with soup, and, after Charlie's resourceful clamber over the rooftops, decisively booted from the back of the truck. The truck driver, alerted to his change of passenger, is routed by Charlie's menacing pretence of pursuit. By this stage, Charlie has earned his right to the film's most unequivocal indulgence of feeling, the tearful embrace of the reunited pair, which figures so frequently in published stills. After the ardours of the loss-and-recovery drama, it registers as a genuinely moving relief.

What is one to say of the dream sequence? Dramatically, it forms a satisfying bridge between the film's crisis (the second removal of Jackie) and its resolution, holding the action in suspense and providing a pause for the accumulated feelings to crystallize, its charm arises from the perfunctory down-to-earthness of its paradisiac setting: heaven is Easy Street with wings. Its best moment is Charlie's strutting assumption of self-importance on donning his angelic gear: he wriggles experimentally and scrapes at the ground chicken fashion—another reminder of the clown's traditional fondness for bird disguises. Thematically, it echoes the main action's concern with the idea of 'paradise lost'. But it departs from the tenor of the film as a whole by giving this theme a moral emphasis. The comedy of temptation and fall acted out in the dream sequence is a disconcerting departure from the feelings that inform both the Charlie and the Edna portions. In these it is the recovery of innocence rather than its loss that is dwelt upon: the loss with which they do deal—the loss of affectionate relationships—is made the occasion not for cynical but for pathetic and regretful feelings. I am not sure how much this is more than a minor cavil: the sequence's dramatic appropriateness is strong enough possibly to nullify its inappropriateness of theme.

The Kid's finale is less equivocally unsatisfying. It takes over from *The Vagabond* a conventional happy ending that depends for its success on our not examining too closely what is involved. Charlie's disappearance into Edna's plush mansion raises more questions than it solves. What are we meant to think of as going on behind that primly exclusive door? The answer is that we are not meant to think anything. The Edna story gathers the Charlie story into its high-minded embrace, politely shutting out all questions. The unreality of this conclusion is brought out by contrast with *Silas Marner*, whose affinities with *The Kid* are suggested above. Like Jackie, Eppie is a foundling brought up in a lowly home whose upper-class parents eventually claim her back. But in George Eliot's fable, the Godfrey–Nancy story is rendered with the same reality as the Silas–Eppie story, and in the final confrontation she is equipped to treat the issues with an honesty that Chaplin, too committed to sentimental evasion, cannot match. Presented with a choice, Eppie politely but firmly elects to stay with Silas, whose affectionate services have given him a claim to fatherhood that her actual father's specious arguments cannot dislodge. It is true that Edna's loss of Jackie is an accidental misfortune, and not, like Godfrey's of Eppie, the product of deliberate and culpable choice, but the contrast instructively demonstrates how the ending of the *The Kid* manages to shirk all the obvious issues. The conclusion is that, at this stage in his artistic progress, Chaplin is still usually unwilling to conceive of happiness in terms of anything other than a rise in the social scale. His power to follow a theme through is disabled by elements of evasive fantasy. It is not until *Monsieur Verdoux* that he is able to look upon questions of class with an eye of sober disenchantment.

For all its weaknesses, *The Kid* is an impressive debut in the feature length field. Its response to the demands of the six-reel format—the framing 'overplot', the gradual elaboration of the central relationship, the crystallizing dream sequence—are structurally successful. It works up a skilful dramatic rhythm. And the uninhibited thoroughness of its treatment of the favourite Charlie situation—its comic utilization of intense and genuine feeling—ensure it a special place in the Chaplin canon.

Chapter 5

Silent Features

A Woman of Paris

Where to make the division between Chaplin's silent films and his sound films is not a simple choice. It is perfectly true that *City Lights* is in important respects a sound film, since it has an integral musical soundtrack and in an early scene offers noises that come very close to being comprehensible speech; and that *Modern Times* is in equally important respects a silent film, since, although it contains music and sound effects, nobody in it except radio and television voices (and Charlie in his stubbornly semi-articulate song) actually speaks. But the 'silent' and 'sound' of my chapter titles are partly terms of convenience, for it seems to me that the films divide themselves up in the way I indicate for reasons that are independent of purist definitions. *City Lights* is in conception and execution wholly a silent film, the burden of whose narrative is borne by its succession of images: the music contributes—in places delightfully—but it is not necessary. But it is hard to imagine *Modern Times* without its bold and minatory musical score; and one feels that it would not harm the film if everybody spoke—were it not (a big exception) that this would destroy the *coup de théâtre* of Charlie's song. More simply, in their use of sound and silence, *City Lights* was at its time of issue a novelty, but *Modern Times* was a curiosity. However, there is a more profound distinction than this. As well as being the last true silent film ever made, *City Lights*, focusing upon Charlie's life of feeling and his fear of rejection and loss, is the last of his films (at least until *Limelight*) to concern itself wholly with his private experience, and it marks the culmination of an important element of his art in a way that makes one continually look backwards for parallels. *Modern Times* on the other hand, deliberately points forward: it is the first of Charlie's strenuous engagements with a recognizable world whose problems are felt to be both threatening and authentic. It is for this reason that my chapter division falls where it does.

Between *The Pilgrim*, the last of the First Nationals, and *The Gold Rush*, the first of his half-dozen feature length comic masterpieces, Chaplin made the only wholly serious film in which (apart from a few insignificant seconds) he does not himself appear: *A Woman of Paris*. Long unavailable, it was reissued with a musical soundtrack shortly before his death. In a study of Charlie's comic art it would be inappropriate to give an extended account of what was in some respects an uncharacteristic (and unrepeated) experiment: but it would be equally inappropriate to omit it altogether. For this strange film, as well as possessing many intrinsic qualities, and considerable historical importance, is integral in a number of interesting ways with the main Chaplin canon.

A Woman of Paris is the story of a provincial French girl who, jilted, as she thinks, by her lover, runs away to the big city, where she becomes the mistress of the most polished and admired frequenter of the *demi-monde*; her old lover inevitably turns up and is pitted in rivalry against the new, with tragic results. Parts of the story resemble D.W. Griffiths's *Way Down East*, and it is clearly this film, and others in Griffiths's non-spectacular sensitive mode— tragedies of the everyday and ordinary—that prompted Chaplin to produce his own example of 'legitimate' cinema. Its virtues are largely a matter of the confidence with which it dramatizes its theme—its directness of presentation, the unhistrionic naturalness of its performances and the subtle economy with which it makes its points—as well as its success in encompassing a wide variety of tones. The expository boldness of its sombre beginning, in which the relationship between the lovers, the conditions of their lives, and the misunderstanding which parts them, are presented with clarity and decision (an effect spoilt only by a dragging sentimental scene between Jean and his parents), gives way to the much lighter, faster and humorous evocation of Marie's life with Pierre. This long central section, in which the *demi-mondaines* quarrel, make up, intrigue and enjoy themselves, contains many of the

subtly suggestive touches for which the film is famous: such as the
man's collar, which, falling from the drawer in which the maid is
rummaging, signals unmistakably both to Jean and to us the relation in which Marie stands to Pierre. Much of the credit for the
success of this section belongs to Adolphe Menjou's swaggering,
dapper Pierre; but Edna Purviance, acting with spirit in her first
demanding dramatic role, contributes nearly as much. With the
re-entry of Jean and his lachrymose mother, the film's impetus fal-
ters: Jean's contradictions of feeling and motive, while important
to the story, are not made real to us, and his suicide provides an
outcome that seems theatrical rather than humanly inevitable. The
forces of conscience and truth in the film seem weak and insipid,
and endowed with none of the attractive liveliness of the forces of
cynicism and sham. The coda, however goes a long way towards
restoring the original balance of tone: the closing image—of Pierre
in his limousine and Marie on her farm waggon with her adopted
brood passing each other without recognition on the dusty road—
beautifully concentrates the film's detached and mocking concern
with life, time, chance and change.

   Some of the well-known effects of *A Woman in Paris* are now
largely of historical interest: the rendering of the departing train
solely in terms of shadow and light passing across Marie's face is in
all the textbooks, but it takes an effort of imagination now to see it
as a bold innovation, so thoroughly has it passed into the 'language'. Yet many other moments, and whole scenes, retain their
power to delight or to shock. The best of them have all to do with
Chaplin's critically observant depiction of the Parisian *demi-monde*
into which Marie has lapsed. The behaviour depicted ranges from
the irresponsible to the vicious, and Chaplin's attitude—and ours
as we watch—from the indulgent to the censorious. At the indulgent end of the spectrum there is the wild party, which Marie is
trying to find when she stumbles upon Jean. The behaviour of the
participants is boorish and prurient, but a certain rough gaiety is
transmitted as well, and a feeling of daring: perhaps it is Charlie's
inveterate love of conviviality that tempers Chaplin's censure. A
more complex example is the quarrel between Pierre and Marie,
in which he tootles away nonchalantly at his saxophone while she
hurls her necklace from the window in a pet, and then scurries
down to retrieve it, breaking her heel in the process. Here our

attitude is detached and humorous: we share partly Pierre's amusement at Marie's feminine folly, and partly her mixture of vengeful-
ness and dismay. At the same time the scene tells us something
significant about his irresponsibility and her moral confusion (for
the quarrel is caused by his inability to take either her or her respectable ambitions seriously, a refusal that the 'good' side of her
knows to be wrong; and her retrieval of the necklace is as much a
concession to a country girl's commendable prudence as to vanity
or greed). In other scenes a telling ironical use is made of medi-
ators, through whom the action is reflected. The most frankly critical note is struck in the early restaurant scene, where Pierre points
out to Marie the grotesque pairings at neighbouring tables—an
old man and his mistress, a gigolo and his patroness. Our reaction
is immediate revulsion, but theirs is worldly amusement. Their
amusement sets them apart, but for us they share in the corruption that they mock. The best use of a mediator is in the famous
massage scene, in which, while the conversation of Marie and her
bitchy friends reveals their shallowness and duplicity, the camera
fastens upon the sceptically impassive face of the foreign masseuse,
restrained from open reaction by the requirements of her trade,
but, in her role of unillusioned observer, doing our reacting for
us. Its use of mediating observers to provide a shifting moral perspective is one of the most striking (and 'modern') achievements
of this remarkable film.

Although *A Woman of Paris* is Chaplin's only 'serious' piece of
pure direction, it is not a freak: its characters and themes bear an
intimate relation to the rest of his work, and it can be seen as an
expression of his characteristic preoccupations in a different form.
It brings to the fore the serious side of Chaplin, which had sought
intermittent expression in earlier films—the projected *Life* and the
sentimental framing plot of *The Kid*—and was to be turned to again
much later in parts of *Monsieur Verdoux* and the whole of *Limelight*.
Chaplin clearly felt the need from time to time to evoke his serious attitudes to life more directly than he felt able to in comic
activity, however strongly grounded and he was never to do this so
successfully, or tactfully, as in *A Woman of Paris*. The dramatic situation—a triangular love story, with the woman torn between
a lover who represents the familiar and known and another
who represents the glamorous and unknown—plainly both echoes

The Vagabond and prefigures *The Circus*: Jean–Marie–Pierre equals Charlie–Edna–Artist equals Charlie–Merna–Rex. Jean, of course, is too passive and insipid a character to be a true representative of Charlie: a lot more of Charlie—his gallantry, amorality and verve —has gone into Pierre, leaving Jean only the familiar feelings of inadequacy and rejection. We can see that one way in which Chaplin has created his story is by splitting himself in two. The theme of innocence and experience is too pervasive in Chaplin to need citing: and the associated equation of country life with peace, independence and simplicity, and of city life with danger, servitude and sophistication, appear, either separately or together, in innumerable of the films. *The Vagabond* suggests itself again here, and the ending of *A Dog's Life*; and the slummy shack in *Modern Times* (associated in that film with the earlier vision of suburban bliss) is invested with qualities of quasi rural tranquillity that set it off against the industrial–urban jungle. In addition to these general resemblances, some particular scenes either repeat or anticipate specific interesting effects in other films. A moment in the final scene of *A Dog's Life*, already mentioned, is repeated in the coda of *A Woman of Paris*. This is the clever trick by which we are led to expect that the unseen cradle contains Charlie's and Edna's offspring, but discover instead that it contains that of Scraps. In the later film this takes the form of the 'father', whose imminent arrival the unexplained (but too easily explainable) children announce, turning out to be the local priest. In both films the joke has the effect both of mitigating the incipient sentimentality and of turning our attention back to earlier elements of the story: in the earlier film, to the importance of Scraps; in the later, with a richness of irony, to Marie's declared desire for 'a home, children, and the respect of a good man'. Another interesting parallel is suggested by the scene in which Marie, scurrying to retrieve the necklace she has flung from the window in a fit of petulance, finds herself having to do battle for it with a bewildered tramp. In its comic use of the ignorant and disorientated onlooker, this moment clearly anticipates Charlie's leaping from his limousine in *City Lights* and engaging with a similarly astonished character for possession of a cigar butt. In each case, the effect is different: in the later film, expressive of Charlie's habitual ambiguity; in the earlier, more complex and relevant to the drama by both exhibiting Marie's feminine prudence and human contradictions and providing material for Pierre's irresponsible amusement. Finally, are not the closing moments of *A Woman of Paris*, when the waggon and the car pass each other and proceed into the distance, when we think about it, yet another of Charlie's favourite balancing acts? What are held in balance are, on the one hand, the life of tranquillity and usefulness that Marie has lost, and, through painful experience, regained, and, on the other, the life of restless and selfish pleasure that Pierre continues to enjoy, and which is immune to the pain of experience. By a gesture that although ironical, is neither sentimental nor cynical, the film invites us to ponder the significance of its witnessed events.

I hope I have said enough to demonstrate both the intrinsic interest of *A Woman of Paris* and the nature of its relevance to the study of Chaplin's comedy. Another reason for its importance almost certainly lies in its providing Chaplin with valuable training in the construction of a feature length film. The structure of *The Kid*, as noted above, tends to the episodic and awkward: it shows signs of being both strung out and tacked together. *A Woman of Paris* is much more of a piece, and more inevitable in its movement: it accommodates a wide variety of incidents and tones into a relatively seamless unity. So it made possible the superior structure, also coherent and inevitable, of Chaplin's first feature length comic masterpiece: *The Gold Rush*.

The Gold Rush

Chaplin was apparently inspired to make *The Gold Rush* by viewing a collection of old glass-plate photographs of Klondyke prospectors. Anyone who has ever seen such photographs will understand their fascination. However, the ones that I have seen do not, in fact, suggest the rather frightening power that the forces of nature assume in the film. They mostly show bleak and inhospitable terrain, with quiet, stoical figures grouped around a sledge or a cabin. I think that what attracted Chaplin was this sense of remoteness and isolation, the absence of civilized apparatus, and the necessity for creating social life and relationships anew. These ideas are strongly present in his film. They are one thing that make it possible for the film, while remaining a farcical comedy, to provoke unusually large questions about the significance of life.

Like *Shoulder Arms, The Gold Rush* confronts Charlie with an extreme form of experience, putting his ingenuity to its severest test. He is obliged to cope not with the hostility of respectable society or the disciplines of war, both of which are governed by rules, but with the random and malevolent forces of nature. Nature in *The Gold Rush* is hostile, vengeful and capricious. Its rigours, and the hardship, privation and madness they produce, are strongly evoked, inducing in the audience a pleasurable feeling of anxiety. There is in this film an especially powerful undercurrent of danger and suspense. We find ourselves braced against the constant threat of violent assault. (Even Charlie's innocent act of supporting himself against the cabin is rewarded by an extravagant avalanche from the roof.) At the same time there is a feeling of hope and new beginnings suggested by the *tabula rasa* of the snowy desolation, and a curiosity about how Charlie will cope. In the face of persistent hostility, and in response to novel conditions, he is forced to make up his own rules. He suffers predictable setbacks. The pattern of defeats and victories evident in *Shoulder Arms* is repeated. How he manages to have the last word is the subject of the film.

The Gold Rush, as well as strong in feeling and rich in significance, is very satisfyingly organized. In this respect it is a great advance on *The Kid*, and it is surprising to reflect that it is only Chaplin's second feature length comedy. What came in between was the experience of directing *A Woman of Paris*. As suggested above, one suspects that working on this, a serious film in which he did not appear, may have given Chaplin a sharper and more objective feeling for dramatic form. Whatever the reason, *The Gold Rush* is excellently constructed. It has pattern, variety of pace, singleness of purpose and, despite the abundance of incident, a clear outline. It resolves itself into four sections. The first, set in the cabin, establishes the qualities of the natural world and depicts Charlie's initiation into its rigours; the second, in the boom town, presents his exploration of the local possibilities of social life; in the third he reverts to the wild for a return match, with renewed vigour; while the fourth is a surprising coda in which conditions are reversed and difficulties overcome.

Plate 4. *The Gold Rush*

Charlie's first reaction to the perils of the wild is one of innocent unawareness. A series of shots of prospectors toiling along a
snow-bound pass is followed, with intentional bathos, by one of
Charlie picking his way gingerly round an icy spur of rock, with
the air of someone taking a morning stroll. A brief comedy of
initiation follows, as Charlie demonstrates his obliviousness, slowly
to be modified, of the dangers that surround him. A huge bear
that lumbers after him disappears into a handy cave as he turns
his head; turning to lean languidly on his cane, he plunges it into
a snow-drift; he confidently navigates his course with a piece of
paper marked with the points of the compass. Charlie's blithe
unconcern plays upon the audience's feeling of vulnerability, and
feeds the growing current of suspense. We know that sooner or
later the danger of the wild is going to make itself unmistakably
felt. But Charlie's innocence is also a manifestation of the traditional clown's immunity from punishment, which enables us to
have confidence in him as well as to fear for him. More specifically, it is in this sequence the innocence of optimism, associated
with his prospector's role, that contributes strongly to the mood
of the film. In *The Gold Rush*, the prospector's quest for gold generates an optimism that provides a powerful counter-current to
the malevolence of the wild. It survives every trial and setback, and
reaps its reward at the conclusion. Both Charlie's vulnerability and
his optimism are expressed by the perfunctoriness of his concession to the prospector's role, which simply consists of a shovel, a
pick and a bag strapped to his familiar costume.

After these preliminary skirmishes, Charlie reaches the cabin in
which so much of the action is to take place. The cabin plays a
complex and suggestive role in the film. Its function is that of a
false friend. It appears to promise shelter, rest and companionship—even whatever the wild might offer in the way of social and
domestic civilities. But instead of a refuge from the irrational hostilities of the outside world, it turns out to be a concentration of
them. Charlie finds himself plunged into an atmosphere rife with
tensions and threats, and has to salvage what civilities he can.

In the first place he has great trouble getting into the cabin, as
the blizzard, which first obligingly prevents him from obeying
Black Larsen's order to leave, next blows him out through the
back door. Once inside, he has to cope with his human compan-

ions, soon finding himself threatened by the malevolence of one and the madness of the other. Human nature proves no more amenable than wild nature. Indeed, in the course of the sequence the two kinds of nature tend to become identified. Their shared characteristic is unpredictable hostility. So, when Larsen is struggling with Jim, his rifle, which with every leap and lurch remains pointing at Charlie's head, displays the same obstinate automatism as the blizzard that forced Charlie to run on the spot; and when, at the climax of Charlie's struggle with the demented Jim, Jim is replaced by the bear, as far as Charlie is concerned the bear *is* Jim—there is no distinction between the threat each represents. Human contact administers numerous raps to Charlie's crust of polite independence, forcing him to feel, act and react. His response to the world of the cabin moves from ingratiation (stroking Jim like a dog, offering him the drum stick, and prudently siding with him against the defeated Larsen) to guilty deception (trying to conceal from Larsen that he has eaten the candle), strenuous self-preservation, and, when the bear is shot, the sudden assumption of an air of brisk and easy familiarity as he polishes the plates and sharpens the knife.

The greatest threat to Charlie's survival is posed by Big Jim's hunger-induced hallucinations, which provide a suspenseful climax to the first cabin sequence. The tension visibly mounts as they metaphorically and actually circle each other, Jim trying to judge, Charlie to anticipate, the moment of the attack. As they sidle in and out of the cabin, feigning innocent business, and reverting when unobserved to attitudes of watchful guile, their movements take on a balletic momentum. Some incidental amusement is provided by Charlie's realistic chicken impersonation—a variant of his angel in *The Kid* and his tree in *Shoulder Arms*, and, like them, an example of the fondness for non-human disguises that he inherits from the wider tradition of clowning. A chicken habit spills over into Charlie's human behaviour when he buries the rifle in the snow by shovelling with his heels. But the chief interest of the scene lies in Charlie's air of wary suspicion, and his prudent stratagems for survival. In particular, the original idea of going to bed with his hands in his boots produces, at the moment when his head emerges from the blanket, a startling sensation of mingle alertness and repose. This gag is a good example of Charlie's creative response to the challenges of experience.

A richer, and more celebrated, example is the eating of the boot. This (together with the dance of the rolls and the tilting cabin) must be one of the three scenes in *The Gold Rush* that everybody remembers. If the random hostilities of the cabin ménage count as defeats for Charlie, the boot-eating is his victory. It shows that, as well as his cunning, Charlie brings his courtesy to the wild. His courtesy is a manifestation of display: represented here by his addiction to the conventions of gourmet dining, it is his reaction to the dehumanizing menace of hunger, a polite but firm contradiction of the indifferent brutality of the wild. The closer starvation stares him in the face, the more Charlie is determined to make a meal (literally) out of manner and performance. In its comic effects the scene is complex. It is full of suggestiveness and surprise. At its heart is the obvious incongruity between the unappetizing boot and the Savoy Grill delicacy with which it is prepared. But Charlie is not content with a single joke. He must elaborate and improvise. So in his hands the dumb boot undergoes a series of swift transformations, as the laces become spaghetti, the ruptured sole a Dover sole, and a bent nail a wishbone. The associations are poetic in their immediacy and appropriateness (and an excellent demonstration of what it means to talk of the poetry of Chaplin's art). Another element of the humorous effect is provided by the act of consumption, in the contrast between Charlie's encouraging display of satisfaction and Jim's glum disbelief in the nourishing properties of the fare. The boot-eating, in fact, marks a stage in the relationship between Charlie and Jim, which is itself important in the film. It shows the strong but simple Jim, under stress of hunger, prepared to defer to Charlie's unorthodox skills and superior optimism.

It is hard to do justice to the liveliness of the cabin sequence. I have tried to suggest its variety of mood, the comic momentum it establishes and its resourceful exploitation of feelings of suspense and fear. But it is more than a succession of incidents. It has a satisfying and significant shape. Its movement from danger to hope is represented by the bear, which threatens the unwitting Charlie in the opening shots, and then returns at the end to become the culminating threat (and also by a neat comic reversal, the means whereby our heroes are fed and all the tensions released). More important in the unravelling of the film's theme is the representative significance that attaches to the three actors in the drama, for each of them is defined in terms of his attitude to the quest for gold. I have spoken of this as a source of optimism. But the total feelings relating to it in the film are actually more complicated. Larsen, beetle-browed and gloomy, is a personification of the malevolence of nature (as we have seen, for Charlie's purposes there is little to choose between him and the blizzard). His quest for gold is selfish and malign. He is not even a proper prospector, but specializes in filching the claims of others. Jim is the embodiment of single-minded energy and purpose, but guileless and simple. His quest for gold is responsible and benign. He and Charlie naturally strike up a friendship. It is not fully developed until later in the film, but is sufficiently established by the boot eating for his subsequent transformation into a menace to seem rather a shocking instance of the cabin's powers of treachery. This is perhaps the point at which to notice how his air of rude energy, which contrasts so well with Charlie's fastidiousness, is qualified by the perplexed and doleful expression of his face—another example of the excellent use to which Chaplin put the talents of Mack Swain. Charlie is more complicated. He shares the benignity of Jim's quest for gold. (He also contrives, with a ready eye for advantage, to share the gold itself.) But his love of riches is not as all-consuming as Jim's. For him, the gold is another form of found money, important largely for the comforts it can bring, but invested, as found money always is with Charlie, with a strong charge of ambitious altruism, a consciousness of the good he can do with it The perfunctoriness of his prospector's kit, as well as a sign of his idiosyncrasy, is itself an indication that he cares about other things in life.

What they care about in life turns out to be an important question for the members of the cabin ménage, since their answers to it determine how they are treated. Despite the pervasive irrationality of natural forces, there is a decided element of justice in the eventual distribution of rewards. Larsen's malevolent solipsism is punished by the crevasse that opens at his feet (representing, by another neat reversal, nature the avenger, and the only natural calamity in the film that we are called upon to applaud); Jim's obsession and simplicity are driven to distraction. Only Charlie's idiosyncratic cultivation of value is allowed to survive unscathed. For the cabin sequence, among more obvious functions, has that of creating an artificial situation fraught with irrational hazards, in which the values its characters live by can be tested. With its villain, madman and fool facing tempest and hunger, one would not be fanciful in thinking of it as a comic version of the storm scene in King Lear, where a disgraced king, a pretended madman and a fool contemplate a life stripped of the pretences of convention. *The Gold Rush*, of course, moves towards a comic (that is, fantastic and optimistic) resolution of its themes, but it would neither be so funny nor so moving if such serious questions did not underlie it.

From the cabin, the action moves to the boom town, where Charlie sets about discovering, or devising, a form of social life that suits his needs. The boom town is raw and characterless, arbitrarily deposited upon the wilderness, but Charlie's instinctive hopefulness, and the unhampered sense of new possibilities that is another aspect of the snowy waste, give grounds for believing that he will be successful. He proceeds to extend the relationships initiated in the cabin sequence. The qualities he looks for are festivity, domesticity and affection. He seeks festivity in the local saloon. Charlie is fond of saloons and restaurants because of the importance he attaches to eating, drinking and dancing as social arts, but he hardly ever has much luck with them. On this occasion he is landed with another of his encounters with the stubborn intractability of experience. Called upon, to his disquiet, to dance with Georgia, he summons to the task all his resources of gallantry and politeness, only to discover that his trousers are falling down. A handy length of rope (replacing the sailor's hitch with his cane) turns out to be attached to a very large dog, who promptly invites Charlie to accompany him on a cat chase—an offer he cannot refuse. This confounding of Charlie's expectations of festivity echoes his humiliation by chewing gum in the Green Lantern. An important difference, to be discussed further below, is that in *A Dog's Life* he is at the time patronizing the unfortunate Edna, while in *The Gold Rush* he is being patronized in more than the neutral sense) by the more fortunate Georgia.

Charlie has more luck in his search for domesticity, when he fetches up at the cabin of Hank the trapper. To gain access to the comforts glimpsed within, he contrives one of his most audacious infiltration tactics. Assuming in the snow an attitude of cataleptic rigidity, he allows himself to be carted plank fashion into the cabin and thawed out with beans and coffee. The comedy of the episode arises both from the audacity of the fraud, and from the nicely judged swiftness of his recovery, as he interrupts his invalidism to sugar the coffee, or signals to the suspicious Hank his need for second helpings. This masquerade is an example of Charlie's unscrupulous habit of manufacturing the conditions that provoke life's pleasures and rewards. As in *The Kid* he sees no reason why he should wait for chance to supply the opportunities for practising his glazier's art, so here he declines to recognize the necessity of having to suffer invalidism's discomforts in order to enjoy its benefits. He soon establishes a secure domestic base in Hank's cabin, which is to prove as true a refuge as the earlier one was false. His new air of settled proprietorship is evident in the pleasant scene of Hank's departure on business, when Charlie's solicitous attention with the brush are transferred, in an overspill of zeal, from Hank's coat to the runners of the sledge.

Charlie's search for affection leads him to fall in love with Georgia. At this point one is forced to stand aside from the film a little and consider it more objectively. Charlie's relations with women in general are open to the charge of sentimentality, and this one is no exception. It is a risk that Chaplin always ran when he embarked on the comedy of feeling. There is nothing irretrievably sentimental about the situation itself. It is possible to make unsentimental comedy about the state of being in love, even unhappily in love. Yet there is a spurious element in this part of *The Gold Rush*. Charlie's relations with Georgia exhibit a mixture of false and genuine feeling, and in justice to the film one must try to distinguish the two. To start with, there is a great deal to be said on the credit side.

Charlie's character, we know, embodies innumerable contrarities. There is hardly any feeling or attitude he expresses that does not at some stage meet with its opposite. His art derives its complexity and powers of surprise from these sudden changes of mood and role. This is true of his pervasive romanticism, which is liable at any moment to a sharp visitation of anti-romantic collapse. It is likely that these deflationary jokes are sometimes not only instinctive expressions of Charlie's plurality but also recognitions that the feeling in question is in danger of getting out of hand. There are more of such jokes than usual in *The Gold Rush*, which is perhaps an indication of the strength of feeling aimed at in the film, and sensed to be in need of containment. Examples that readily come to mind include the occasions when Charlie, in a state of romantic euphoria, opens the door of the cabin to greet Georgia: first, to be rewarded with a snowball in the face; later, on the night of the party, to encounter a strayed mule (which, adding insult to injury, and distracting Charlie's inevitable disappointment, barges in and consumes a serviette). The effect of these moments is to qualify any tendency towards romantic indulgence.

There are other comic moments, not deflationary in intention, which seem to me to express the genuine feeling in the film. One is the occasion when, in the saloon, he appropriates the discarded photograph of Georgia and, finding himself observed, feels constrained to temper his curiosity by an elaborate pretence of unconcern. Another is the moment when Georgia returns to the cabin to retrieve her gloves, to find Charlie seated on the floor amid the debris of his jubilant and gymnastic bout of pillow-bashing. There is nothing sentimental about such moments, although they result from Charlie's love feelings. What Chaplin is doing with them, as so often in his mature comedy, is appealing directly to our experience of life. There is an interesting difference of emphasis between the two examples. In the first, the feeling involved is Charlie's embarrassed reluctance to acknowledge publicly his private preoccupation, and it registers a kind of compunction that everyone must have known. In the second, the equally recognizable embarrassment belongs to both parties, as Georgia witnesses, and Charlie is unable to conceal, his private ritual of celebration. They have in common a deliberate confusion of the public and private in our behaviour (making the private public, to our mingled pleasure and discomfiture), which is one of the functions of comic art, though rarely achieved with this delicacy.

If Charlie and Georgia only were involved in the love relation, there would be less of a problem. Georgia is unusual among Chaplin's heroines in being experienced and self-reliant, a woman rather than a waif. The intention of the film is that she should at the same time be sensitive enough to be irritated by her companions and surroundings, and gradually discover in Charlie the possibility of something finer. This does more or less happen. But it means that, in the early part of their relationship at least, it is the passively lovelorn rather than the actively protective Charlie who is most in evidence. And the lovelorn Charlie is more prone to indulgence, and less productive of comedy, than the protective Charlie. So there is an irreducible element of sentimentality in their relationship itself. What augments the problem is that Georgia, for the sake of realism and dramatic complication, is endowed with friends. The attitude of these friends towards Charlie is patronizing and contemptuous. This would not matter so much if the friends were themselves stylized figures of comedy, like most of Charlie's earlier persecutors. But Georgia's admirer Jack, at least, is not a comic heavy, but a realistic figure. So the force of his contempt has a blunting and diminishing effect on Charlie, reducing him to the status of laughable victim. Jack's baiting of Charlie in the saloon is painful not only in itself but also because of the obviousness of its dramatic intention. It is in scenes such as this that the sentimentality of the film resides, and not in the love interest as such. Something similar can be said of Georgia's giggling girl-friends, and the occasion of their visit to Hank's cabin (though here at least Charlie derives innocent revenge, in a moment of abstraction, from placing his burning foot under the fat girl's seat). By exposing Charlie to their patronizing attention, Chaplin threatens to rob him of his subversive force.

But there is one scene, not yet mentioned, that prevents the sentimental element in the sequence from upsetting its balance of feeling. This is the famous dance of the rolls. It is a beautiful and memorable scene, but its effect is a matter of poetic suggestiveness rather than any obvious dramatic intention, and so it is difficult to discuss. It takes place in a dream, when Charlie falls asleep awaiting his truant guests. That he is obliged to dream about a happy outcome to his party suggests, if we do not already know, that he is going to be disappointed. Despite the appearance of jollity, a current of sadness and disappointment runs through the scene, deriving not just from the occasion but from all Charlie's doubts and fears about his love relationship. Yet there is no trace of self-pity. When the dance happens, it is photographed close, in a subdued light, without distracting reminders of its fictional audience. It

seems to be addressed directly to us. It is an extremely witty and
enjoyable piece of display, reproducing with the fidelity of precise
observation the style and rhythm of a vaudeville dance number,
complete with applause acknowledgment routines (reminding us,
like the alfresco recital in *The Vagabond*, how readily Charlie trans-
lates his experience into theatrical terms). And it has the effect of
transforming the feelings from which it issues: as well as of the
combined simplicity and audacity of the idea, we are conscious
while watching of Charlie's losing himself in the intentness of his
performance. Sadness, self-pity and anticipated disappointment
are fed into the act, and emerge as self-forgetful absorption. It is
one of Chaplin's subtlest creations, and takes the comedy of feeling as far as it will go.

As if conscious that it has reached a limit in one of its directions,
the film now abruptly changes mood. Big Jim wanders into town
and yanks Charlie off to renew the search for his claim. The action
gathers momentum as the climax approaches. They return to the
lone cabin, and we are immediately struck by the new confident
ease and familiarity with which they take possession of it (demonstrated by Charlie's casual but compulsive tippling as he carts in
the provisions). There is a brisk air of purpose and bustle, a feeling of manly camaraderie, and a strong reassertion of the optimism associated with the prospector's role. Thus the stage is set for
the cabin's final act of treachery. By slyly getting itself deposited on
the verge of a huge ravine it manages to revive the fear and insecurity of the first cabin scene, subjecting our heroes once more to
the hazards of irrational forces. Charlie and Jim contrive at first to
remain ignorant of their plight, and there is a brief comedy of
perplexed unawareness when they stamp from side to side, fortuitously preserving the cabin's poise, and Charlie imputes its shud-
ders to the aftermath of intoxication. Alerted at length to their
peril, they register alarm, a feeble pretence of calm practicality,
and finally desperation. As they cling to the floor, their show of
purposeful cooperation gives way, at each lurch, to a case of every
man for himself. This exciting climax is Chaplin's most famous balancing act, outdoing the earlier scene in its evocation of danger
and threat. (Like Harold Lloyd's building-climbing exploits, it
gives a freshly literal force to the notion of 'suspense'.) With the

cabin and Charlie at the point of collapse, Jim chooses to delight our sense of pattern, and contrive another comic reversal, by discovering his mountain of gold, which, we suddenly remember, is the *raison d'être* of the whole proceedings.

Jim's gold makes possible the surprising finale, which shows the rich and famous prospectors travelling home by liner. This scene has been criticized as fantastic and discordant, but it strikes me as a very attractive and appropriate way of ending the film. It does have a pronounced element of fantasy: but then so do most comic conclusions. Fantasy is an important means by which the conflicts of comic drama are resolved. Its very discordance is a virtue, as I hope to show. The attractiveness is mostly a matter of the relish with which Charlie and Jim perform their new role of millionaires. There is a self-conscious theatricality about their assumption of wealthy ease, and a superfluous extravagance in their dress (even Charlie's fur coat has its own fur coat). At the same time, to add to the complexity of the effect, they remain their familiar selves. Their old habits are liable to reappear from under the trappings, as when Charlie makes a sudden grab for a discarded cigar butt. There is a new joshing familiarity in their relationship, evident by the playful cuff with his foot that Charlie administers to Jim to discourage him from taking liberties with the manicurist. Altogether it is a vivid and lively scene, and one can understand Chaplin's disregarding whatever misgivings he may have had about including it. It may owe its qualities to an autobiographical origin. A few years earlier Chaplin had travelled by sea on his first visit home to England, had been an admired object of interest and had dressed in his tramp costume for the benefit of photographers, as Charlie does here. Anyone seeing the newsreel of the occasion must find themselves reminded of the ending of *The Gold Rush*.

The appropriateness of the scene is a matter of a number of factors. One of its functions is to provide an enlivening contrast to the mood and manner of the rest of the film. Wealth is set off against privation, ease against hardship, civilization against nature. More important, the scene enables two of the film's outstanding issues to be resolved. The first of these is Charlie's optimism. This, I have suggested, is associated with his role of prospector (or finder of money), and provides a powerful counterbalance to the prevalent feelings of danger, fear and hardship. As the film progresses the optimistic undercurrent becomes more pronounced, and imperatively seeks an outlet. The luxurious conclusion enables it to take over the action entirely, to our great satisfaction. Charlie's optimism is rewarded, and his dream of wealth and ease given its most explicit realization. The second issue is Charlie's love for Georgia, declared but left unresolved upon his departure to the cabin. Their relationship as always an uncomfortable one, characterized by disparity, doubt and uncertainty. It hardly ever looks a promising match, and its being left hanging in the air is perhaps an acknowledgment of the difficulty, as well as a device for prolonging suspense. How are they to come together? The question is solved by a neat piece of symbolism. By reassuming his old costume, Charlie reverts to his former self, and by inadvertently tumbling to the steerage deck he literally comes down in the world. This pretended reversal of fortune allows Georgia, who believes Charlie is a stowaway, to imagine she is protecting him, before he elevates her—again literally—to his wealthy status and cleverly bridges the new gap between Charlie and Georgia that his success has created. It also avoids the sentimental unreality that the lack of such a device produces at the conclusion of *The Kid*. We are made to feel that he has earned Georgia as well as his gold.

The Gold Rush is Chaplin's most popular film; the one by which he is most often remembered. It is also his finest, as he himself consistently recognized. He never again achieved such profundity of effect, or devised a situation in which all his impulsion's and interests come together in so satisfying a dramatic whole. It would not be so warmly admired if it were not more than a piece of comic entertainment. It ultimately owes its appeal to the largeness of the questions it poses (can any comic film ever have posed larger?) and the quality of the answers it provokes. It strikes a responsive chord in the audience because of the way it dramatizes a widely held fear that our lives are governed by indifferent or hostile natural forces. Its challenge takes the form: if nature is brutal and irrational, and death the end of all, then what is the significance of life? But rather than counselling despair the film induces hope by indicating the benign aspect that nature's indifference can wear. Destructive power is balanced against creative potential. As well as oblivion, the snowy waste also powerfully suggests the shedding of the old and the possibility of the new. So the question becomes rephrased: what aspects of life can we cultivate in order to create significance?

Charlie's answers are: food, money and love. These are, of course, the perennial Charlie values. Upon analysis they turn out to be more complex than they seem thus baldly set down. As much as for their obvious benefits, each of them is valued for the opportunity it provides for gentlemanly manner and display (or what I have called Charlie's courtesy). Food means the rituals of gourmet dining; money (which must be providentially discovered, not lusted for or earned) means the dignified deportment of, and the respect owing to, a member of the leisured class; love means both the informality of companionship and the gallantry of infatuation. Charlie's values are a blend of the material and the non-material, and it is to demonstrate the mix that the film's considerable artistry is devoted. The most vivid demonstration is the boot-eating scene, where the food consumed is really non-food, its nutritional benefit being nil, and the entire satisfaction is a matter of display. Faced with the threat of starvation, Charlie stubbornly refuses to acknowledge its authority to modify his customary way of doing things. He may be dead, but he'll be damned if he'll lie down before it suits him. His stubbornness is not rigidity, but the reverse: it is a poetical logic, brought from beyond the 'boundary', that emancipates him from the actual rigidities of our logic, and it saves him. (Our logic says, If you are starving you will die.) Charlie's non-material values enable him to survive when simpler souls, for whom food is just food, are in danger of perishing. But it is important to emphasize that he is far from despising material satisfactions, which he seizes every opportunity of indulging. *The Gold Rush* is in many respects a paean of praise to the manifold pleasures of money, food, drink, love and conviviality. It is from the tension between the two kinds of value dramatized in the film—material and non-material—that Charlie derives his adaptability and resilience. His answer to the film's looming question can be said to read, you can live on old boots if you have to, but should enjoy the good things in life when you can. It may sound an obvious recipe, but it is harder, and wiser, than it seems.

The Circus

Although it is highly enjoyable, and takes its place in the canon of great Chaplin films, *The Circus* is not one of the best, or even most likeable. I think that everyone, without necessarily being able to define it, is conscious of the sense of something lacking in the film. I will discuss later my reasons for thinking that this is not a mistaken impression. The most obviously surprising feature of *The Circus* is the choice of subject, which does not seem to offer the same comic opportunities as the earlier films. Comedy thrives on contrast, and the Charlie figure particularly seems to call for situations in which his incorrigible oddity can be exploited to the full. A circus setting seems insufficiently incongruous. However, Chaplin manages to extract a remarkably varied range of comic effects from his chosen subject. More important, the feelings of restriction and enclosure imposed by the setting are themselves essential elements in the theme. For *The Circus* is about the idea of enclosure as it relates to comic performance. By depositing Charlie in an enclosed world of professional performers, it enables him to examine his own performing role, and to make some discoveries about the nature of performance.

Chaplin, in devising his major features, extensively cannibalized the situations and subject matter of his successful shorts. So much is obvious. Both the chief elements in *The Circus*—the love theme and the comic performance theme—clearly derive from earlier material. The love relationship between Charlie and Merna is established by an alfresco meal before a caravan, involving instruction in table manners and personal hygiene, that calls to mind the similar domestication of Edna in *The Vagabond*. The unhappy development of the relationship, in the form of a handsome intruder whose superior skills Charlie attempts to imitate, reminds us of the same film. But the love interest in *The Circus*, although it provides such motivation as the story possesses, is subsidiary to the theme of comic performance. Here, too, an obvious ancestry is apparent. Charlie's blundering intrusion into *The Circus* acts of others, and his own unfortunate attempt to reproduce time-honoured routines, recall those early shorts set in film studios where he contrives to reduce theatrical performance to a state of unseemly disarray. There seems to be a particular reminiscence of

Behind the Screen in the scene-shifters' strike, common to both films, that results in Charlie's engagement as factotum. But to compare *Behind the Screen* and *The Circus* is to realize that Chaplin's borrowings from himself were not simply a matter of thrifty elaboration and refinement (and that, despite the prominence of such borrowings in *The Circus*, they do not indicate any poverty of invention). The comedy of drama-confusion in *Behind the Screen* issues solely from the derangement of dignity and the subversion of order. In *The Circus*, while no less humorous, it is made the pretext for a quite unusually thoughtful investigation of the notion of comic performance.

It is some time before Charlie is allowed actually to enter *The Circus* itself. There is a long preliminary scene set in the fairground outside, in which he is obliged to undergo a succession of trials. If the length of this sequence did not suggest that it was important, and not a mere prelude, the quality of its comedy would. It is a virtuoso Chaplin opening: hectic in pace, rich in incident, full of suspense and surprise. It also establishes, wittily and economically, the themes of the film. The comedy of the sequence depends upon the systematic confusion of the distinction between reality and illusion. Charlie is thrust abruptly into a series of situations in which nothing is what it appears, and anything seems likely to happen. He is subjected to a crash course in disorientation, as his reasonable expectation of what will ensue is persistently confounded. Life takes on the unpredictability of a kaleidoscope. The result is a massive feeling of insecurity (delightedly shared by the audience, and, because of the normality of the context, even greater than that induced by the behaviour of natural forces in *The Gold Rush*), and a chronic uncertainty about identity and role. Charlie, who takes nothing lying down, needs all his resourcefulness to salvage what stability he can, as the tide of treacherous illusion threatens to engulf him.

Found money is an early casualty of the assault upon Charlie's certainties. It takes the form of loot, which, planted by a canny thief upon the unsuspecting Charlie, provokes a series of insecurity-inducing reversals of condition. When the thief is discovered in the act of retrieving from Charlie's person the stolen wallet and watch, Charlie is persuaded perplexedly to accept them as his own, only to find himself accosted by the owner for flaunting them with

a swaggering assumption of wealth, at the hot dog stall. The double chase that follows—of Charlie by the owner, of the thief by a
cop—culminates in a neatly symmetrical shot of Charlie and the
thief as the objects of parallel pursuit: with Charlie, wholly at a loss
but unfailingly polite, tipping his hat to his fellow fugitive. The
complicated comedy of mistaken intentions can rarely have been
extended so far, or so fruitfully. At each successive shock to his expectations, Charlie's reaction alternates between false confidence
and unwarranted guilt, until he eventually abandons all pretence
of knowing what the right reaction is. Charlie usually trusts found
money, and accepts it without question. He can only resolve this
situation by emphatically handing back the loot to the bemused
cop, leaving him and the thief to sort it out between them.

Charlie's disorientating trials in the purgatory of the fairground
continue in the maze of mirrors, where he is driven by the cop, and
where, suddenly confronted with multiple images of himself, he
has trouble sorting out the true from the false. Reality is fragmented, and the evidence of the eye cannot be trusted. Even the
simple action of retrieving his hat exposes him to unlooked-for
thumps on the head. However, Charlie derives advantage from
the confusion by realizing that he is not the only victim of it. The
same fragmentation of reality enables him to boot his pursuer's
backside and make his escape. His resourcefulness is carried over
to the next episode, when the pursuit leads to a carnival tableau of
Noah's Ark dummies. Charlie evades capture by smartly taking the
place of a retired automaton, and swivelling on the spot with gestures of paralytic precision. A characteristic, though still surprising, non-human disguise, the imposture enables him plausibly to
improve the occasion by walloping the thief, who has been forced
to join in. Here, perhaps on the 'if you can't beat them' principle,
Charlie *becomes* an illusion. Finally he is chased into the circus ring,
where he tangles involuntarily with the magician's act, in an amusing piece of drama-confusion. In faint perplexity, he emerges from
the magic box in place of the vanishing lady: providentially vanishing himself before the cop can grab him.

Each of the episodes that make up the fairground sequence illustrates the reality–illusion division in an interestingly different way.
The mix-up over the watch and wallet could be called a natural
illusion, caused by a complication of reality. The illusory element

derives from the participants' misinterpretation of what they experience, and the confounding of their expectations is the more
violent for the context's being so normal. The mirror maze is an
artificial illusion, recognizable as such but given dramatic significance by being made to intrude upon a 'real' situation. The
automaton imposture is a functional illusion, improvised by Charlie for his immediate advantage. For the purposes of the theme,
the vanishing lady episode, while probably not the funniest, is the
most interesting of all. The vanishing lady act is itself a deliberate
illusion and the significance of Charlie's intrusion varies according to whose point of view you take. For the magician, it represents a disastrous element of meddlesome reality that ruins his
illusion. For Charlie, it is all real, however unaccountable and per-
plexing. For the audience, it is a conventional illusion suddenly
endowed with the unexpectedness of reality. One cannot help
being conscious of all these attitudes when watching the scene,
and they make for an enjoyable complexity of response. By the
end of the whole sequence, reality and illusion seem to have become indistinguishably confused.

It is the presence of the audience that gives the vanishing lady
act its status of art-illusion. And the nature of art-illusions, which
The Circus exists to promote, is what the film proceeds to examine.
At this point we have to take into account the character of *The Circus*. Circuses occupy an affectionate place in the popular imagination. They are traditionally images of freedom, vagabondage,
courage and skill. They are enterprises that adventurous youths,
by convention, run away to join. The most important literary example is Mr Sleary's horse-riding in *Hard Times*. Dickens endows the
circus folk with the additional virtues of spontaneity, conviviality
and natural kindness, setting them against the disagreeable utili-
tarian philosophy of fact. However, Chaplin's circus is in sharp
contrast to this image. It is more like a circus run by Mr Gradgrind.
A depressing institution, its spirit is exemplified by the blankly
miserable faces of the clowns, briefly glimpsed as they are being
harangued by the moustachioed ringmaster; or by the picture of
the same gentleman walloping his daughter for flunking one of her
tricks. The most prominent qualities of the circus world are its enclosure and its unreality. It is literally and metaphorically enclosed
in a circle (and, within the film, enclosed between two images of a

paper star stretched over a hoop), and is devoted to the fostering of illusion by means of carefully circumscribed skills. Charlie, his sense of secure identity shaken by his fairground experiences, attempts to find a role in the circus world in which chance has deposited him. His attempts involve him in, and genuinely illuminate, a special aspect of the reality–illusion problem: the relationship between art and life.

Charlie's wrecking of the magician's act, so unexpectedly popular with the audience, earmarks him for the role of comic performer, and he is invited to participate in the official comedy of the circus. Two venerable routines, the William Tell act and the barber-shop act, are paraded for his imitation. It soon becomes clear that the circus's spirit of unreality has infected its comic art. The routines, laboriously performed and wearily predictable, are examples of paralyzed convention: made up of boorish aggressiveness and pointless acrobatics. Charlie is instructed to do likewise. But with the best will in the world (he earnestly *wants* to learn) he cannot help reducing the proceedings to an ignominious shambles. He is prevented from gobbling the apple by the presence of a worm, indicated in the famous finger-wiggling piece of mime, and helpfully proffers a banana as a substitute. In the barber-shop, the severe lathering to which he reluctantly submits rendering him sightless, he daubs myopically at everything within reach.

The humour of Charlie's versions of the routines is partly a simple matter of confusion-drama, provoked by his innocent literal-mindedness. But the reasons for the havoc he wreaks are very interesting. Charlie's inability to participate successfully in circus art is caused by his strong sense of reality and personal advantage. The worm in the apple is very real to him, as is the lather that plasters his face, and he doesn't see why he should undergo either if no tangible benefit is the result. He cannot reproduce, because he cannot understand, the conventions of circus art, and so meets the situations of art with the reactions of life. He further muddies the distinction between art and life by involving the ringmaster and other bystanders in the lunatic confusion. His chief impediment is his failure to appreciate any illusion that is not devoted to a practical end. He is himself a manufacturer of illusions, but his own—each improvised for the occasion and with an immediate purpose in view—have all the spontaneity and urgency that the circus's lack. (A good example of Charlie's familiar mastery, and the only pre-circus gag in the film, is his unscrupulous enticement of the acquiescent child's hot dog during the fairground preamble.) Charlie does eventually perform in the circus. But the irony of his performing career is that he is acclaimed as a performer for behaviour that, to him, is uncalculated and involuntary. The circus's art is Charlie's life. He repeats his success only when he is chased into the ring, as he was the first time, clutching a pile of plates, by a rampaging mule (who represents the irrational hazards of life). He can only maintain it by reproducing its provocation: so the mule has to professionalize his instincts and be on call to chase Charlie at every show. Charlie seems to need at least the sensation of entering art direct from life. To create illusion, he requires either a practical aim or the incitement of the fortuitous.

Charlie in performance, in fact, suggests a number of fruitful reflections. These deductions from his behaviour can be given a larger application to the general question of the relationship between art and life. Chaplin seems to be proposing that no art is profitable that does not have a vital relation to life, in the form either of a real-life incitement or a real-life aim. Without such a relation, the energies of art will slacken and its products wither. Against the rigid segregation of art and life implied by the enclosure of the circus, Chaplin sets the idea of a subtle interpenetration of the two. When at the end of the film he scrunches and discards the paper star, he is rejecting the limitations of circus art as well as the frustrations of circus life. Charlie's failure to perform circus art is an indication of his actual success, as his destruction of circus routines is really a higher form of creation. His protest is an instinctive recognition that creativity comes from life. Chaplin's own certainly does, as his great films abundantly testify, and not least in the wealth of ways in which his comic business appeals directly to our experience of life. (There may even be in these routine-wrecking scenes an autobiographical reminiscence of Chaplin's struggle to render sensitive and human the crude comedy of Karno and Keystone.) The thoroughness with which *The Circus* examines the theme of art and life would justify our regarding the film as Chaplin's critical credo. It is his comic-drama version of *An Essay on Criticism*. The treatment is all the more subtle and inward for itself being in terms, not of discursive argument, but of creative art.

If in one respect circus art is too controlled, in another it is not controlled enough. The debate does not end with the routine-wrecking scenes, but continues in those of Charlie's attempts, provoked by jealousy, to emulate the art of the tight-rope walker. Charlie usually enjoys, and profits from, the challenge of the un-predictable (it is for him a necessary ingredient of the creative), and this is what the tight-rope act, representing the circus's com-mitment to skill and courage, would seem to provide. This may appear to indicate a discrepancy in the proposed view of circus art. Can it be both closed to life and open to danger? The con-sistent element, for Charlie, is unreality: to him, it is as unreal to ignore the existence of danger as to manufacture unprofitable illusions. Charlie's flirting with danger (as well as being a matter of seized opportunities rather than constant exposure) is always balanced by his strong sense of prudence and instinct for survival. It is these that lead him to seek the benefits of heroism without incurring the risks: by practising on a rope two feet above the floor, or, when thrust into the ring, arranging to be supported by a safety harness. His prudent tipping of the scales in his favour can also be taken as registering a qualification of his idea of art, which is after all not so much like life that it involves tolerating open-ended hazards.

The tight-rope act is the culmination of Charlie's performing career, and the climax of the film. It is one of Chaplin's great balancing act finales. As well as providing a familiar element of suspenseful danger (Charlie's safety harness soon becomes disen-gaged and dangles tantalizingly before him), it is clearly intended to be a cathartic scene in which the themes of the film unite and are resolved. The tight-rope represents the courageous skills of the circus, and Charlie is impelled to attempt them by his love for Merna as well as his need for performing success. We are to see him as holding in balance the pleasures and the frustrations of circus art. That it does not quite work out like that is due to the weakness of the love interest (to be discussed below), which is too undeveloped to register much in our reaction to the climax. The art theme, however, is amusingly extended. Charlie finally tri-umphs in that he really does walk the rope unaided. Irony is provided by his temporary unawareness of the defection of the harness (rendering his confident shimmies on the rope much more audacious than he supposes), and suspense is augmented by his invariable talent for complication, resulting here in the released swarm of monkeys that attach themselves to his face and divest him of his trousers. His triumph is modified by the scene's neatly symbolic conclusion, when, cycling dementedly down the wire, he overshoots the net and ends up in the street outside, soliciting in bewilderment from life the applause denied him by art. The confusion of art and life is complete, and Charlie can no longer distinguish the two. He has no option but to give up. This fine scene extends the theme further by suggesting the necessity for a judicious blend of safety and danger, the predictable and the unpredictable, in life as well as in art.

I have indicated that the weakness of *The Circus* seems to me to lie in its love interest. Charlie's love for Merna is part of his attempt to find a role in the non-art area of the circus world. The early scene establishing their relationship is very well done in the affectionate-protective manner of *The Vagabond*, with Charlie showing the famished Merna how to eat without gobbling. (Their breakfast is provided by a hen that gingerly crosses the screen from side to side under Charlie's interested gaze—an unusual instance of Chaplin's comic use of the film frame.) At a later stage the love theme is integrated with the art theme: Charlie's belief that Merna loves him turns out to be an illusion. The trouble starts with the coming of Rex, the tight-rope man. Rex introduces a jarring element of normality and niceness. He is joined in this, outside the feeding scenes, by Merna, and together they force Charlie back into the sentimental situation of pathetic victim that he occupied in *The Gold Rush*. Rex is even worse than Georgia's Jack, because he hasn't the advantage of being a lout. He is so nice that Charlie is only allowed to take a fantasy (or illusory) revenge—in the compelling double-exposure scene when he imagines kicking the dust over his defeated rival. The feeling in this scene is so surprisingly violent that it is perhaps an indication of the extent to which Rex is a cipher, arousing Charlie's frustration as much as his jealousy. But the predominant feeling is sentimental. *The Circus* is the only film in which Charlie, as well as accepting the frustration of his love, actually contrives to bring the girl and his rival together.

Plate 5. *The Circus*

It would not be so bad if the love interest were not just about all that the film has to show in the way of story. The benefits of an energetic story-line are apparent in *The Gold Rush*, where the search for gold, even though remaining in the background, gives impetus to the events. In *The Circus*, Charlie is not significantly impelled to action by anything outside his love feelings. This robs the film of dynamism, and leaves a vacuum where our interested attention should be. It also leads to the central section's being padded out with irrelevant jokes—the cleaning of the goldfish, the doctoring of the horse and Charlie's heroics in the lion's den. These are amusing in themselves (Charlie's pleading with the dog not to disturb the lion by barking is an especially nice touch), but even regarding them as stages in Charlie's attempt to find a role in the circus world does not redeem their miscellaneousness. Nor is there any compensating scope for the comedy of feeling: Charlie's love, which is over almost as soon as it has begun, is not allowed to generate much business. The weakness infects even the tight-rope act, which is not *for* anything, except possibly to please Merna. It is really an elaborate imitation routine, Charlie's customary reaction to the superior skills of his rivals. Although a major test of his resourcefulness, it does not, like similar scenes in other films, result from his instincts for advantage or survival.

It would be a pity to leave the stress upon the sentimental element of *The Circus*. The film is about Charlie's (literal) disillusionment, and an unhappy love affair, however embarrassing, is at least appropriate to the theme. Also we are meant to feel, and do feel, that his final rejection of the circus, with its sealed-off art and deficient life, is both necessary and inevitable. (Though could he not as plausibly have been allowed to carry off Merna as Georgia?) *The Circus* asks in the end to be remembered for its analysis of the theme of reality and illusion (which in subtlety of interest goes beyond anything that Chaplin, or any other comic film-maker, had so far achieved), and for the wealth and variety of the comedy with which the theme is realized. It demonstrates with beautiful clarity that, however unremarkable Chaplin's conscious reflections of his art may have seemed, at the deeper level of instinct he knew exactly what he had to do, and how.

City Lights

This film was the occasion of more intense public interest even than any of Chaplin's earlier films. A silent film released at a time when talk, after a transitional period, had completely driven silence from the cinema, it came as a revelation of forgotten pleasures to filmgoers surfeited with indiscriminate chatter. It is understandable that contemporary reviewers should have dwelt upon this aspect, at the expense of any serious examination of the film's meaning. But the silence of *City Lights* no longer has this novelty interest: today it looks no different from those of Chaplin's earlier films to which synchronized soundtracks have been added. Free from the distraction of historical accident, we can perhaps try to determine more exactly what the film is about. For the conventional account of *City Lights* does not explain why it should be thought of as a great film.

That it *is* a great film, one of Chaplin's most successful, is generally agreed. But its greatness is usually described in terms that make it sound both sentimental and miscellaneous. There is to start with the question of its 'pathos', a term that is invariably employed in accounts of the film. I don't myself like the way this word is used, without definition or qualification, to describe the love interest in Chaplin's stories, and it is one that I prefer to avoid. Pathos suggests sentimental self-indulgence, a dishonest appeal for pity. This is an offence Chaplin certainly cannot always be acquitted of. But, as I tried to suggest in my account of *The Gold Rush*, the pathetic element in his films is often qualified by a genuinely realistic rendering of sensitive feelings, and of the behaviour dictated by feeling. Both sentimentality and real delicacy sometimes reside in the same material. I think that this is true of *City Lights*. It is often hard to distinguish the genuine and the corrupt in Chaplin's treatment of feeling: but the task of criticism is to try, and language that cannot convey the distinction is best left alone.

Whatever one calls them, feelings of love, unhappiness and fear clearly figure large in *City Lights*. It has even been suggested that they are more important than the moments of 'pure' comedy. Paul Rotha wrote, at the time of the film's first appearance, 'The humour lies there on the surface, easily picked up and not long-lived, but the pathos...is too deep down to be lightly forgotten.' And

René Clair, at the time of its reissue in 1950: 'In *City Lights*, Chaplin appeared for the first time in sentimental scenes that were
more important than the purely comic scenes.' These observations seem to me to be both right and wrong. They are right to
recognize the prominent part played in the film by feelings, but
wrong to regard these feelings as something distinct from the
comedy. If feeling and comedy were quite separate elements, we
would hardly be justified in thinking of the resulting mixture as a
great film, which should surely be distinguished by more unity of
effect.

The structure of *City Lights*, it is true, lends support to the idea
of a separation between comedy and feeling. There are two distinct strands to the narrative. The story of Charlie's love for the
blind flower-girl, which contains most of the feeling, runs parallel
to, but rarely combines with, the story of his involvement with the
eccentric millionaire, which contains most of the comedy. They are
linked by the demands of the plot: it is from the millionaire that
Charlie must obtain the money needed to cure the flower girl's
blindness. But a film consisting of two largely unrelated stories
would be no better a candidate for distinction than one in which
the comedy is wholly divorced from the feeling. It is unlikely to be
the coherent artistic success that *City Lights* is undoubtedly felt to
be. My own interpretation of the film is based upon two premises.
The first is that the two stories that form its narrative are linked by
more than the accidents of plot. For one thing, although their
atmosphere and setting are clearly intended to be in sharp contrast, they are not as distinct as they seem: not all the comedy is on
one side, nor all the feeling on the other. For another, they are
strongly linked by common themes in a multitude of ways. This
point will be developed at length below. The second premise is
that comedy and feeling are not separable elements. In Chaplin's
best films, there is no such thing as pure comedy: everything is significant, and serves an end. *City Lights* is a great film partly
because of the way in which the comedy defines and examines the
feeling. Rotha's observation, in fact, looks better when stood on its
head: it is the pathos (in the pejorative sense) that lies on the surface, and the humour, that with a little coaxing, reveals the depths.

City Lights is remarkable for the suggestive power of its comedy.
An example that will serve to introduce the film's main preoccu-

pation is the scene in which Charlie subjects a nude statuette in a shop window to a covert examination. This scene comes early in the film, and is not related to either of the two stories. It forms part of a preliminary 'warming up' sequence (which, despite its apparent randomness, contrives to establish all the chief characters, settings and themes), and doesn't, at the point it happens, seem more than gratuitously funny. Charlie, his eye caught by the statuette, pretends to be examining the picture that stands next to it. His manner is one of disinterested connoisseurship, and he moves back and forth on the pavement in his search for a juster estimate of form and perspective. But his eye keeps straying to the statuette, to which he eventually transfers his attention. A complication is added by the underground elevator being operated unawares behind him, on whose platform he manages providentially to land each time he steps back. The tension is resolved when, barely saved from a tumble down the shaft, he turns to sternly berate the slowly surfacing workman, who turns out, however, to be of a height and girth that make argument seem rash.

This scene takes its place in a long line of statuary gags, mostly in the short films, in which various representations of the female form arouse Charlie's more or less covert interest (examples include the voluptuous statue to which he doffs his hat in *A Night at the Show*, and the miniature version that he keeps tinkering with in *His New Job*). The humour that lies on the surface is the same in all instances, and derives from the contrast between Charlie's pretended interest and his actual interest. But the comedy of this scene is more extended, and more serious in its implications, and is not only devoted to the exposure of human weakness. One element that is emphasized is the clandestineness of the operation, which suggests the momentary indulgence of feelings that are normally suppressed. Another is the powerful attractiveness of the feelings that are denied, and the relish with which they are indulged. And the effect of the introduction of the elevator is to transfer its suggestion of danger and suspense to these same feelings, so that Charlie's eroticism comes to be felt as something at once suppressed, attractive and dangerous. Finally, there is a social implication in the contrast presented between public and private behaviour: Charlie's art critic act is seen as a socially acceptable expression of the erotic feeling he denies.

The statuette scene handily encapsulates the themes of *City Lights*. Its dramatization of the distinction between acknowledged feeling and suppressed feeling is central to the film. This idea is part of a general preoccupation with contrast and division. The structural division of the narrative into two distinct stories has already been noted. And the two stories, which take place in separate worlds, embody a social division. The poor, industrious, and self-respecting world of the flower girl is contrasted with the rich, idle and irresponsible world of the millionaire. It is possible to exaggerate the social aspect of the film, and, in particular, to attribute to it a more pointed significance than it possesses. There are no villains in *City Lights*. One kind of division it does not exhibit is moral division, and there is no sense of a divisive society as hostile or threatening. We are not back in the dog's world. In this respect, the opening scene, with its suggestion of social satire, is a trifle misleading. What is satirized here is simply social pretension, the studied denial of inconvenient feeling. This is the dominant habit of the top-hatted types who attend the unveiling: represented by the pompous monumentality of the statues they have come to see, which Charlie, planting his bum upon one outstretched hand and converting the solemn salute of another into a cocked snook, endows with a suddenly ribald life. Charlie's function is to introduce some human crudity into the dignified proceedings: he represents the class of feelings which the high society set pretends to ignore. He plays a similar role in the later party scene, when the respectful hush that precedes the vocalist's recital is interrupted by the whistle that he has inadvertently swallowed. The satirical target of these scenes (and one implication of the statuette scene) is the unreality of social convention.

City Lights is more concerned with the dramatic aspect of social division, the opportunities it offers for ironies of contrast and comparison, than with its moral aspect. Charlie accepts social division as a fact of life, and exploits it for his own ends. He relishes, as always, his fraudulent and insecure tenure of the high society world. Another indication of the film's central interest is the way it begins. Instead of the virtuoso opening scenes of the two preceding films, which firmly engaged the attention and elaborated the theme at length, there is an apparently random succession of short episodes, with only a temporal connection. This 'progress of a day' sequence is actually far from random: it does establish the theme, with subtlety and wit. What its form suggests is an offer to generalize from a wide range of experience. The theme being generalized, which cuts across the structural and social divisions, and that pervades the whole film is that of psychological division.

Despite its air of outward excitement and activity, *City Lights* looks inward to the human mind, to its obscure compulsions and motives. It finds in the mind a complex drama of cross-purposes, whose actors are fears and desires. On the one hand are the feelings we acknowledge, which are public, predictable, safe and respectable. This is the life that is lived on the surface. On the other hand are the feelings we suppress, which are private, unpredictable, dangerous and inclined to be disreputable. This is the life that is lived in the depths. Each kind of life is both desired and feared. The attraction of the surface life, which preaches the security of restraint, is countered by the attraction of the submerged life, which urges the pleasure of release. But at the same time the frustration of restraint is balanced by the terror of release. *City Lights* is one long balancing act, in which every quality encounters its opposite, and every impulse meets its check. Chaplin's treatment of this complicated material is inventive and masterful. His film owes its tension to this multiple conflict of feelings, its aesthetic pleasure to the opportunities for patterning they provide, and its energetic life to the variety of dramatizations to which they are submitted. The psychological drama is played out in terms of Charlie's relationships with each of the other main characters, the flower girl and the millionaire (whom I shall call Virginia and Harry, after the names of the performers), and of his experience independent of either. The two halves of the narrative are linked by the different ways in which they embody the common theme of the dangerous and attractive submerged life.

The most important instance in the film of feeling that is both desired and feared is Charlie's love for Virginia. This is, even at the obvious level, what the film is 'about' and most of the other instances serve to enforce it. Charlie's dilemma is that only love can give him happiness, but that to submit to love is to court near-certain grief. Virginia represents to him both the temptation and the terror of giving way to feeling. Charlie fears love because it carries the threat of rejection, betrayal and ridicule. (His proneness to ridicule is established by scenes in which he is baited by a pair of vindictive street urchins.) The crucial factor in this relationship is Virginia's blindness. Charlie can't deny his love, but Virginia's blindness saves him from the consequences of it (she can't witness his insignificance and delivers him from fear by enabling him to play the role of lover without danger of exposure. The irony of his situation is that love impels him to devote his creative energy to Virginia's recovery of sight: an end that, accomplished, will reintroduce the danger. That he is aware of this thought, but buries it and dislikes to be reminded of it, is neatly registered by the brief hesitation and careless shrug with which he marks Virginia's reaction to the prospect of sight ('Then I'll be able to see you!'). His deliverance is only is only temporary, and the irony supplies a dramatic tension that builds up to the inevitable moment of exposure.

Her blindness is no less protective for Virginia herself. It enables her to be deluded into thinking Charlie is a grand and wealthy suitor, and to remain ignorant of her degree of destitution, and of her mother's sacrifices on her behalf. Her blindness is inner as well as outer. The limitation of her understanding is comically rendered by those moments when her blindness is made to seem faintly ridiculous: when she unsuspectingly sloshes the adoring Charlie with dirty water, or unravels his vest in mistake for her ball of wool. (Her affliction, while respected, is not immune to comic treatment.) Virginia's insulation from reality is more complete than Charlie's. She is not, like him, troubled by a consciousness of duplicity, or by any premonition of disappointment, and her disillusion comes all at once. Although she is happy in her blindness, which represents the predictable surface of her life, she longs for sight, which represents the unpredictable depths. She doesn't fear the depths because she can't imagine their danger, but we fear them for her.

Before asking whether this pattern of feeling is in fact successfully conveyed, I want to consider how the same ideas recur, and are extended, in Charlie's other important relationship, and in his own behaviour. Charlie's dealings with Harry are unquestionably successful, and give rise to some of the best comedy in the film. The first thing to notice about Harry is that he is, in his comical way, a 'tragic' figure. Like Charlie, he is a refugee from feeling.

He has suffered a massive unhappiness, related, we gather, to his ruined marriage and absconded wife. We first meet him in the act of trying to drown himself, and he introduces into the film a note of suicidal despair that threatens Charlie's safety as well as his own. He doesn't have Charlie's protection against the painfulness of his feelings, and can only take refuge from them in drink.

Harry is a very complex case. If he resembles Charlie in his fear of feeling, he resembles Virginia in the psychological division that rules his life. As Virginia, without really knowing it, is torn between blindness and sight, so Harry is torn between drunkenness and sobriety. With this comparison, the complications multiply. A common-sense view would imagine that Harry's sobriety corresponds to Virginia's sight, both being states of lucid understanding. And they do correspond in that both involve confronting, and coming to terms with, painful feelings: just as both Harry's drunkenness and Virginia's blindness provide insulation from pain. But there is a more powerful consideration for which the comparison must be stood on its head. Harry's sobriety resembles Virginia's blindness in being a frustrating and inhibiting condition of restraint, while his drunkenness, like her sight, stands for the perilous pleasures of release. The important difference is that Virginia finds satisfaction in confronting her problem, Harry only in avoiding his.

Harry in his cups is a man who abandons all restraint. To increase the complication, his psychological division has its own subdivision. When drunk, he switches into a manic-depressive cycle of behaviour, alternately suicidal and festive. It is this division that creates the greater problems for Charlie. To read many accounts of *City Lights* before being able actually to see it, which was my experience, is to imagine that the humour of the Charlie–Harry relationship lies in the disorientating effect upon Charlie of Harry's changes from hospitable drunkenness to unresponsive sobriety. In fact, this reaction is made very little of. Charlie comes to accept Harry's periods of perplexed non-recognition, just as he accepts the division of society into rich and poor, and simply contrives to extract the maximum advantage from the periods of recognition. He is more flummoxed by the manic-depressive habit. To Charlie, Harry represents both the danger and the excitement of giving way to the promptings of the submerged life. The obvious danger comes from Harry's depressive half. Charlie expends

Plate 6. *City Lights*

much effort in trying to frustrate his friend's suicidal drive: dredging him from the river, confiscating his gun, assuming control of his car in mid-spin. An associated danger is the pair of thugs who raid the mansion and attempt to nobble Charlie's hard-extorted loot. In Harry's company, there is an oppressive feeling of the need to stave off threats, and Charlie's talent for survival is tested to its limits.

Harry's alternative appetite, for the excitement of riotous conviviality, Charlie is only too glad to go along with, but it turns out to be hardly less dangerous. Harry's euphoric half seeks its satisfaction in the city's night life. The cabaret scene that results is the most inventive passage of comedy in *City Lights*. From the moment the companions enter, with that combination of limpness and self-importance that intoxication confers, the proceedings erupt into vivid life. The action visibly accelerates and a feeling of nervous excitement takes command. Charlie, his eyes glazed but his reflexes alert, is subjected to a sustained demonstration of the disorientating effects of total release. Drink doesn't affect his quickness of reaction, but misdirects its application by blurring the reality of what he perceives. In a boisterous warming-up exercise, both Charlie and Harry aggressively misinterpret the innocent behaviour of waiters and guests, removing their jackets and squaring up for battle at imaginary provocations. Arrived at their table, across a dance floor whose surface deprives his legs of their normal rigidity, Charlie is no safer. The menu thrust at him suggests a hymn book, and he rises dutifully to participate in the unexpected rites. Harry's cigar, gestured towards his mouth, he repeatedly lights in the belief that it is his own. The spaghetti he is served, whose constituent strands he nibbles individually, transforms itself, by a remorseless progression, into paper streamers attached to the ceiling. And the behaviour of the apache dancer, who uses his attractive partner to polish the floor, suggests to Charlie's gallantry the need for urgent intervention. After dinner, Charlie, his feet tapping, is infectiously attracted by the dance. Impulsively grabbing the nearest woman, he launches on to the floor, exchanging her shortly for a passing waiter, who, in his state of euphoria, serves his purpose just as well.

Charlie's drunken relationship with Harry, with its air of camaraderie and companionable ease, calls to mind, in conjunction

with the action and business of the cabaret scene, such earlier
night-on-the-town two-reelers as *The Rounders* and *A Night Out*. Part
of the intended effect is that we *should* be reminded of the simple
comic exuberance of these earlier films. The obvious difference is
that the cabaret scene, unlike the earlier films, is set within a serious framework that gives both emphasis and point to its image of
festive abandon. Also, while the comedy of the two-reelers consists
mostly of the disturbance of order and dignity, that of the cabaret
scene arises from Charlie's befuddled perception of a world from
which, together with conventional restraints, conventional expectations have vanished. Charlie's adventures in the cabaret express
the theme by demonstrating that, in abandoning ourselves to the
life of instinct, we abandon our power to make reasonable predic-
tions about our experience. The actual moment of abandon is
beautifully caught in the image of Charlie's eruption onto the
dance floor. At the same time, so powerful is the liveliness of the
scene, and so exhilarating its picture of release, that the total
effect is far from admonitory. The attractiveness of the psychological underworld is as much in evidence as its danger. The theme is
qualified by the suggestion that it is only in the lower reaches of
the mind that creative energy is generated.

For Charlie, Virginia and Harry represent different versions of
the problem of how to cope with dangerous and attractive suppressed feelings. With Virginia, the problem is held in suspense;
with Harry, the feelings are let loose. Charlie's own role in the
film's conflicts is usually the unenviable one of pig-in-the-middle.
Although hazardous, the role allows him to display his familiar
mastery over circumstances. His dilemma is dramatized by the
structural division of the film: Virginia is the respectable surface of
his life, Harry the disreputable underworld into which he periodically descends. He spends much of his time shuttling between the
two. He inhabits both of the social divisions of the film, and contains within himself its psychological division. He is both rich and
poor: a fraudulent member of Harry's world, and a genuine member of Virginia's (where he pretends to be a member of Harry's).
His richness and poverty are wittily fused in the moment when,
leaping from his limousine, he battles with an astonished tramp
for possession of a discarded cigar butt. He is both respectable and
disreputable: elevated to the best society by Harry's patronage, he

jeopardizes his position by ruining the singer's performance, and commits such solecisms as mistaking a bald head for a cream pie.

Charlie's experience independent of both his friends is not padding or gratuitous clowning, but can be seen to embody the psychological division of the film. I have suggested that the deceptively modest statuette scene expresses his nervous awareness of suppressed feeling, especially of its attractive aspect. Something similar is true of one of the obviously major comic passages in the film: the boxing match. This is one of the highlights, surpassed in the richness of its comedy only by the cabaret scene. It is hard to credit that at so late a date anyone could create a boxing comedy that is wholly original and surprising, yet Chaplin succeeds. Like the cabaret scene, its effect depends partly upon our remembering Chaplin's earlier treatment of the same material (in this case, *The Champion*), but, this time, in order to confound our expectations. The big surprise in the boxing scene is that next to no boxing actually takes place. Charlie, his prospect of an easy bout upset by a substituted opponent, solves the problem by turning the proceedings into a dance. The whole match is taken up by an agile but delightfully relaxed sideways prancing, clearly derived from observation of the kind of movements that boxers make before actually engaging. But no engagement happens, if only because Charlie contrives to keep the referee between himself and danger. The effect is of a needle stuck in a groove, or of an important announcement that consists only of a repeated introduction. Charlie's insistence upon going through the motions of boxing without actually doing any eventually mesmerizes both his opponent and the referee into participating in the game, which takes on an absurdly self-perpetuating momentum. These are delights of social comedy, but it must be stressed that *City Lights* is Chaplin's most deliberate engagement with the comedy of feeling, and the risks are clearly large. Many elements in the situation—Virginia's blindness, their common protection from reality, the moment of exposure—risk inviting sentimentality by their obvious appeal for the audience's pity. A large part of their effect certainly is sentimental. The tormenting of Charlie by the street urchins, which marks him as ridiculous and pathetic by 'normal' standards, is a further distasteful inducement to pity. Chaplin, in fact, sets up Charlie as a pathetic victim in a pretty thoroughgoing way. Yet I hope I am not alone in feeling able to salvage something genuine from all this. It would be a shame if our distaste for the sentimentality left us immune to whatever is really felt and communicated. I feel that a number of aspects of Charlie's relationship with Virginia are genuine in this way, and that, as usual, they establish their credentials by a direct appeal to an experience of life.

For one thing, Charlie's affection for Virginia communicates itself in a number of delicate ways that we recognize as forming part of our experience of similar situations. The delicacy is a matter of the compunction with which he treats the embarrassment of her handicap. At their first meeting, Virginia imagines that he is a rich man alighted from a limousine (which he has actually been using as a thoroughfare): she sells him a flower, and, hearing another car door slam, thinks he has left without his change. Charlie, fearful of destroying the illusion, tiptoes away. Later he endures, in the same cause and with admirable stolidity, a drenching with flower water and the piecemeal removal of his vest. The need, at the risk of our own embarrassment, tactfully to connive at fictions in order to spare the embarrassment of another is one we must all have felt. These episodes also help to endow Virginia's character with rather more reality than it possesses for most of the time. She is in general rather limp and lifeless: a more vigorous and attractive characterization would have done much to qualify the sentimentality. Her limpness may be due to the inexperience of the actress, or to the difficulty of acting blind; it is probably designed to contrast with the much greater animation she displays at the end, when she has regained her sight.

For another thing, Charlie's predicament is genuinely interesting. Fear of rejection in love is a sufficiently common and important experience for the irony of his situation—the knowledge that by serving the object of his love he invites its rejection—to engage our sympathetic interest. We do care about the progress of Charlie's love affair, and, like him, both desire and fear its outcome. The resolution of his love feelings, long held in suspense, is the moment towards which the whole film inexorably moves. About the success of this moment, when both Charlie and Virginia are forced to shed the protection of blindness, there is general agreement. Although it is potentially the most embarrassing moment in the film (and has been described by some advocates in terms that seem to me exaggerated), its effect, by virtue of tactful acting and timing, is not sentimental but delicately honest. Virginia recognizes Charlie by the feel of his hand, and her ironical words ('Yes, I can see now ') express not cheap disillusion but perplexity and wonder. Charlie's shy smile (*not* 'foolish grin', *pace* Walter Kerr) beautifully registers his mixture of hopefulness and fear, and is the image we are left with as the film fades away. The outcome is that there is no outcome, in simple narrative terms, but it is nonetheless a satisfying conclusion to the theme. Charlie and Virginia are obliged at last to face the reality of feeling: all the conflicts of the film are concentrated in their expressions, and held in ambiguous tension.

City Lights is perfectly enjoyable on the surface as a story of love and comic misadventure. But I hope that I have shown, without straining credibility, that it can be made to yield depths. Indeed, the film could be regarded as an endlessly resourceful demonstration that there are such things as depths, and that they cannot be ignored. The film is remarkable, perhaps unique, in comic drama, for the extensiveness with which its central theme, as well as being directly dramatized, is re-enacted metaphorically in other parts of the action that don't, to the casual eye, appear to relate to it. As I suggested at the beginning, the effect of this, as well as redeeming the film from the charge of miscellaneousness, is to generalize Charlie's predicament by placing it within a larger context of fears about feelings and their violence. So his familiar hopeful and fearful love relation is at last given the prominence and dignity it deserves, and brought to the forefront of the drama without risk of sentimentality by being presented as one aspect of the unpredictable and hazardous quality of life itself. And I very much doubt whether the complex pattern of significance I have proposed was the result of Chaplin's conscious devising. It was much more probably unconscious and unbidden: evidence, surely, that the theme and its resolution had themselves arisen from the depths.

Chapter 6

Sound Features

New Challenges for Charlie

The three films treated in this chapter form a kind of trilogy. Each is very different from the others, but they are linked by the common challenge of sound and speech, and the common aim of confronting Charlie with the anxieties of modern life. It is to Chaplin's credit that he recognized, and did not flinch from, both the challenge and the aim. The task of meeting them involved him in a huge effort of consciousness. I have suggested that consciousness was not an unmixed blessing to Chaplin, and that he easily descended into bathos and facetiousness when he neglected the deeper promptings of instinct. So it is not surprising if, in discussing these films, one finds oneself more engaged in sifting the true from the false, and more often moved to qualifications and disclaimers. Yet they constitute a striking original achievement. We are always conscious of the effort involved, but the assimilation of different dramatic traditions that the effort produced (that of clown comedy and that of social satire) resulted in a treatment of the themes that is highly individual in its mixture of fantasy and acerbity. These three films now look like a natural development, but it would have been impossible to predict that Chaplin would develop in this way. They are a true, if unexpected culmination of Charlie's art.

They are not the only sound films that Chaplin made, and once again an explanation of the omissions seems called for. After *Monsieur Verdoux* appeared *Limelight*, and it is this that has a fair claim to be considered Chaplin's last truly distinguished film. I do not discuss it at length partly because it is largely a 'serious' film rather than a comedy, and partly because so much of its intended effect remains at the level of intention, and so is not really discussible in the terms it proposes. *Limelight*'s faults are fairly obvious: it is verbose, sententious, sentimental, exaggeratedly acted and sluggish in movement. It is a long film, and seems even longer than it is. The chief barrier to taking it totally seriously is the fact that our appreciative sympathy depends so much upon our consciousness of Chaplin the man and of his by then legendary career, and upon the film's relation to these. The feeling of nostalgia and retrospection, which it is the film's main achievement to evoke, belongs to Chaplin as much as to Calvero, and the tribute of our sympathy is to him. In other words, too much of Chaplin's personal prestige is invested in Calvero, whose story, without it, is not endowed with enough substance to make it seem more than pathetic. Chaplin is not Calvero, of course: for one thing, Chaplin was a phenomenal success. But the film does have an unmistakable autobiographical resonance, especially in its depiction of Edwardian London and of theatrical life. The careful recreation of houses, streets and clothes is clearly derived from Chaplin's memories of his youth (his autobiography reveals his observant eye for details of dress). There is a specific reminiscence in the character Postant (played by Nigel Bruce) of the actual theatrical manager William Postance whom Chaplin had known as a young actor. These personal factors serve both to emphasize the identification of Chaplin and Calvero and to soften our reaction to the film's faults.

Yet *Limelight* also has real virtues, and to a certain extent can be taken seriously on its own terms. It is a study, in the figure of Calvero, of demoralization as a result of old age, failing creative powers, thwarted emotion and cynicism; and of recovery of morale by the adoption of an object of dependence and by the hopeful example of youth. At the centre of the drama is the relationship between Calvero and Terry (Claire Bloom). As with all Chaplin's love relations, there is a genuine element in this that is not wholly obscured by the undoubted self-indulgence. What gets in the way is not so much sentimentality as verbosity and weakness of dramatization. Chaplin seems unable to let his story speak for itself, but must put his verbal oar in, at tedious length. Yet the intention is clear enough; and there *is* something touching in their familiar

protective-dependent relationship. Particularly striking is the irony
that, after Calvero has forced Terry back into life, she has similarly
to force him; and that her fame coincides with his decline. This
pattern rescues the film from shapelessness, despite its length. An
added poignancy is the love that Calvero reluctantly feels for Terry,
which leads him in the end to relinquish her to her younger admirer. A triangular love situation, like the principal's protective-
dependent relationship, is an ingredient that conjures memories
of many of Chaplin's past achievements (one thinks of *The Vagabond*, *The Kid*, *The Circus* and *City Lights*), and so solicits even more
of our sympathy. What has come in between *Limelight* and these
earlier films is *Monsieur Verdoux*, with its predominantly cynical
tone. It is likely that the reluctant attraction between Verdoux and
the Girl, which his cynicism cannot overcome, was the inspiration
for the story of Calvero and Terry, where the same theme is developed at much greater length.

There is another theme in *Limelight*, handled very interestingly,
that issues in the film's most memorable scene. This is the theme
of comic performance. Calvero lives only in performance, and his
exclusion from it is a kind of death. We see some imagined episodes, in flashback, from his performing life. His solo acts, which
are conventionally competent, have a strangely isolated air, as if
taking place in a closed room, with neither sight nor sound of an
audience. The oddity is explained when the camera at length
draws back to reveal an empty theatre: they are Calvero's night-
mares. His one piece of indubitable performance, with which the
film concludes, is no less baffling. This is the famous double act
with Buster Keaton in which, as would-be *salon* musicians, their
efforts to produce music are repeatedly frustrated by the malevolence of their instruments, or of their own bodies. This scene has
a more vivid life than Calvero's earlier performances, and has
always been recognized as crucial to the film. It is difficult now to
place it *within* the film, so direct is its real-life appeal. Keaton complicates the effect by adding his own particular nostalgia (which
may have been less potent, and was certainly different, at the time
of issue than now when he is so well-known). He is certainly very
good, but his present-day celebrity probably has the effect of disturbing the scene's balance: his function here is largely to be Chaplin's foil. It has often been remarked how each clown behaves

characteristically: Keaton private and self-absorbed, desperately shovelling up the sheets of music that keep collapsing into his lap; Chaplin, as his foot disappears into his trouser-leg, turned to address the audience (whom he mutely invites to share his perplexity at the untoward event).

The Chaplin–Keaton duo is a virtuoso exercise in comic frustration. It is a self-contradictory performance—one in which the idea of performance is defeated and denied. In this it resembles Charlie's equivocal song at the end of *Modern Times*, where our reasonable expectations of orderly performance are thwarted by its semi-comprehensibility. In the present case the performance fails to begin. There are a number of other reminiscences of earlier films. For one thing, Chaplin is a violinist, as in *The Vagabond*, a fact that alerts us to the art theme. And the physical indignity that plagues him, and which he spends the greater part of the scene helplessly attempting to rectify—the self-elevation of his foot—is a reminder of those moments in earlier films when Charlie appeared to disclaim responsibility for the extremities of his body: his foot, lifted for a kick, would, caught in the act, be examined curiously, readjusted with his cane or brushed with his cuff. The most significant reminiscence comes at the conclusion of the scene, when Chaplin falls from the stage and lands in the drum. This suggests Charlie's characteristic leaps from art into life (such as his backward tumble into the washtub in *The Vagabond*, or his demented overshooting of the high wire in *The Circus*), except that for Calvero it is a leap into death. This performance is a final one, a circumstance that casts its shadow back over the whole episode and makes us reflect that it is, for Chaplin, a performance afflicted by a dismaying degree of paralysis. This is the theme of a long account by William Willeford, in which he discusses the scene in terms of the conflict between chaos and order, and as a demonstration of the ubiquitousness of sickness and death. An especially telling point is his detection of a kind of unadmitted collusion between the performers and the malign forces that overwhelm them. I think that Willeford exaggerates the macabre element, but it is certainly present, and his analysis is characteristically subtle. For my purposes I would stress how different the double act seems, for all its fascination, from Charlie's impudent acts of transformation.

Calvero's death is, for practical purposes, the death of Charlie
too. There are glimpses of Charlie in *A King in New York*, but he
is never again an effective force. The glimpses include the clever
'caviar' and 'turtle soup' mimes in the restaurant scene when
Shahdov's order to the waiter is drowned by the noise of the floor
show; his familiar attitude of coy propitiation on his discovery in
the act of keyhole-peeping at Dawn Adams (followed by the business-like enlistment of a stool for more comfortable viewing, and
the pulling of rank on his elderly aide, who wants to look too);
and the moment when he registers that, in a fit of pique, he is tearing up a cheque for a sizeable sum. More generally, Shahdov exhibits a pervasive Charlie-like play of expression and attitude in
his reactions to objects and to people (in particular, a first-Char-
lie-like sensitivity to insult). We recognize all these glimpses with
pleasure. But the point about them is that, except possibly for the
first, they are all marginal and gratuitous. The only funny and
familiar moment that bears any relation to the theme is the whisky
advertisement scene, when Shahdov's paean of praise for the spon-
sor's tipple is ruined at its climax—the moment of tasting—by an
energetic choking fit. This is a standard piece of drama-confusion,
but it is also the last example we are to see of Charlie's difficulty in
distinguishing between art and life. For his involuntary reaction to
the disgusting product is successful, and he is forced to watch it
reproduced on television night after night, just as Charlie in *The
Circus* had to repeat his spontaneous entry into the ring as if it
were a routine gag: Shahdov's life is the advertiser's art. The scene
is relevant because the theme of *A King in New York* is the vulgarity
and materialism of American life. But in general the treatment of
the theme is characterized by neither subtlety nor wit. The film's
method of procedure is to drown the absurdities of modern life
with ridicule; and ridicule of an obvious and childish kind. We can
applaud the simple generousness of the intention, but hardly the
way in which it is effected: Charlie's true art is missing from the
centre, where it ought to be. It doesn't help that the only positive
value that Shahdov can oppose to the way of life he attacks is a
naive Wellsian vision of the beneficence of nuclear power. One
brief satirical moment early on—when Shahdov nervously negotiates the lurid and crowded hubbub of Times Square at night, while
a syrupy voice on the soundtrack (his own?) croons, 'When I think

of a million dollars/Tears come to my eyes'—has always struck me, in its telling economy, as the best joke in the film.

A Countess from Hong Kong is short on jokes, and on everything else except tedium and embarrassment. Here the brief glimpses we get of Charlie are literally that: moments when a door opens to find him standing there, in the guise of a seasick steward, with his hand to his bilious mouth. Two hours of boredom is a high price to pay for a few seconds of pleasure. Only love of Charlie could make anyone sit through it, and even then the pain of the experience outweighs the consciousness of loyalty. It is never pleasant, though it may be profitable, to contemplate genius in decline. All one can say for Chaplin's final enterprise—interminable, miscalculated and miscast—is that it forces one to remember that he nonetheless *was* a genius, and to turn one's attention to the many films in which that genius is expressed.

Modern Times

Chaplin's earliest films are neither dependent upon, nor limited by, being set in any particular time or place. There is no attempt to disguise the setting, which the costumes and decor reveal as pre-1920 America, but it is not important in itself. It did not strike any contemporary audience, and does not strike us now, as distractingly alien. The spirit of these films is theatrical rather than realistic. The houses, hotels, restaurants and parks in which the action takes place are the conventional background for the conventional complications of farce. This stylized element makes the occasional intrusions of the unmistakably specific (such as *The Jitney Elopement*'s car chase along the wet rutted roads of developing California) all the more startling. It also both allows Chaplin to emphasize the human aspect of his comic dramas and encourages the universal identification upon which his popularity is based.

Their timeless quality meant that these films were to a certain extent insulated from contemporary reality. In the films made during the war this did not especially matter, since their confident energy reflected the stability of the prewar world. The postwar world was markedly unstable, restless and confused. But Chaplin's films made after 1920 do not register this change in spirit. They are just as indeterminate in time and place. In *The Kid* this vagueness is turned to advantage: the city where Charlie lives, which in the high-life scenes is obviously on the west coast of modern America, is in the low-life scenes able to suggest, as has often been noticed, the squalid London of Chaplin's youth. *The Gold Rush* and *The Circus* both have specialized and exotic settings, which do not need a realistic context; and the city of *City Lights* is deliberately made anonymous and representative to highlight and generalize the drama of human feelings. So the problem of Charlie's relation to the modern world is repeatedly avoided.

After *City Lights* it could be avoided no longer. There were three factors that made it a problem, and one which to Chaplin must have seemed increasingly urgent. The first factor has already been suggested: the nature of the postwar world. This, which is still our own world, was characterized by political ferment, industrial unrest and accelerating social and economic change. In such a world the figure of Charlie seemed an anachronism: an Edwardian gentleman down on his luck, reflecting the niceties of social distinction that had started to vanish. How could what he represented be brought into a living relation with the changed conditions? The question was to preoccupy Chaplin for many years. His ingenuity in finding ways to avoid it is perhaps an indication of the uneasiness it caused him. The second factor, closely related to the first, was the increasing refinement and ambition of Chaplin's art. He had progressed from the unsophisticated farce of the earliest films to a realistic mode of comedy, based upon the subtle observation of human behaviour, which admitted a new range of feelings and gave them dramatic shape. He looked for new and challenging subjects, and the new conditions of the modern world seemed to offer them. The third factor was technical, but momentous: the demise of the silent film, and the universal adoption of speech. *City Lights* was an anachronism by the time it appeared, although the conventions of the silent film must still have been fresh in the minds of the audience. But *City Lights* could not be repeated. Charlie's eloquence was essentially mimic and silent: but to remain silent was to risk seeming even more of an irrelevance. Sooner or later, Charlie had to speak.

Chaplin's answer was to make *Modern Times*, in which Charlie is thrust unceremoniously into the modern world and left to his own devices. The story of the film is the story of his efforts to survive.

So there are really two problems: Chaplin's and Charlie's. The film is in the nature of an experiment for both. Chaplin's problem of artistic survival, or how to make films reflecting modern conditions, is paralleled by Charlie's problem of physical survival, or how to cope in a world whose malevolence has suddenly taken an alarming new form. The fictional problem dramatized the actual problem, and the sympathy of the audience, whether it realizes it or not, is engaged equally in the solution of both. A consciousness of multiple suspense, of Chaplin's having as much at stake in the outcome as Charlie, is what gives *Modern Times* its tension, rather than any accident of plot. But it makes the task of criticism difficult when one comes to sort out the kind of success or failure involved. Equally, the knowledge that both Chaplin and Charlie were to face unprecedented challenges was one factor that made *Modern Times* eagerly awaited. Another was the knowledge that Charlie was, finally, to speak.

Modern Times announces itself as 'a story of industry, of individual enterprise—humanity crusading in the pursuit of happiness'. This epigraph is impressive but vague, and seems uncertain whether or not it is meant to be ironical. In this it is symptomatic of the film as a whole, and so strikes a truer note than it intends. However, like the title eventually chosen (the first was *The Masses*), it alerts us to the prospect of a departure from Charlie's familiar themes, in the form of an involvement in realities hitherto avoided. We are meant to feel, and do feel, that *Modern Times* is Charlie resolutely confronting the twentieth century. This feeling is conveyed by the opening shots, with their overtly satirical intention— the huge clock face, the linked images of sheep and commuters, the factory boss with his gadgets, jigsaw puzzle and comic books— and by the, sternly portentous music, whose cadences now seem so characteristic. The chief impression of the opening is one of menace. It soon becomes clear that the modern world is highly uncongenial and conceals as much danger and threat as the wilderness of *The Gold Rush*. Charlie finds himself deposited in a different kind of wilderness: a vast, anonymous, modern industrial state, where he is shunted from place to place—factory, jail, store, swamp—in his search for security. It is like the dog's world, but impersonal and organized. The danger is psychological rather than physical: harassment is transformed into a principle. The

Plate 7. *Modern Times*

modern world is seen as a powerful and oppressive servitude. The atmosphere is genuinely painful and frightening: the film owes its disturbing power to the way it dramatizes widely held feelings of fear, anonymity and frustration in the face of modern life.

Work is one of Charlie's favourite modes of operation, and it is appropriate that the film should find the hostility of the modern spirit concentrated in the image of the factory. Charlie values work for the opportunities it offers for creative satisfaction: the modern spirit regards it as a merely functional, rather than a human, activity, and an obvious candidate for the discipline of mechanization. It is the machine, and all that it entails, that introduces the element of anxiety, and makes a crisis for Charlie inevitable. For machines don't recognize creative satisfaction: they are reductive in intention and effect. They counter the natural human tendency to diversify and complicate by imposing uniformity and simplicity. Their virtues are speed, regularity, repetition, predictability, efficiency and accumulation. Harmless enough if kept in their place, which is that of a means to an end, they are too readily elevated to ends in themselves. Their effect upon work is to change it from a source of immediate satisfaction into a fragmented and self-perpetuating chore whose end product is so remote from the performer as to lose all reality. (What Charlie's factory actually produces is never divulged, and doesn't really matter: as far as the workers are concerned, it could be anything or nothing.) And machine work is a process justified not in terms of human fulfilment but of economic obligation, though champions of the system try to confuse the two. As René Clair's schoolmaster, to whom I will return, speciously intones, 'Le travail est obligatoire, car le travail est la liberté ('work has to be done, for work is freedom'). In the pragmatist's comfortable double-think, bondage is a truer kind of liberty.

Charlie isn't concerned with theory, but he has a lively sense of practical realities. When the camera pulls back to reveal Charlie's frantic absorption in his assembly line task, the incongruous spectacle induces in us a familiar pang of anticipation, at once delighted and apprehensive. We know that something has to give. Charlie sets about demonstrating, politely but firmly the inadequacy of the machine principle as applied to work. Part of his strategy is to counter the mechanical virtue of predictability with his own brand of unpredictability—the inspired art of the random and arbitrary. The relentless automatism of the conveyor belt doesn't allow, as Charlie must, for the unforeseen hazard of a predatory wasp, or the discomfort of an itching armpit; nor can it wait while he mimes to the foreman the cause of the resulting confusion. Charlie himself is not invulnerable: the machine habit invades his nervous system, reducing him to a twitching automaton who mindlessly wields his spanners on the buttons of a bending secretary's dress, and slops a plate of soup over his mate's trousers. He isn't even allowed the basic human privacy of a quiet smoke in the wash-room: the spirit of scientific omnipotence extends even there, in the form of a television screen that erupts with the President's hectoring image.

Charlie's rebellion, when it comes, is directed against the whole ethic of work as a mere frustration and social obligation that underlies the imposition of machine methods. For him, work is more a matter of aesthetics than of ethics: it must both have an evident purpose and be a self-sufficient pleasure. He is concerned to restore work to the status of a human activity, which need not exclude the larger interests and promptings of life. He challenges the discontinuity between work and play by turning work into play (and, later in the film, play into work). So, in the delightful finale to the sequence, he reverts to a state of child-like irresponsibility, a prelapsarian innocence: skipping from machine to machine snapping switches at random, squirting oil at the assembly line slaves (who dutifully stop chasing him and return to their stations when he reactivates the conveyor belt), and coyly shunting the huge lever, his leg daintily uplifted, in a shot that provides the film's most memorable image. In these exhilarating moments, Charlie achieves his most thorough transformation of work into dance.

Work is not the only area of life invaded by the machine. The conveyor belt comedy, we know, was inspired by Clair's *A Nous la Liberté*, from which Chaplin lifted an episode and expanded it into a sequence. But something wholly original, and a bolder flight of fancy, is the business of the Billows Feeding Machine. The mechanization of food consumption constitutes an even greater violation of what might be called the Charlie sanctities. For Charlie, eating is an act charged with a variety of significances—social, amatory,

aggressive, role-playing—according to context. It is never routine.
Just as the conveyor belt scene insists that living is not something
that one does in one's spare time, the feeding scene insists that
eating is not something one does simply to stay alive. What the
feeding scene illustrates is the mindless automatic persistence of
the machine habit: the machine can't distinguish between pieces
of cake and nuts from its own innards, but crams both indiscriminately into Charlie's captive mouth. When it starts to exhibit
human tendencies by going beserk, even its unpredictability is
tempered by reminders of forsaken habit: when the corncob on its
revolving spit has finished grinding Charlie's face, the mouth
wiper, mindful of its cue, swivels delicately round to dab at his lips.
The dominant feeling is one of revulsion at the standardizing
degradation of a creative activity. But the total feeling is more
complex. It is not a simple matter of Charlie versus the machine.
We can't but feel an impenitent relish when the machine, in its
moment of madness, takes on a defiant life of its own, to the discomfiture of its inventor. If the world of *Modern Times* is one in
which men are conditioned to behave like machines, it is also one
in which machines are liable to behave like men.

Chaplin's attack upon the idealization of productive labour, the
mainstay of the capitalist system, lent support to the view of him as
a dangerous political agitator. But the view could not be more
wrong. It is true that he feels, and expresses in his films, a warm
sympathy for the outcast and despised. But this sympathy is easily
made to seem more sentimental than it is: it is usually directed
towards particular cases rather than a class, and, in Charlie's case,
is always balanced by his strong sense of personal advantage, which
is likely to operate at the expense of his fellow outcasts. And it is
true that, shortly after leaving the factory, Charlie is involved in a
left-wing demonstration and becomes a victim of police brutality.
But the point of the episode is the innocent and unwitting nature
of his involvement: the red flag he is arrested for brandishing has
fallen from the back of a lorry, and has nothing to do with the
occasion. The parading strikers and the police are equally factions
from which he is anxious to dissociate himself. Similarly, in the jail
to which he is consigned, so far from identifying with his fellow
prisoners, he wins enviable comforts and privileges by foiling their

attempt to escape. Charlie is a natural aristocrat rather than a tribune of the people; a blackleg rather than a martyr.

Charlie's jealously preserved independence of action prompts two important reflections. The first is that Chaplin is not really concerned with the sort of practical solutions that are the province of politics. He doesn't see the problems of life in terms of rectifiable injustices or abuses. The frustrating unreality of machine labour is a social problem, but Chaplin doesn't suggest an answer. His concern goes deeper than any political remedy, to the rationalizing and dehumanizing spirit that underlies the adoption of machine methods. The second reflection is that what Charlie represents is the priority of the individual life. Both the factory president and the political reformer who would oust him see people in terms of docile and manipulable units in a mass: Chaplin sees only individual lives, and the responsibility for individual choice. Charlie, in this film as in others, spends much of his time cultivating his distinctiveness and avoiding the contamination of the mass.

Modern Times is not only about the mechanization of work, but about the plight of civilization. Our civilization has been characterized by F.R. Leavis as 'technologico-Benthamite', an expressive coinage that links the automatism of the machine habit with the facile idealism of social engineering. Machines are agents of standardization, and the target of Chaplin's indictment is the crippling naivety about the ends of life that makes standardization seem desirable. As important to his case as the conveyor belt comedy are those scenes that generalize the theme by revealing the pervasiveness of the standardizing habit: the image of sheep-like commuters that combines the ideas of uniformity and aggregation as twin evils of modern life; the interruption of Charlie's skive in the lavatory, which shows that an economic unit has no right to privacy; the enforced humiliation of the feeding machine that denies the possibility of relaxing social ritual. The conception of life's meaning implied by these scenes is only suitable for a life lived at subsistence level. (The feeding machine implies that subsistence is all that food is for.) Charlie embodies a deeper sense of human need than machine civilization can conceive. His rebellion challenges the assembly line slaves to ask for what end they are required to perform their deadening tasks. They don't stop to think, but the answer can only be: for the good of the aggregate, the mass. But 'what *is* the "social condition" that has nothing to do with the "individual condition"?' asks Leavis, picking up a phrase of C.P. Snow's. Chaplin's film demonstrates what Leavis argues, that it is only in the individual that society has life. Charlie salvages his individual's right of responsible choice, and holds that those who forfeit it to the service of the anonymous mass deserve the misery they endure. His message to his fellow-workers is, You are fools if you do not live.

The factory sequence must have dispelled any fear that Chaplin's bold entry into the twentieth century would entail a loss of comic invention. It is one of the most resourceful passages of comedy he ever created. But as well as lively and exhilarating, it is strongly disturbing. It owes its considerable suspense to the unusually threatening nature of the forces with which Charlie takes issue. Charlie is accustomed to danger, but the factory's automatism and regimentation impose a greater strain than any to which he has so far been subjected. The anxiety of the audience is especially keen because the threat that Charlie faces—the oppressive spirit of modern life—is what they were used to coming to Chaplin films in order to forget about. Probably the most frightening moment is when Charlie is actually swallowed up by the monstrous machine. His subsequent smooth passage around its entrails, which is both a comical relief and invulnerability, can't entirely dispel our disquiet at the sight of his disappearance down its gullet. A significant indication of the intensity of the pressures he endures is the fact that they send him mad, something that no previous ordeal had succeeded in doing. His madness, of course, is cathartic and creative, and an irresistible invitation to exhilarating release. But it is nonetheless only a temporary solution, and something of a defeat. Altogether, it is a great relief to everybody when Charlie leaves the factory behind him.

It is when the film leaves the factory that one begins to have doubts about the direction it follows. The trouble is that both the length of the factory sequence, and its disturbing quality, cast a shadow forward, modifying the meaning and success of the events that ensue. The length of the sequence upsets the balance of the film, making it difficult for a new feeling to be established that will counter the depressing influence of the factory. The remainder of the film is taken up by a series of much shorter scenes, which have been criticized as miscellaneous, and as appearing to have only a temporal connection (a view that seems to me only partly just). And the sequence's disturbing energy has consequences that I don't think Chaplin is completely conscious of. It results in a feeling of exhaustion, and an overriding desire for release from the painful pressures of the factory world, which cannot help communicating itself to the rest of the action, infecting parts of it with something like paralysis. I have suggested that *Modern Times* is Chaplin's artistic, as it is Charlie's emotional, engagement with modern realities, entered into by both with every expectation of success. But I will argue that in both cases there is a discrepancy between intention and performance that reveals itself increasingly the way that events turn out.

It would be unfair not to acknowledge that the post-factory section contains much of the film's most memorable comedy. Its picaresque shape, the picture of Charlie shuttling distractedly from home to home and from job to job, can be justified, and made to seem more than arbitrary, if one sees it as Charlie's search for security and satisfaction in the inhospitable wilderness of modern life—for anything that will counteract the baneful influence of the factory. He finds security in the company and affection of the lake front gamine (Paulette Goddard), whose truancy from official custody provides such narrative suspense as the rest of the film possesses. Their relationship is the familiar comradely and protective one, rather than the idealizing. It is reminiscent of the Charlie–Edna relationship in *A Dog's Life*, being attractively established by two vignettes of companionable domesticity that call to mind the charming conclusion of the earlier film. In the first of these, the sight of a commuter being despatched to work by an extravagantly doting wife prompts Charlie to imagine his own version of domestic comfort. This involves a bright and chintzy interior that Charlie parades with lordly ease, wiping his hands on the curtains and back-kicking his apple core out of the window. A handy cow deposits her milk directly into Charlie's jug, and trees obligingly dangle their fruit at the doorway, in a manifestation of natural largesse that recalls Marvell's garden ('The Nectaren, and curious Peach/Into my hands themselves do reach'). The second domestic vignette, which is intended to provide the contrast of actuality, is the shack in the swamp that Paulette finds for them to squat in. Here the comforts are minimal: the table legs penetrate the rotting floorboards; at the least vibration the lintel fetches Charlie a whack on the head; and the stream into which he plunges for his morning dip turns out to be six inches deep. But their touching pleasure in acquiring a domestic base, and their tolerance of makeshift compensate for the squalor. His talent for domesticity is one thing that enables Charlie, however precariously, to colonize the modern wilderness.

Charlie also seeks opportunities for creative satisfaction, both the incidental ones that life throws up, and the more formal ones offered by his occupational pursuits. An excellent example of the first is what happens when, after emptying the shelves of a cafeteria and treating himself to a good blow-out, he politely declines to pay. The cop who is called, and to whom he is shackled, pauses at a phone booth to summon the police waggon. This is conveniently close to a cigar stand, where Charlie, his captive condition unnoticed, does his wealthy patrician act, sampling the cigars with an air of disdainful ease, and, with discovery imminent, hastily distributing candy to the neighbourhood kids. This impudent masquerade is a delightful expression of Charlie's familiar mastery, conducted at a brisker pace than any description can convey, and deriving its suspense from our pleasantly anxious awareness of the inevitability of discovery. It wittily fuses the notions of freedom and constraint, and demonstrates the pleasure in theatrical imposture that Charlie can never resist indulging. But as well as the pleasures of gratuitous display, Charlie needs the solider ones of work. In *Modern Times*, if the film is to have any shape, one would especially expect his appetite for professional roles to produce some civilized alternatives to machine drudgery. We get one in the department store scene, when Charlie gets appointed as night watchman. This scene is important because the profusion of material goods enables Charlie and Paulette, in a brief period of release, to combine with work the taste for luxury and comfort that the factory world denies them. There is a feeling of blissful sensuousness about the image of Paulette perched model-fashion on the bed, swathed in expensive furs. Charlie's formal duty of punching the time clocks is hardly onerous, but he discovers that with the assistance of roller skates he can discharge it with exemplary expedition. The roller skates suggest non-functional pleasure, and he is soon entertaining Paulette by describing blindfold arabesques around a deserted mezzanine (edged, unknown to him, by a precipitous drop). Charlie's skating is really stylish and graceful, and the danger of his familiar balancing act doesn't stop us from admiring his skill. Work is once again converted into dance, and into relaxed and idiosyncratic enjoyment.

There is no doubt that our response to the non-factory section of the film corresponds in some degree to the account I have given of it, and I think that something like it was Chaplin's intention. The threatening regimentation of the factory life is countered by an evocation of freedom and optimism in which Charlie regains his mastery. But it is a strangely qualified mastery. It is qualified by a number of constraining and inhibiting factors that limit the success even of the scenes I have described. Charlie's relationship with Paulette, for example, while free from the sentimentality that afflicts his unhappy and idealizing romances, is embarrassing in a different way. An affectionate note is struck by their scenes of domesticity, and about half-way through a nice reversal of roles takes place, when Paulette starts being protective about Charlie and doing all the arranging. The trouble is with Paulette herself. Her winsomeness is too contrived, too obviously set up for our pitying approval. The contrivance is symbolized by the exaggerated smut on her cheek, which speaks more of the make-up room than the lake front (Chaplin has recorded that his future wife disliked even this disfigurement). Paulette's attractiveness is too much a matter of such conventional devices, and not sufficiently the sort of full humanness that would win our unsolicited sympathy. A similar objection could be made to the shack where they set up home, whose picturesque dilapidation has a decidedly studio-made air. It is really just as fanciful in its effect as Charlie's suburban dream.

However, the shack points to another pervasive quality of this section of the film. This is the presence, persisting from the factory sequence, of a feeling of constraint. The shack is not really a very successful haven. Marooned in a muddy and dismal swamp, it is only half a mile from the dreaded factory, whose elaborate structures can be seen in the distance. The factory casts its psychological, as well as its actual, shadow across Charlie's refuge. He is never really free from threats to the equilibrium of his inner life. Something similar is true of the department store scene, except that in this case it is a feeling of artificial insulation that empha- sizes Charlie's vulnerability. Despite the sense of creative release that it generates, the store scene is circumscribed by its peculiar conditions. Charlie's release does not take place in the real world, but in one put together for the occasion. The deserted night-time store performs the function, and has the artificiality, of a theatri- cal set. So the danger threatening Charlie is avoided, not faced. This robs his beautiful performance on skates of some of its power, and lends it the appearance of desperate jesting rather than con- fident mastery. It is in any case nearly as frightening as it is exhil- arating. The department store idyll cannot last: the real world must eventually intrude (as it does in the shape of Charlie's bibu- lous cell-mates).

A related feature of this section is a feeling that the problem of modern life is being evaded rather than faced, and that Charlie is seeking refuge from its uncongeniality in the reassurance of famil- iar situations. For example, the café stratagem discussed above is Charlie's attempt to get himself returned to prison, whose com- forts are decidedly superior to the outside world he was reluctantly dumped upon. That for Charlie prison should mean safety rather than servitude is, of course, deliberate comic irony. But the irony serves to blunt the force of the fact, and makes us find it less sur- prising than we should. That prison should represent for Charlie a womb-like haven to which he strives to return is, quite as much as his factory-induced madness, an indication of the oppressive power exerted by modern life. A different, but more interesting, indication is provided by the scene in which Charlie returns to the hated factory (having secured a job by elbowing his way smartly through the crowd besieging the gate). Here the surprising thing is how the factory, which had formerly seemed so threatening, has entirely lost its power to terrify, and seems tamed and amenable. It is as if Chaplin were trying to demonstrate, to Charlie and to us, that there is no cause for alarm: the monster is harmless, its vi- ciousness an illusion. But isn't it rather an unreal demonstration? The action is a partial reprise of the first factory scene, this time with Chester Conklin being swallowed up by the machine. But the sight of Chester toppling into the cogs and wheels doesn't arouse

the elemental panic induced in us previously by Charlie's disappearance down the same gullet. It is simply a humorous misfortune. There is, it is true, a variation that makes a neat point and is
wholly successful. This is when the machine seizes up with Chester
still trapped in its innards. It is lunch time, and Chester has to be
fed the contents of his lunch pail: a task Charlie performs with
delicate eccentricity, stuffing a stalk of celery and a whole boiled
egg into Chester's mouth, but wiping his lips with tender concern,
and, in a brilliant improvisation, using the chicken as a funnel for
the coffee. This is Charlie's answer to the feeding machine, demonstration of humanized forced feeding. But its functional success
doesn't alter our sense of the flatness and unreality of this second
factory scene. One can try to justify it by saying that Charlie has
purged himself of the terrors of the factory and no longer needs
to fear them. But the factory, and the dehumanizing spirit it represents, have not essentially changed: what has happened rather is
that Charlie can no longer bear to face it, and so reduces it to
a farcical rather than a real menace; one that he can deal with.
Rather than a display of mastery, the scene is an evasion of threat,
and an unconscious indication of how much the threat is feared.

If I am right about these suggestions of constraint, unreality and
evasion, then the post-factory sequence is afflicted by something
like a loss of nerve. Here there is some point in invoking the distinction made earlier between Chaplin and Charlie, and the nature
of their involvement with modern realities. For both, *Modern Times*
is intended to mark a resolute confrontation with the modern
world. But in both the desire for confrontation battles with revulsion. Charlie the character, driven to distraction by factory work,
seeks refuge from its menace in a succession of reassuring situations (which, as has often been said, resemble a series of Keystone-
to-Mutual routines): Chaplin the author, exhausted by exposure
to unpleasant realities, reduces the menace to manageable size,
and sets up reassuring situations for Charlie to retreat to. Creature
and creator can't in the last resort be as clearly distinguished as
this: but the point to be made is that the confusion that character-
izes the film's performance is the result of an unconscious deflection of impulse that has modified its original intention. However
one accounts for the fact, the promise of resolute confrontation is
not, after the factory sequence, fulfilled: and the action offered by

way of fulfilment is actually an expression of a different intention. *Modern Times*'s oddness of form, which so many have commented on, may be explained by being seen as Chaplin's unconsciously acting out the desperation it is part of his conscious intention to express. In other words, the film is both Charlie evading modern times and Chaplin evading the problem of Charlie's involvement in them. Its amorphous shape and uncertain tone are both overt demonstrations of its theme—the uncongeniality of modern life— and covert symptoms of Chaplin's perplexity in face of that theme: failures, one might say, uneasily doubling as virtues.

It is instructive at this point to compare *Modern Times* with Rene Clair's *A Nous la Liberté* (1931), mentioned above. It is well known that Clair's conveyor belt joke provided the germ of Chaplin's fac- tory sequence, and it is hard to resist the belief that the whole of the earlier film was the chief source of inspiration for the later. *A Nous la Liberté* is also about the innocent soul in a dehumanized world. But it is much more in control of itself than *Modern Times*, and more thorough in its investigation of its theme. It demon- strates, for example, in the joint hero's progress from convict to capitalist, that behind the dehumanizing process is a corrupt human intelligence, an atrophy of feeling that can be opposed. Further, by inter-cutting the scene of the tramp-hero being march- ed to the factory for compulsory labour with shots of a classroom of children dutifully reciting 'Le travail est obligatoire/Car le travail est la liberté', Clair conveys that submission to machine habits is partly a result of educational conditioning. Structurally, too, the French film is superior. It has a satisfying and carefully wrought shape. Its end returns neatly upon its beginning when the tramps-turned-plutocrats revert to vagabondage. And interest is sharpened by a pattern of ironies: Clair's jail, for instance, is not, like Chaplin's, an opportunity for isolated comic effects, but is linked ironically with the factory, whose punitive regime makes it difficult to tell the difference between the two. Finally, the pos- itive values that Clair sets against the oppressive regimentation of modern life are conveyed by the relationship between his protag- onists, whose affectionate and larky camaraderie is more authentic and likeable than Chaplin's idealization of simple goodness in the figure of the waterfront waif.

It would be wrong to maintain that all the advantage lies with *A Nous la Liberté*. One could argue that Chaplin's version of modern servitude gains power from not being explained: it presents itself as an unaccountable but inescapable fact, which is after all how it seems to most people. *A Nous la Liberté* is hardly ever actually frightening, as *Modern Times* certainly is: Clair's habit of ironic perspective and manipulation of comic effect, ensure that there is always a certain distance between us and the unfolding events. And *A Nous la Liberté* itself (though this is not the place for a critical account of it) is not free, in its final version of a world where machines do the work and people play, from an element of fanciful evasion. (In this respect it must yield advantage to a later example of the *genre* that clearly owes much to both the earlier: Jacque Tati's *Mon Oncle* [1958].) Less happily constructed than the Clair, less ominous than the Chaplin, its comic invention more laborious than either, Tati's masterpiece nonetheless is more candid and sardonic than its progenitors in its censure of the rigidities and absurdities of modern life. The target of its ridicule is larger—modern cleanliness comes under attack, as well as architecture and furniture—and its positive values are much more realistically embodied in its evocation of the vanishing Paris of *le quartier* and *les copains*.) The point of the comparison is not absolutely to elevate one film at the expense of the other so much as to indicate what Chaplin's film may have lost, in terms of significance and shape, by his not being wholly conscious of what he was doing.

Like so many Chaplin films, *Modern Times* builds up to a strong ending, and one which, without resolving the suggested confusions, goes some way towards offsetting them. The final scene provides Charlie with his least qualified triumph. After so many frustrations, he ends up as a waiter in a cabaret, the most familiar and reassuring of all his roles (Chaplin, we remember when barren of ideas for a short, would instruct his carpenters to knock together a restaurant set). The confident ease with which he inhabits the cabaret world communicates itself to the action, which moves with a quickened pulse, and leaps into energetic life. There is nothing in this scene that can quite match the manic abandon of the cabaret scene in *City Lights*, but it does express a similar sensation of being swept up and carried along by events (as Charlie literally is when trying to convey a duck dinner to his customer). The lively pace; the comedy of the duck, the swinging doors and the hand-drilled Gruyére; and the convivial atmosphere combine in a valiant attempt to dispel uncertainty and unease.

It turns out to be a kind of whistling in the dark, for the stiffest test is yet to come. Charlie is not just a waiter, but a singing waiter (his ability to sing having been vouched for by Paulette in a nicely mimed interview with the proprietor). So with his waiter's role he combines that of performer: the most practised of all his roles, now once more made official. As in *The Circus* the prospect of officially playing the clown induced a kind of paralysis, so now he is afflicted by first-night nerves, and has to be anxiously coached by Paulette. But the tension of the scene does not, of course, spring primarily from this genial pretence of nervous amnesia: it comes from outside these fictional circumstances altogether, from the direct relationship between Chaplin and his audience—our fearful consciousness that Charlie can no longer defer opening his mouth and speaking. The actual situation bears hard upon the imaginary one, multiplying the sense of expectation. This is the real significance of the prolonged, teasing preamble.

He finally sings his extraordinary and baffling song. It is a very equivocal business. Dramatically, it is a culmination, something like the recognition scene in a play. It is Charlie fulfilling himself by an act of energy and will, with the bonus of being heard to speak for the first time in a film. In the event, our carefully built-up expectations are confounded at every level by Charlie's mis-laying his script and resorting to inspired gobbledegook. The result is certainly a beautiful performance. The catchy ballad of amorous intrigue is translated into incentive polyglot and embroidered with dependably skilful mime. His nonsense gives the song a sharper and weirder life than any sense could do. But it is a bit like turning on the radio for a vital announcement and getting an earful of static. The laugh is on us, The conclusion is irresistible that the song is Charlie speaking directly to us, in a calculated act of defiance. It is his answer to the clamour for speech, a demonstration that we can't presume to possess him, but that he remains in the end, as ever, elusive.

Charlie's cabaret life and nonsense song count as successes in his battle with modern times. But overall, he must be judged to be worsted. If the constraint and confusion that I sense in the way *Modern Times* evolves are covert admissions of defeat, as they seem to me to be, then the answer to the question that Chaplin originally proposed to himself is that there is no place for Charlie in the modern world. His unfitness for the times, I have suggested, is unwittingly demonstrated by the shapes into which the film resolves itself. This does not mean that there is no place for Chaplin, and Chaplin in fact went on to make films in which Charlie played little or no part: or, at any rate, assumed more thoroughgoing disguises than any he had known in the past. So there is a very real poignancy about Charlie's disappearance, with Paulette on his arm, down that endlessly receding road; his spirit doesn't vanish, but he never reappears in the same form.

The Great Dictator

With *The Great Dictator*, Chaplin continues his analysis of contemporary realities. Although one has to use such words, 'analysis', with its prosy associations, doesn't adequately suggest his poetic and intuitive method of proceeding. And the disturbing realities with which he deals are (in the form of Hynkel) quite as much psychological as political. However, it is obvious that, as *Modern Times* issued from the misery and industrial unrest of the depression, so *The Great Dictator* issues from the ominous political atmosphere of the immediate prewar years. In the first film Chaplin was moved to a radical questioning of the function of work in life; in the second he is led to an equally basic scrutiny of the psychology of power. Once again he compels his audience's involuntary involvement by basing his drama upon a widely held anxiety: *The Great Dictator* (completed in the course of the war, but planned before its outbreak) is dominated by the ubiquitous fear, and expectation, of war. The experience of Hynkel reflects the rise of the dictators, the deceitful diplomacy and the international tyrannizing that made the stuff of headlines: the experience of the Jewish barber reflects the arbitrary oppression, clandestine resistance and struggle for survival that comprised the world of the dispossessed.

Hynkel and the barber divide the narrative between them, in two interweaving strands. (I shall call them, for convenience, the

Hynkel section and the Charlie section.) By concerning itself with
both the world of the powerful dictator and that of his humblest
citizen, the film is able to profit from the dramatic contrast between extremes of experience: between high life and low life, freedom and servitude, the public and the domestic. By playing both
characters himself, and emphasizing their physical resemblance,
Chaplin enlists the powerful mixture of fascination and fear that
invariably attends the idea of the double life, as well as the suspense that precedes the inevitable moment of substitution. *The
Great Dictator* is a *doppelganger* comedy which, unlike many examples of the type, doesn't rely for its effect upon the repeated confusion of its two protagonists, but reserves its moment of substitution for the very end. (This feature, by prolonging the suspense,
has consequences for the ending that aren't, I shall suggest, entirely happy.) The film is not one of Charlie's familiar imposture
dramas. As a matter of fact, very little attempt is made to exploit
the irony of the resemblance between Hynkel and Charlie, whose
lives follow their separate courses; or, except in the case of Hynkel's calculated relaxation of persecution in the ghetto, to show
the effect of one world upon the other. This may seem surprising.
It does not mean that there is no significant connection between
the two halves of the film. As in *City Lights*, the connection is made
by the theme, which operates at a deeper level, and in a less mechanical fashion, than the complications of plot. My own procedure will be to examine each section in turn, and then to consider
the relation between the two.

   I have said that the familiar Charlie figure disappears at the end
of *Modern Times*, giving an added poignancy to his dwindling progress down the endless road. It has to be admitted that he reappears in *The Great Dictator*, although in a modified and muted form.
To all intents and purposes, the Jewish barber *is* Charlie, and is
able to draw upon the huge fund of sympathetic attention that the
very appearance of Charlie evokes in the audience. There is a
striking sense of familiarity and possession, a brisk confidence, in
the scene of the barber's homecoming to his deserted and cobwebby shop, where he snaps up the blinds and shoos out the cats,
registering only a faint perplexity at the evidence of neglect. I
don't think it is fanciful to see an extra-fictional reference in our
reaction to this moment: our expectant pleasure is partly that of

recognizing that Charlie the character has returned. But in the event his role is reduced and his possibilities of action limited. The barber is only half of the film, and the less important half. And the dramatic situation in which he finds himself gives perhaps the least scope he has ever been permitted for his flights of creative virtuosity. Like the Charlie of *Modern Times*, the barber is a casualty of modern life, whose terrors drive him mad. But the shell-shocked barber emerges from his sanatorium into a world even more soulless and regimented than any he has known. In the industrial desert, Charlie was able to imagine, and partially create, his domestic ideal: in the ghetto, which he cannot leave, all his energy is devoted to fending off attacks. Nonetheless, it is appropriate to call this part of the film the Charlie section, for it is Charlie virtues and Charlie values that the barber contributes to the total effect.

Another reason for the muted effect of the Charlie section is that it has more than its share of the film's weaknesses. The obvious of these is the pervasive facetiousness. Chaplin's films, as I've already suggested, operate at two levels: the conscious and the unconscious. The ideas of comic art that he is able to articulate are not remarkable for their subtlety, and his effects at the conscious level are often relatively crude. It's to his unconscious art—the products of the instinctive clown—that we must look for finer effects and deeper meanings. We find ourselves often having to invoke this distinction in watching *The Great Dictator*, too many of whose jokes issue only from the surface of Chaplin's comic imagination. The facetious names—the most glaring example—belong mostly to the Hynkel section. But equally superficial, and a serious weakness, is what offers to be Chaplin's version of the Nazi menace. This consists of a bunch of amiably oafish storm troopers with jarring American accents, whose idea of depravity is to belt Hannah with vegetables, and whose punishment to be sloshed with paint and walloped with frying pans. They introduce a note of vaudeville that slackens the tension where it ought to be tightened. There is more real terror in the earlier montage of headlines and contemporary events that mark the passage of Charlie's amnesia, in which a Jewish shopkeeper's son is murdered before his eyes. Charlie's old Keystone-to-Mutual antagonists were more frightening than this. It is probably the storm troopers that critics of the

film are first thinking of when they deprecate its bad taste and miscalculated levity.

The best ghetto comedy is reserved for the subsequent scene of
the pudding. This is probably too long, and slows down the action,
but it is a good example of ensemble clowning. The coin in the
pudding is designed to select Hynkel's assassin, who will himself
face certain death. Schultz explains that he cannot take on the
job himself ('Why not?' pipes Mr Mann), and the others confront
the meal with expressions of glum foreboding. There follows a
series of startled discoveries, as coins turn up in all the puddings,
to be promptly and covertly transferred to a neighbour's plate. Mr
Jaeckel's honest admission breaks the circle: Hannah's subterfuge
then revealed, Charlie improves the occasion by pocketing the
evidence. The scene owes its tension to the very human conflict it
dramatizes between self-interest and self-esteem. It also, unusually,
demonstrates two of Charlie's standard preoccupations—food and
found money—in reverse: on this occasion the food is not rel-
ished and the money not sought.

Charlie's relation to the ghetto is defined in the best scene of
the Charlie section (and one of the most memorable scenes in the
film): the shaving of Chester Conklin to the music of Brahms. No
description of this simple but inventive piece of clowning can do it
justice. It is yet another, even more surprising, example of work's
being turned into dance. A beautiful self-contained accomplishment, with nothing false or redundant, its isolation from the rest
of the action is emphasized by the abruptness with which it begins
and ends. Its shape is wholly determined by the music. But this air
of virtuoso performance doesn't mean that it is an irrelevant
bonus, and it relates in a number of interesting ways to the main
concerns of the film. For one thing, it is a splendid, if rather
quixotic, demonstration of professional skill. Charlie's professional role of barber is important in our view of his function. It is
worth recalling that barber-shop routines are one of the oldest
kinds of clowning: William Willeford, calling them 'typical...of the
bond between clowns and their audiences', cites the *commedia
dell'arte* and various early English plays.[1] Charlie had not been a
barber in any previous film, surprisingly enough, but it as a barber-shop act that Chaplin chose to demonstrate the superiority of

1.   Willeford, *The Fool and his Sceptre*, p. 16.

Charlie's 'improvised' style of clowning over the circumscribed skills of the circus. As already suggested in regard to the scene of his return to the shop, Charlie takes to the role with an appearance of confident familiarity, and a sense of its rightness is part of our reaction to him here. Another significant feature of the scene is its function of social ritual. Barbers minister to intimate personal needs, which gives them a social role, at once desired and feared, that is similar to that of the dentist (another perennial comic figure). Barber-shop comedy requires a customer-victim, and its enduring fascination probably stems from the audience's ambiguous relation to this figure, whose inevitable humiliation is awaited with a mixture of distress and relish. But here the tension has a different source. A feeling of threat is certainly present in the scene of Chester's shaving: but the threat is contained and regulated, so to speak, by the music; and in any case is a threat as much to the element of benign neighbourly ritual in the occasion as to Chester's person. A lot of the pleasure derives from Chester's expression of muted astonishment, of concern held in check by unwillingness to make a scene. Chester's tactful forbearance helps to mitigate Charlie's air of demonic possession: together, they provide another fine example of ensemble clowning. The full significance of these remarkable few moments becomes apparent when they are compared with their opposite number in the Hynkel section.

Charlie's most successful relationship is with Commander Schultz. Schultz's contribution to the political drama is that of the highly placed renegade, the liberal whose scruples force him to turn against his former companions. He is also the only character who appears in both sections of the film, between which he acts as a necessary bridge: finally escorting the disguised Charlie to the scene of his public substitution. He and Charlie develop into an excellent comic team, his affected upper-class twittery being played off against Charlie's innocence, cunning and instinct for survival. Schultz is unthinkingly brave, loyal and decent: but his courage runs to histrionics, his idealism to drippy sentimentality and his class pride to a pettish concern for creature comforts. He provides a number of hilarious moments. We first meet him in the World War I prologue. This amusing but somewhat uninspired assembly of gags (which looks concocted in comparison with *Shoulder Arms*) has two redeeming features. One is the moment when Charlie drops a live grenade inside his tunic (instantly raising the tension several notches). The other is the advent of Schultz, who, staggering from his abandoned plane, invests the proceedings with an air of theatrical menace and doom. When, back in the air, they discover that the plane's fuel tank is empty, Schultz enlivens the seconds of accelerating descent with an inopportune rhapsody about Romania in the spring and Hilda's daffodils: interrupted by the almighty crash, he continues rhapsodizing from the ground, while Charlie struggles from a nearby morass. Later in the action he reappears in time to save Charlie from a lynching (Charlie being lugged into the frame by the neck and then, at Schultz's command, unceremoniously dropped); and, finally, turning his coat after a dispute with Hynkel, ends up taking refuge in the ghetto. Here he is the occasion of the pudding scene described above, after which the approach of storm troopers forces him to escape to the roof with Charlie. On this occasion Schultz acts admirably true to character by insisting on taking with him into exile a suitcase, a hat box and his golf clubs. By teaming his stiff-lipped idealism with Charlie's canny realism, Schultz generates some of the best comedy in the Charlie section.

Despite its weaknesses, the Charlie section must have seemed familiar and reassuring to its contemporary audience, and there is no bar to anyone's enjoying it. But the Hynkel section is something different. Chaplin breaks decisively with his professional habit by creating and performing a dramatic role with few of the familiar attributes, and none of the costume. It is true that Hynkel retains expressions and mannerisms that are strikingly reminiscent of the old long-loved clown figure (it could be argued that he is more like Charlie than the Charlie of *The Great Dictator* is), but the shock of his sudden first appearance must have been (as it still is) considerable. As I hope to show, he richly repays study as a character in his own right. However, although he has been enjoyed and praised, his section of the film has consistently provoked critics to express doubts and misgivings. The burden of complaint is that the film trivializes serious and distressing actual events by making them matter for low comedy: Hitler was too evil, and caused too much suffering, to be turned into a figure of fun. So persistent has been this line of argument that Chaplin himself has finally come to share it, conceding in his last book (*My Life in Pictures*)[2] that he wouldn't have made the film in its present form if he had known about the horrors of the concentration camps. Chaplin can't be blamed for what he didn't know, and there are certainly aspects of his rendering of Nazi persecution that, with hindsight, he might legitimately regret. But in general I believe that these criticisms are both confused and misconceived, and that Chaplin has very little to reproach himself with. The Hynkel section seems to me the most brilliant and richly suggestive portion of the film, and a major development in Chaplin's art.

It is true that the Hynkel section has more than its share of the pervasive facetiousness that is one of the film's principal weaknesses. This facetiousness is partly a matter of punning names and references and partly a matter of a few feeble verbal jokes. The mistake the critics make is to assume that the film's whole conception of its serious subject works at this shallow level. For a sounder judgment one must invoke the distinction made often above between Chaplin's conscious and unconscious art. The crude and mechanical elements in the comedy are the obvious product of an uncritical and loosely hospitable mind. But the parts that seriously move us and engage our feelings come from the depths of an imagination that has grasped and possessed its subject. A great deal of the Hynkel section, I suggest, affects us in this way.

There is nothing half-hearted or embarrassed about our response to Hynkel's first appearance, for example. A common reaction (if mine is not wholly untypical) must be a mixture of shock and delight at the audacity of the impersonation. Even those otherwise hostile to the film tend to concede the authority of Chaplin's performance. This mesmeric first appearance gives us Hynkel at work, being a dictator. His histrionic role-playing before the vast crowd is a version of the real Hitler, made comic by additions, exaggerations and refinements. The impersonation is in terms of speech and mannerism. The gutteral, half-intelligible gobbledegook, with its graduated descent into a coughing fit, that issues from his mouth suggests, insolently, that this is all Hitler's speeches *are*. The effrontery is augmented and our laughter sharpened, by the slightly shocking breach of the polite taboo

2.   Charles Chaplin, *My Life in Pictures* (London: Bodley Head, 1974).

against making fun of the way people talk. And Hynkel's platform
manner, with its curt dismissals of applause and air of scarce-con-
tained frenzy, catches and improves upon Hitler's quality of strutting self-importance. Chaplin's creative and surprising addition is
the rigmarole of water application—to the back of the neck, and,
with particular relish, down the front of the trousers. This disconcerting eccentricity, of which there are later interesting vari-
ants, appears in this case to have a self-fortifying function, and to
be a kind of involuntary overflow of nervous energy. The sequence
concludes with Hynkel subjected to the first of many indignities by
being accidentally butted down the staircase by Herring's oversize
rear end.

In appealing to the authority of this sequence I am trying to
suggest that those who criticize *The Great Dictator* on the grounds
that the reality was too dreadful to be made fun of are under-
estimating both the resources of comedy and the seriousness of
Chaplin's reaction to Hitler. For, as L.C. Knights concludes in
well-known essay, 'Comedy is essentially a serious activity'.[3] That is,
it is not inherently trivial, but can be a way of coming to terms
with serious issues. We habitually joke, after all, about our deepest
anxieties. Hitler is, and was, no joke: to turn him into a joke is one
way of overcoming our fear of him. Not that the process is an
evasive one: it is more a matter of putting dreadful matters into
a human perspective. Comedy insists that the immediate, vulgar
and humdrum in experience are as real and valid as the dangerous and fearful. Hynkel is Hitler judged and diminished by
being referred to a world of wider values: the humourless self-
importance of fanaticism is enveloped by comedy's largeness.

Hitler, for all his wickedness, was not a monster but a man. And
the guarantee of Chaplin's seriousness is the way Hynkel is made
not a farcical butt but human, and even likeable. He represents an
illuminating criticism of his original, a sort of demonstration of
dictatorhood rendered in terms of comic art. At the heart of his
character is a conflict between his irritable sensitivity and the
demands of his heroic public role. Hynkel's official life is seen as a
façade constructed of public ostentation, hypocritical idealism and
ruthless self-assertion: and the commonest type of comedy in the
film is that in which this façade is punctured by the vulgar vindic-

3.   'Notes on Comedy', *Scrutiny* 1 (1933), pp. 356-67.

tiveness of circumstances. An early example, already mentioned, is the way his successful rabble-rousing session, in which he strenuously asserts himself in his role of dictator, is ignominiously concluded by a shove down the stairs from Herring's bum. Other examples are the baby, who, dutifully held and kissed, ungratefully soils her leader's hand, necessitating the surreptitious use of his handkerchief; and the desk set of pens that however vigorously shaken, refuse to be parted from their mounts. A brief, but especially telling, instance is the shot of Hynkel, in self-important abstraction, striding across a huge palatial vestibule and stumbling over a carpet in the middle: this moment registers with beautiful directness and economy his chronic vulnerability to indignity and setback. Hynkel desperately wants to live up to the heroic part in which he has cast himself, but his nature and the malice of events repeatedly conspire to frustrate him.

The greatest blow to Hynkel's desperate self-esteem is inflicted by the visit of Napaloni. The part this episode plays in the plot—being Hynkel's attempt to neutralize Napaloni's threat to his proposed invasion of Austerlitz—is less important than its further revelation of Hynkel's character. Its function is to multiply the humiliations by bringing pressure to bear upon Hynkel's vulnerable points. Napaloni, in complete contrast, is brash, extrovert and cheerfully overbearing. Hynkel, in collusion with Garbitsch, devises nervous plans to extract the maximum advantage from his interviews with his awkward ally: but all his stratagems to ward off loss of face go wrong. Their first carefully posed encounter, with Hynkel placed commandingly at the end of a long room, is upset by Napaloni's entering unexpectedly from the rear, and giving Hynkel a friendly wallop of the back that brings his chin into sharp contact with the top of the desk. As well as his self-esteem, Hynkel's fastidiousness is offended by Napaloni's hearty and oblivious vulgarity: Napaloni mitigates the boredom of the military review and fly-past by munching peanuts, chucking the empty shells into Hynkel's lap. The climax of their encounter is the lavish buffet-banquet at which the treaty is to be signed. Here the aggression induced by a last-minute disagreement spills over on to the food, which is seized on for use as ammunition. Hynkel, threatening 'I'll tear you apart like this!', attempts to dismember the spaghetti by way of illustration: but it displays a degree of intransigent elastic-

ity that he spends the next few seconds, forgetful of the row, dementedly trying to overcome. This beautiful moment, which recalls
Charlie's similar struggle with the length of dough in *Dough and
Dynamite*, is an example of Chaplin's habit of giving old gags a new
life. Not all the humour of this episode arises from the relationship between the dictators: a comic bonus is the callous mistreat-
ment of Madame Napaloni, who, inadvertently abandoned in the
crowd on arrival when the cavalcade moves off, is manhandled
when she protests; and is later diplomatically selected to dance
with the gallant but disastrously lightweight Hynkel. Altogether,
the Napaloni episode charges the Hynkel section with new life,
prolonging the film's momentum, and gives Hynkel a partnership
founded on comic contrast that matches the Charlie–Schultz relationship in the Charlie section.

  Hynkel is at the mercy of his own public image. It is in the interest of this image, his idea of himself as dictator, that he compartmentalizes his life with such absurd precision: posing for his
artists for a minute at a time, in the interval of more urgent business; and, in the middle of a fit of snorting lust, dropping his
acquiescent secretary at the call of public duty. Such watchful self-
regulation (only departed from in moments of abstraction, as
when the act of saluting suggests an opportunity for idly scratching his armpit) indicates a determination to preserve the public
façade, and a near-desperate reluctance to reveal what lies behind
it. Understandably, for in fact nothing lies behind it. Hynkel's
problem is that he is a cipher. His confidence and strength are a
sham, his dignity and orderliness continually undermined, his
control over events nonexistent. At the heart of his character is a
fear of his own insignificance: a fear that is realized at the end,
when he is ignominiously carted off in mistake for the Jewish barber. Deprived of his façade, he has no protection against the
malice of events. This is where the importance of the Charlie
section comes in. For in Charlie we have a character with a strong
sense of himself that is proof against the assaults of experience. In
the fine scene of his homecoming to the cobwebby shop, Charlie,
accosted by the Jew-baiting storm troopers, doesn't understand
what they mean: he can't relate their categories of distinction to
his own. 'Vegetarian' he later echoes in perplexity, when Schultz
asks if he is Aryan.) Momentous changes have passed him by: but

one feels that, even if they hadn't, he would still behave as he does. The ignorance of amnesia is indistinguishable from the innocence of conviction. Fortified by his ignorance, Charlie is impelled to action—albeit sneaky and circumspect—by his strong sense of identity. Hynkel, by contrast, doesn't have an identity, only a fear of what underlies his façade. The difference between them is the difference between that which the self derives from inner conviction and spontaneous life and that which derives from public role and mechanical assertion of will.

Hynkel defines himself most thoroughly in the famous scene of his dance with the globe. This is provoked by Garbitsch's gloating prediction of his master's assuming the dictatorship of the world. 'You make me afraid of myself!' protests Hynkel, and, in a fit of that which is at once absurd and appropriate, skips across to the window and shimmies up the curtains. Like the self-fortifying rigmaroles in the opening speech (and like Charlie's petulant dive into a dustbin when his night out with Hannah is interrupted by the storm troopers), this odd behaviour is the result of nervous feeling spilling over into instinctive and ludicrous action. Back on the ground, he toys abstractedly with a huge geographer's globe, while pondering the idea of world domination. The eccentric behaviour of Hynkel that follows is one of Chaplin's great creative flights. Detached from its stand, the globe exhibits a balloon-like buoyancy, and Hynkel proceeds to keep it cleverly bounced aloft with his hands, legs, head and, for one vulgar but solemnly unconcerned moment, his behind. This dance-like scene is delightful and compelling. Its entranced rhythm, its visual beauty, and the feeling of an eavesdropped private ritual combine to create a strange tension, which evaporates when the balloon-globe twangingly bursts. In this bathetic outcome there is an obvious reference to the pride of power: but equally in evidence are the attractively casual playfulness and the elegant jugglery of Hynkel's performance. That is, we are allowed for a few moments to enjoy with Hynkel his dreamy and poetic megalomania before reality catches up with him and us.

We can't properly appreciate this scene without relating it to the equivalent set piece in the Charlie section: the shaving of Chester. The difference between them resides in the feeling that each expresses. The shaving of Chester is an example of Charlie's friendly social relationships, and a demonstration of his awareness of others. Chester's involvement in the performance is an affectionate tribute, not a slight: as I've already suggested, the element of threat in the routine is subordinated to the element of neighbourly ritual. The shaving testifies, however eccentrically, to Charlie's membership of the ghetto community. The dance of the globe, on the other hand, is private and clandestine, almost onanistic, and firmly excludes the participation of others: unlike Charlie, Hynkel is largely unaware of other people except as rivals or obstacles. The dance testifies to both the isolation and the unreality of his chosen role. Charlie's performance is creative and outward-directed, Hynkel's self-frustrating and self-enclosed: Charlie feeds on others, Hynkel on himself.

So one way of seeing *The Great Dictator* is as a dramatized argument about the possibilities of life. The contrast in character between Charlie and Hynkel is a moral contrast. The theme of the film is not just the hatefulness of arbitrary and oppressive political power, but its inhuman emptiness. Charlie's world is the human world of domesticity, affectionate relationships and creative activity: Hynkel's is the moral vacuum of hatred, isolation and desperate self-assertion. However, it would be unfair to see the film too simply in terms of black and white. Not all the advantage is with Charlie. Hynkel has an obstinate and compelling life of his own. Like Milton's Satan, he has the best lines and the best scenes, and he tends to hog the limelight. One effect of Chaplin's success in getting inside Hynkel's skin is to convey the relish and exhilaration, as well as the hatefulness, of dictatorial power. Chaplin's enjoyment of the role communicates itself to us, and helps to establish a sneaky affection for Hynkel, as well as building up the nervous euphoria upon which he, and we, are borne along. So the contest between Charlie and Hynkel is a real one, with the forces they represent held in a precarious (and typically Chaplinesque) balance.

Charlie represents the sanity of human relations and affections, the normality of private life. Perhaps it's for this reason, partly, that the film's theatrical conclusion, the long final speech delivered at the rally, strikes such a false note: high-minded exhortations are not what Charlie stands for, here or elsewhere. It is hard to see, it is true, how the speech could have been avoided without a radically different scenario. The structure of the film leads relentlessly towards it. By withholding until the end, and pinning his total effect upon the moment of public imposture, Chaplin was committed to a large theatrical gesture, and committed to speech.

One can say for the harangue that it gives the film a strong dramatic curtain, and that it is delivered with passion and conviction. Chaplin clearly *wanted* to do it, and no sense of presumption or incongruity was allowed to deflect him from his purpose. (He is reported to have said, 'They had their laughs, and it was fun, wasn't it? Now I wanted them to listen': a remark which, while creditable to his good intentions, says little for his trust in his own art.) In his defence one can admit that Charlie's love-inspired exhortation provides a fitting contrast to Hynkel's hate-inspired rant, and that a climax composed of action rather than words would, in the film as it stands, have been evasive. In the interests of dramatic satisfaction there has to be a public recognition of Charlie's imposture, and a public assertion of his values: somebody has to *say* something.

Yet when every allowance has been made, the final speech is painful to watch. It is probably the most embarrassing thing Chaplin ever did, and committing himself to it was a major misjudgment. The words he utters are trite and sentimental, and their high-minded unreality is a denial, as much as an assertion, of the real spirit of Charlie. Charlie—the real Charlie—doesn't believe in anything so impossible as the indiscriminate love of humanity. And though the speech starts with some unexceptionable sentiments it deteriorates as it goes on, and its end contradicts its beginning: the Charlie of *Modern Times,* while agreeing that 'machinery that gives abundance has left us in want', might be puzzled to understand how this produces the conclusion that 'science and progress will lead to all men's happiness'. There is little point, and less pleasure, in subjecting the speech to a detailed examination: its recital of clichés and truisms doesn't pretend to the consistency of an argument. Perhaps its greatest offence is to abandon the fictional context entirely, and leave it dangling in the air. What is one supposed to imagine as happening after the speech is concluded? Nothing that can be plausibly related to what has gone before. As Chaplin's quoted remark betrays with such unconscious candour, in embarking upon the speech he released him-self from any further responsibility for bringing the fictional events (the 'laughs') to a satisfactory conclusion.

Luckily, *The Great Dictator* doesn't have to stand or fall by its last few minutes. The final speech comes from the conscious, crudely calculating, side of Charlie's imagination, like the facetious names and the weak jokes, and can be regarded as an aberration: much of the rest, including the rendering of quixotic but fortified inno-cence, and of Hynkel's glum insecurity, comes from the uncon-scious depths of Chaplin's great art. The film's finest moments have the unpredictability and nervous life of Chaplin at his best. Its cheeky ambition (Charlie outdoes his Kaiser-catching exploits in *Shoulder Arms* by playing the Kaiser himself—or the Kaiser's suc-cessor) is indicated by the result. From the point of view of his development, *The Great Dictator* provides a workable solution to the problem of what to do without Charlie by creating a Charlie substitute, a distinctive and lively dramatic character who gives full scope to Chaplin's comic art. This lesson is learned and improved upon in the great film that follows, when the old Charlie seems to be finally abandoned.

Monsieur Verdoux

Yet it is too soon to bury Charlie. He shows remarkable powers of resurrection not least in *Monsieur Verdoux*, Chaplin's next film, released after an interval of seven years. On the face of it, Henri Verdoux is a complete break with the past: a specific dramatic character, with his own name, history and credentials. Yet with his fastidious elegance, studied politeness and habit of amorous dal-liance, it has often been remarked how close a resemblance he bears to the familiar Charlie—both the lordly first and the playful second, to invoke our classification. The smirking face he wears in the photograph that is our first glimpse of him is like Charlie's at his most amiable and propitiatory: and the guarded mask-like ex-pression he offers to the world when we see him in the flesh, tending his rose-garden, is Charlie's too. In appearance, he is an elderly and dandified Charlie: perhaps what Charlie would have become if he had married Edna and settled down

Plate 8. *Monsieur Verdoux*

Verdoux's behaviour, and the things that happen to him, are full of echoes of the earlier films. Perhaps the most striking thing about *Monsieur Verdoux*, after the prosiness and rhetoric of *The Great Dictator*, is the abundance of its visual comedy. It is strewn with sight-gags that refer us back directly, with a pang of delighted recognition, to the world of the Keystone-to-Mutual shorts. Most of them arise out of Verdoux's amorous and marital intrigues (which, being his vocation, take up a large part of the film). The wooing of Madame Grosnay, which engages Verdoux's most earnest efforts, is particularly productive of such gags. It provides what is probably the film's most memorable moment when Verdoux, interrupted in the middle of his ardent attentions to the nubile widow, pretends instead to be chasing a bee, and, in a guilty excess of enthusiasm, tumbles backwards out of the open window, disappearing from sight. It is a classic role-switching gag, like the rose-plucking in *The Pilgrim*, and the plate-brushing in *A Dog's Life*: its effect here is augmented and topped by the neatness of the unexpected acrobatics. Another surprising incursion of the physical occurs at a later encounter with Madame Grosnay, when Verdoux, impulsively renewing his attentions, lurches accidentally from the sofa to the floor, managing adroitly to retain the contents of his tea cup. Of the further numerous manifestations of the old Charlie, the most familiar is the pose of coy propitiation—face smilingly bent, hands crossed on knees—that he adopts when noticed by Annabella in the act of securing the rock that is to hasten her drowning: this is Charlie's standard method of disguising a guilty intention.

It is not only Verdoux's person, and his comic business, that contribute to this striking sense of continuity, but also his professional activities, and the dramatic situation in which he finds himself. The legacies from successively departed wives that are the basis of his fortune are, after all, a kind of found money—Charlie's regular standby. No more than Charlie does Verdoux worry about its provenance; and he shows a similar tenacity in retaining it. The method of acquisition, of course, is slightly different: Charlie's windfalls are usually genuinely providential, while Verdoux believes in sending providence some polite reminders. Yet even here there is a respectable precedent. Isn't Verdoux's habit of hastening the dispatch of inconsiderately surviving wives basically a work

creation ploy? Something of the same order as Charlie's enlistment of Jackie's stone-chucking powers to invigorate the window-
mending trade? Just as Charlie doesn't see why the supply of
broken windows should be left to chance, so Verdoux's tidy business sense is offended by having to wait for important lives to take
their natural course. (The ethics of the matter, although crucial,
can be left until later.) The most significant resemblance of all is
that *Monsieur Verdoux* is, like so many of Charlie's escapades, an
imposture drama. Indeed, it outstrips its models in being a multiple imposture drama, in which the tension inherent in the type
is complicated and intensified. The tension is that between the
imposter's real, and his assumed self: in this case, between Verdoux the murderer and Verdoux the family man, one could say—
if it weren't for the difficulty (which is Verdoux's difficulty too) of
establishing which of his selves is real and which assumed. There
is more than one contradiction in his character. For the moment,
however, the point is that much of the comedy of the film issues
from ironies of role-playing that are, to Charlie watchers, wholly
familiar.

The more one examines it, in fact, the more *Monsieur Verdoux*
strikes one as not a Chaplin anthology, which is what *Modern Times*
is often called, but a Chaplin distillation, in which familiar ingredients contribute to a brew of unusual richness and strength. As
suggested, some of Chaplin's favourite themes—found money,
work creation, imposture—come together in this film. So do Charlie's perennial concerns, the staples of his life, which here associate themselves in a state of remarkable concentration. For Money
and Women, one could say, are Verdoux's Work: interestingly,
Food plays virtually no part, and Drink is almost always lethal—
facts whose significance I'll consider later. There is a case for regarding *Monsieur Verdoux* as a kind of summation of Chaplin's
work, both in the ordering of its themes and in the complexity of
its art.

If this is true, it didn't stop the film from being, in commercial
terms, a failure. It met nearly everywhere with incomprehension
and hostility, and in some places was actually banned. Theodore
Huff gives some dispiriting statistics of engagements forfeited and
income lost. The film's failure to sell itself prompted Chaplin to
withdraw it prematurely from circulation. Yet at the same time it

was a remarkable critical success. It called forth serious critiques of a standard far higher than those usually accorded to Chaplin's films. In particular it attracted literary critics like Robert Warshaw and Eric Bentley, raised in a more rigorous school of debate than that which obtains in film reviewing, who contributed eloquent defences. What was the cause of this, for Chaplin, unusual combination of public hostility and critical esteem?

The cause of both was probably the same: the film's matter and style. Its matter is unpleasant and its style is ironic. These qualities are common enough now and should not have seemed so novel then. But irony is an acquired taste. And perhaps there is truth in the speculation that Chaplin's personal unpopularity, after years of contentious and unsavoury law-suits, influenced the reception of his film. So perhaps it is not surprising that the same film should have incurred both the distaste of middle America and the plaudits of the sophisticated. What is surprising is that the distaste was not qualified by appreciation of the film's consistently vivacious comic surface.

Monsieur Verdoux is subtitled 'a comedy of murder'. Both halves of this equation deserve equal weight. The comedy is as important as the murder: indeed, the murders themselves are comic—or at least the preparations for them, which are all we are usually allowed to see. So at the outset we are challenged with the task of reconciling the comedy and the murder. Most of the comedy results from the impostures of the film's eponymous hero. Henri Verdoux is a respectable, long-serving bank clerk, whose callous dismissal at the onset of the great crash renders him sceptical of the benefits of respectability. As he explains, 'I was forced to go into business for myself.' His business turns out to be the marrying and subsequent murder of rich widows. In addition to his succession of professional false wives, he maintains a true wife and child, to whom he is deeply attached, and in whose interest his business is conducted. His true ménage is carefully kept in ignorance of his false ones, and protected, as far as is possible, from the dangers of his hectic and volatile 'business' life.

From such an account one might imagine that the story is a sort of comical *Jekyll and Hyde*, and its centre of interest the ironies of the double life. But the film's emphasis is not upon the contrast between Verdoux the genial family man and Verdoux the mass killer (though this obvious discrepancy is allowed to play its part, as in the dutiful father's fireside lecture to his son about cruelty to animals). Verdoux is outwardly not a divided but a remarkably consistent character: his murderer's manner seems to be a theatrical and animated version of his real manner. He is consistently and genuinely courteous, winning and thoughtful in his dealings with others; and in himself dapper, elegant and fastidious. Verdoux's seductive charm is Charlie's incongruous charm turned sinister (and, I shall argue, sour), which accounts for the uncanny familiarity of the performance. So the film's comic tension arises in the first instance from the conflict between his courtesy and his criminality. The criminality is nicely under-emphasized—being largely a matter of the mouth-pursings, eyebrow-raisings, hand-clenchings and finger-flutterings with which, deliberately or involuntarily, Verdoux registers his duplicity—but no less powerful for that. The resourceful energy of his seductive manoeuvres is accompanied, and continually checked, by the consciousness of a dark undercurrent of murder and deceit.

But this friction between courtesy and criminality, although continuous, is not the only source of tension in the film. Even more suspenseful, and productive of comedy, is the conflict between Verdoux's insolent mastery and his fear of discovery. The instigation and maintenance of his professional amours are creative endeavours: artistic in spirit, ingenious in execution. He enjoys his work, and communicates the enjoyment. But the continual fear of discovery gives the proceedings a sharp edge of suspense. The more his impostures burgeon and multiply, the greater the feeling of peril. His working life teeters exhilaratingly between triumph and disgrace. We share the exhilaration, and the fear. Verdoux is so attractive, his stratagems so impudent, that at the moments of crisis our sympathies can't help being largely engaged in willing him to succeed. As well as a multiple imposture drama, *Monsieur Verdoux* is a multiple balancing act. And the balance continually having to be struck is between—to use the terms we applied to *The Pilgrim*—the power-conferring aspect of imposture and its danger.

Leaving aside, yet again, the ethics of the matter, I want to consider in more detail Verdoux's relationships with his false wives, for they form largely the substance of the film. Verdoux, as befits his business training, believes in the benefits of the assembly line. He achieves his high rate of productivity by keeping several wives on the stocks at once, and shuttling energetically between one and another. So his wife relations develop intertwined, in a kind of dramatic counterpoint. The film's rhythm, its moment-to-moment suspense and surprise, derive from the changes of mood as we switch from wife to wife—from false to false, and from false to true. To disentangle the pattern, and examine the wives severally, is perhaps to do injury to the film's skilful structure. But it is a good way of getting closer to the comedy, and hence, one hopes, to the film's central, interests. Verdoux's false wives, in rough order of importance, are Thelma Couvais, Lydia Floray, Marie Grosnay and Annabella Bonheur.

Thelma Couvais, as has often been remarked, never appears except as a column of smoke. Nonetheless she is a palpable presence in the film, and exerts a powerful influence upon Verdoux's fortunes. Her presence is that of a silent accuser, and her retributive influence is conveyed, necessarily, by proxy. She is the ultimate cause of Verdoux's downfall, and while he has no immediate reason to fear her memory, the uneasiness of his behaviour, while her shadow is still on his life, is perhaps an unconscious premonition of disaster. We first see Verdoux as he prunes his roses in his sunny villa garden—abstractedly working his scissors barber fashion between clips, and pausing to rescue an injudicious centipede —while the incinerated remains of Thelma smoke voluminously behind him. This image neatly encapsulates the moral drama of the film—the innocent outward activity, the darkly criminal backdrop. Inside the villa, to which he presently resorts, Verdoux's behaviour is an odd mixture of jauntiness and disquiet: when the doorbell rings, he starts exaggeratedly, as if in guilt; and the rapping on the window that interrupts his frenzied (recuperative? self-fortifying?) session at the piano seems to his bemused perception to emanate from the instrument itself. Verdoux's nervousness suggests that Thelma, who can make pianos talk, represents the inescapableness of his moral dilemma. She is even able to take a more substantial form. One of her surrogates is the fat tailor's dummy (an indication, perhaps, of her own physical dimensions), which, encountered during Madame Grosnay's tour of the villa, has to be hustled behind a screen: it later turns up at Verdoux's

Paris storehouse, where it attracts the surprised interest, rather
than the suspicion, of the police inspector ('What's that?' 'I can't
imagine.')

Thelma's influence on events is exerted chiefly through her
quarrelsome and objectionable relatives. It is the long scene in
which they wrangle over what to do about her disappearance that
opens the film. This scene has been criticized for being static,
outmodedly theatrical and crude in its humour. I have always felt
such strictures to be unfair. It is true that it is shot picture frame
fashion, from a fixed point of view, in the manner of the earliest
films. But no other part of the film is shot in this way, so why
should not the effect be functional, rather than anachronistic?
Chaplin never seems to be given any credit for technical compe-
tence. Although the point of view doesn't change, except for a few
inserted close-ups, the camera does move restlessly from side to
side, in a way that emphasizes the claustrophobic meanness of the
room and the oafishness of its inhabitants, and makes us positively
want to escape. Distaste and discomfort are the feelings the scene
is intended to generate, and which the static set-up helps to create.
The scene strikes me as a definite success. As well as conveying
necessary plot information, it provides, in its image of vulgarity
and truculence, a good introduction to the sophistication and
charm of Verdoux. Verdoux's scenes are, by contrast, all light,
elegance and rapid movement. (This last quality, together with
nervous restlessness, is well suggested by another device that has
come in for some, to me, undeserved criticism—the 'train wheels'
motif that punctuates each section.) The opening scene is not the
last we see of the Couvais family. They double as furies and chorus,
setting the police on the trail of the imposter, and turning up
fortuitously at the restaurant where Verdoux is dining the outcast
girl, newly enriched, whom he befriended. By this time Verdoux
has no stomach for further concealment, and after giving his pursuers a little run for their money, happily turns to meet his rather
farcical Nemesis. Here the panic of the Couvais on recognizing
him contrasts nicely with his gentlemanly willingness to assist: at
one point, when Lena Couvais faints and a crowd collects, he is
forced to become a spectator at his own capture.

While Verdoux remains only marginally aware of the threat
posed by Thelma, he is roused into thorough alarm by that rep-

resented by Lydia Floray, the next false wife we meet (not counting Madame Grosnay's preliminary appearance). Lydia is an early
setback, introduced to vary what might be called the film's development section. Delivered to the brink of financial collapse by the
vagaries of the stock market, Verdoux reaches about for some
assets to realize, and Lydia is the asset that is closest to hand. To
survive, he must persuade Lydia to empty her bank account by
four o'clock, when the banks close. The interview that ensues is a
stiff challenge to his professional skill, as well as a nerve racking
reminder of his perennial insecurity. The circumstances give the
scene its suspense, and its comic richness is provided by the tension between discordant elements that all Verdoux's propitiatory
charm cannot quite reconcile. There is the contrast between Verdoux's pretended mission and his actual one. He brings to bear a
practised rhetoric of persuasion, conjuring up an imaginary financial crisis to panic Lydia into doing what he wants: but he cannot
resist, in the intervals of his lucid exposition, an agitated glance at
his watch. There is the even funnier contrast in temperament between Verdoux and Lydia: he suave and hypocritically insinuating;
she hatchet-faced and frumpish, sceptical of his mendacious alarm-
ism, and scowling ill-naturedly as he improvises at the piano.

His purpose accomplished, Verdoux sets about the inevitable
sequel: the elimination of Lydia. This final professional duty
provides, appropriately, some of the film's blackest humour. The
best remembered, and most often cited, moment is when he bus-
tles briskly downstairs the following morning, alone, and absent-
mindedly sets the breakfast table for two. A pause for reflection, a
smirk at his own forgetfulness, and one place setting is discreetly
spirited away. This is an excellent sick joke, and one of the moments where the film's feeling of moral ambiguity is at its keenest.
But a moment I find stranger, and more eerily disturbing, is the
evening before, when he climbs the stairs to join Lydia, already
retired to bed clutching her money. He pauses on the landing to
gaze at the moon through the window, and launches into an extraordinary flowery rhapsody: 'How beautiful this pale Endymion
hour!' ('Come to bed!' is Lydia's waspish reply). It is a gothic
moment of crisis, at once absurd and serious. For Verdoux's rhapsody is not cynical but moved and reflective: the evident discrepancy between his deed and its setting pleases him and, so far from

deflecting him, steels him to his purpose. To aim for effects of this kind is to take risks, and to burden the narrative with complexities of feeling that not everyone can appreciate. It was too much for some of the first audiences to stomach.

If Thelma and Lydia represent the difficulty and danger of imposture, the Marie Grosnay 'job' is, until its unforeseen conclusion relatively plain sailing. Its importance lies in its being the only one of Verdoux's seductive manoeuvres that we are allowed to follow from the beginning: from the first swift appraisal of possibilities, through the ardours of courtship, to the slap-up wedding beano. The Grosnay sequences are Verdoux at work, confidently, if quixotically, practising his art. For the chief impression left by these sequences is one of a mixture of gallantry and oddity. Verdoux's confidence supplies the gallantry and his nervousness the oddity. It is not hard to understand why he is genuinely popular with women. There is his delicate hesitation over Madame Grosnay's age ('Why, life begins at—' before rapid calculation concludes the sentence with an embarrassed smirk). There is his soft-sell wooing by telephone from the flower shop, when his murmured protestations render the flower girl misty eyed. He maintains a well-tried repertory of seductive charades. More interesting, and more comic (because less predictable) is the oddity. Verdoux's professional tasks seem to release in him a large fund of energy, whose frequent overspill takes the shape of unexpected behaviour. It is not a coincidence that most of the film's memorable sight-gags are to be found in the Grosnay sequences. At his first meeting with Madame Grosnay, Verdoux, scenting a 'killing', and perhaps wishing to keep his hand in, plunges with ludicrous promptitude into a passionate declaration of attachment. The famous backward somersault out of the window that follows (so surprising at every viewing) is as much a result of this initial eagerness as of a role-switching tactic to avoid detection. It registers the wholeheartedness of his application to his purpose, which in turn suggests the seriousness with which that purpose is pursued. A similar over eagerness compels the series of fatuous misidentifications that Verdoux commits on entering Madame Grosnay's house: affectionately saluting first the maid, and then the society friend, before alighting on the lady herself. This scene leads to the equally impetuous tumble from the sofa in mid-spiel, already alluded to, that ends with Verdoux slumped on the floor, clutching his unspilt teacup. Like Charlie's and Hynkel's, Verdoux's oddest behaviour is the result of nervous energy uncontrolled or misdirected.

Madame Grosnay, a normal, pleasant and susceptible woman, eventually succumbs. The consequence is the fashionable wedding that coming late in the film, proves a watershed in Verdoux's fortunes. The factor that gives the wedding scene its comic suspense is, of course, the presence at the shindig, unknown to Verdoux, of Annabella Bonheur, his fourth false wife. The irony of the situation is nicely managed. Both we and Verdoux are adverted to her presence by her familiar braying laugh, which he decides to pass over as a delusion. But we know better, having seen her, and can only sit back and await, not without relish, the inevitable outcome. At one point their rear ends bump and each turns to apologize without registering. The mention of Annabella's name finally seals Verdoux's doom, causing him to spew the contents of his wineglass over neighbouring guests. Amusing as all this is, it is not the only claim the scene has upon our interest. The sequel is even funnier, and in a less predictable way. Most of Verdoux's encounters hitherto have been with individuals or small groups of friends or acquaintances. But the wedding is a public crowd scene, in which he is surrounded by strangers. The interest of what follows resides in the opportunities that are taken of extending and complicating the comedy. Verdoux's new task is to avoid Annabella without exciting the suspicion of guests and host. The proprieties of the occasion forbid outright flight, and the tension of the scene shifts to the conflict between his fear of discovery and his fear of causing a scene. The desperate expedient to which he resorts is that of doubling over, as if in agony, whenever Annabella heaves into view. To his sceptical host this odd behaviour is explained as a sudden attack of cramp. To a kind elderly gentleman who discovers him crawling under the table, Verdoux pretends to be searching for a sandwich: this seems a perfectly natural course of action to the obliging guest, who promptly offers to help. This involvement of an innocent and uncomprehending bystander in his hero's lunacy is an unusual example of Chaplin's availing himself of a wider comic tradition (specifically a convention that has been dubbed 'the comic onlooker'). The result is as if René Clair, who is said to have borrowed so much from Chaplin, has finally given something back. The wedding scene ends with another unusual feature when Verdoux eventually throws caution to the winds: a single frame tableau of the house. This contains, in one shot, the host peering out of the front window in search of the errant groom; Madame Grosnay descending the stairs to the lobby in her bridal outfit; and, through the open back door, Verdoux hot-footing it over the garden wall. It is a shot in which is concentrated all the various frustrations to which the episode has led.

In turning up at her husband's wedding, Annabella Bonheur is acting true to form. It is wholly appropriate that it should be she who opens the sealed compartments of Verdoux's life and muddles the contents. For Annabella is the wife who got away. She offers the only sustained challenge to Verdoux's insidious mastery. If Madame Grosnay represents to Verdoux, until the unfortunate outcome, the satisfaction and success of his criminal role, Annabella represents its frustration and failure. She gets away by living, for Verdoux's purposes, in a distant and inaccessible world; by arming herself, in innocence, with a moral and psychological insentience that his trusted weapons cannot harm. As Robert Warshaw says, she is more like a natural force than a person. She defeats him, without realizing it, by sheer vulgar force of being, and can be said to represent the obstinate intransigence of life, the existence of an order of experience beyond the reach of his cynical calculation. Vulgar, scatter-brained, impulsive, simple-mindedly energetic, gullible but capable of instinctive scepticism ('Music on a cargo boat?' she objects, in the middle of his incautious rhapsody about the nautical life), Annabella is proof against both Verdoux's cunning and his menace. He is forced continually to interrupt his plans to rescue her from indiscretions, such as buying glass jewellery or investing in a company that professes to turn salt water into gasoline. He cannot even kiss her neck, in an act of calculated propitiation, without getting a mouthful of fluff. Obstinately indestructible, she reduces his seductive homicidal routines (so successful with Thelma, Lydia and Madame Grosnay) to an unruly shambles.

Verdoux makes two disastrous attempts to eliminate Annabella. His first idea is to make her another victim of the lethal but undetectable poison employed so successfully upon the police inspector. At this stage, his experience of Annabella has not been so

punishing as to unsettle his habitual confidence, and he sets
about his gruesome preparations with untroubled briskness. His
plans are overturned not by Annabella, but by the unforeseen return of the dismissed maid, who muddles Verdoux's poison with
her own bottle of peroxide. As a result of a series of absurd complications, Verdoux mixes his wife a peroxide cocktail and waits,
with polite impatience, for her to collapse. Unnerved by her immunity (she quaffs the swill with every sign of relish), and by the
apparition of the maid whom his poison has rendered bald, he
takes an incautious gulp of the laced drink himself: and launches
promptly into a splendidly theatrical death throes act, staggering
about the house in incoherent search for an antidote. Where
Annabella is concerned, Verdoux can do nothing right, and is
liable to find himself at any moment victimized by circumstances:
she, for her part, remains throughout entirely unaware of what is
going on. Her blithe unconsciousness is her shield, and Verdoux's
doom. For his second attempt he lays on something more crude
and direct: a drowning accident on a fishing trip. For this he swops
his dapper suit for a holiday outfit. His soft trilby hat and lightweight jacket have the strange effect of diminishing him: he looks
mean and dispirited, and nothing like a successful criminal. The
boat trip is a predictable farce: Verdoux succeeds only in chloro-
forming himself and dumping himself in the lake, while Annabella
devotes her energy, with muscular concentration, to landing her
catch. Aimed at Annabella, Verdoux's homicidal stratagems turn
back upon himself, and his resourcefulness takes on the impetus
of desperation. The tension of these scenes is not, as before, between his civilized suavity and his criminal guile, but between his
desire to act with spirit and style and his disintegrating hold on
events.

I hope I have been able to convey something of the remarkable
liveliness, as well as the dramatic point, of these false wife sections.
They contain the film's most spirited comedy, and also give rise to
the sharpest questions about its meaning. They each dramatize
different aspects of Verdoux's imposture: its power-conferring satisfactions (Madame Grosnay), its skilful surmounting of obstacles
(Lydia), its frustration and defeat (Annabella). What they have in
common is that they derive their tension from certain standard
conflicts. For Verdoux, these conflicts are chiefly practical and

expedient—he is caught between his determination to survive and the imminence of ruin, or between his enjoyment of imposture and his fear of discovery. They are all these things to the audience too, but something else as well. Verdoux's vicissitudes pose a painful dilemma to the sympathies of the audience. We share both his pleasure and his alarm, and are anxious for his survival; but unlike him we are troubled by the moral discrepancy between his courteous behaviour and his criminal occupation. We can't help admiring Verdoux the adroit financier, and warming to Verdoux the graceful amorist, but the unorthodox way he earns his money keeps inconsiderately obtruding itself. *Monsieur Verdoux* is subtitled 'a comedy of murder'. As I have said, the fact that it is a comedy, and a very funny one, challenges us to reconcile the murder and the comedy, as well as to recognize that the comedy is inseparably dependent upon the murder.

Actually, it is misleading to say that Verdoux is not troubled by his own criminality. It is true that, rather than parading it in our view, he politely consigns it to the closed rooms of his life. The smile on his face as he enters Lydia's bedroom is that of a man who excuses himself from company to perform an unpleasant but necessary chore. But, as his continual nervous susceptibility demonstrates, he is certainly aware of the discrepancy. And when he is finally unmasked, and on trial for his life, he is at pains to justify his behaviour. Unfortunately, his explanations tend to muddle the issue, rather than clarify it. *Monsieur Verdoux* has often been somewhat misinterpreted on the basis of its hero's tendentious and evasive self-vindications. Chief among these are his assertion, in the dock, that the world's war habits encourage mass killing ('I'm an amateur in comparison'); and, in his cell, 'One murder makes a villain; millions a hero. Numbers sanctify!'. This line of argument has led to the film's being described as 'an untimely sermon against the unscrupulous business of war', and, although I can see why, it strikes me as the wrong emphasis. After all, many wars are entered into for perfectly creditable motives, and have been known to produce good as well as evil: the satire would be on shaky ground if it contested only this issue. More important, to be regarded as the theme of the film, war would reasonably be expected to play a part in the action, or to register itself as a focus of interest independent of what anybody merely says: as it is, it only crops up in Verdoux's excuses. His introduction of the war idea seems to me a self-serving irrelevance.

Yet Verdoux does have a case. And it is things he says, though not always in self-justification, that point to what it is. In his voice-over introduction, describing the collapse of his legitimate career, he explains, 'I was forced to go into business for myself.' Agreeing with his wife's concern at his overzealous devotion to 'business', he concedes, 'If I lose one job, I can always get another.' To the girl he has temporarily rescued from the streets he asserts, 'This is a ruthless world, and one must be ruthless to survive.' And the most telling pun in the film is provided, unconsciously, by an acquaintance encountered at the cafe: 'You must have made a killing!' Even without these ironic suggestions, it is obvious enough that the primary target of *Monsieur Verdoux*'s satire is the ruthless amorality of competitive business. Verdoux's justifiable defence is that he is the victim of a social ethic whose only yardstick is material success: so that his work creation ploy is simply an act of self-preservation ('I was forced to go into business for myself'), and his unorthodox choice of career is sanctioned by society's indifference to any motive but the profit motive. His false wives are jobs, chosen with calculation and instantly expendable, and valued only in terms of the income they yield. He asks, by implication: if the only important objects in life are practical, financial and material, and if the realm of practical affairs has no relation at all to the realm of moral choice, why isn't my chosen method of enriching myself as valid as yours? This challenge is not unanswerable (I suggest some answers below) but one must grant its logic. If life is indeed a jungle, the predators who survive are those with fewest scruples.

At this stage I want to dissent from the idea, suggested by some accounts on the above lines, that *Monsieur Verdoux* is simply a kind of anti-capitalist tract. There is certainly a sharp anti-capitalist edge to the satire. The money theme is a crucial one. The experience of the depression seems to have communicated its nervousness to the film: there is a sense of civilization's being always at the hazard of arbitrary economic fluctuations. Verdoux is a manufacturer of found money, but he cannot control its capriciousness and it defeats him in the end. The possibility of ruin casts its shadow over all his business dealings: he is once threatened with it, and eventually visited with it (and is not above frightening others with the prospect of it). The danger of wizardry combines with the danger of imposture to feed the film's suspense. Yet the issue is not clear-cut. For one thing, Verdoux's insecurity should be seen in the context of Chaplin's habit of presenting life itself as chronically insecure. After all, the providential finding of money presupposes the arbitrary losing of it. The hazards of the financial life resemble those of nature in *The Gold Rush*, or of war in *Shoulder Arms*, in being felt as the product of impersonal forces rather than of human calculation. If Verdoux's attempt to create a life free of struggle comes to grief, like Charlie's unrealized fantasies of do-mestic bliss, it may be because his object is not more realistic than Charlie's. For another thing, there are no identifiable villains in *Monsieur Verdoux*. Its battle lines are not rigidly drawn but vague and misleading: we are rarely sure where, or even who, the enemy is. The trouble is that Verdoux himself is both the hero and the villain of the piece. His confusing quality is his niceness. I have suggested before that he is genuinely, as well as designedly, nice: his extravagant professional courtesy strikes us as continuous with a courtesy that is not feigned. His niceness has the effect both of partially excusing him and of implicating us. Involuntarily identi-fying with him, we are forced to face the implications of his crimes, and so are seen to be just as guilty of them as he: we are Verdoux. His last words at the trial—'I shall see you all very soon'—sinisterly suggest, not only the inevitability of death, or perhaps the likeli-hood of a global catastrophe, but also our complicity in his career.

The moral ambiguity of *Monsieur Verdoux* has the effect of gen-eralizing the issue it presents. The target of the satire is a personal and cultural condition rather than an economic system. The film's irony indicts, not the wickedness of a class, but a pervasive failure, or blindness, of modern civilization. In the world at large, the equation of happiness with material well-being; in the individual, an atrophy of the moral sense: these are symptoms of the failure. The failure itself might be called, to enlist a still serviceable phrase, a dissociation of sensibility: a nearly complete divorce between en-ergy and will and the ends that they should serve. F.R. Leavis, enlarging on this, his constant theme, has written, 'Significance is a profound human need, like creativity, its associate. The thwart-ing of the need, or hunger, has consequences not the less catas-

trophic because of the general blankness in face of the cause.'
Monsieur Verdoux offers a grimly comic demonstration of these
consequences. And the distinction of the film is to show, by examining a significant case, how the private and the public sickness
are related.

The significant case is Verdoux. The ethical and spiritual blindness of modern civilization is a contradiction that, by satirical
means, he demonstrates. But there is another contradiction of
which he is the victim (it is really the same one). For Verdoux is
not simply a stylized instrument of satire. That is, he is not like
Jonson's Volpone, a comic monster whose function is to draw out
the wickedness of others; or like Stroheim in *Foolish Wives*, a cynical monster who preys upon the weakness of others (and whose
punishment is to be casually dismembered and thrust into a sewer
by the father of the girl he has deceived). Nor, except briefly at
the beginning, is he a comic self-ingratiator like Louis Mazzini in
Kind Hearts and Coronets, whose voice-over commentary provides
the ironic tone by which we are invited to judge the events. He *has*
a satirical function, discharged with considerable élan in the false
wife sections, but he is also intended to be a fully human, even
sympathetic, character, deserving of our interest and concern, and
himself a victim of the very contradiction that he demonstrates. In
the parts of the film we haven't yet considered, a private theme
takes over from the public.

The burden of the public part of *Monsieur Verdoux*, the indictment of the dehumanizing tendency of modern life, is borne by
the false wife sections. The private part, the examination of one
example of spiritual corruption, is borne by what might be called
the true wife sections. Verdoux has only one true wife, of course,
but there is reason for regarding the girl he rescues from the
street as a surrogate true wife, since she is the only other woman
in the film with whom he is seen to have a genuine relationship,
free from the artifice of his imposter's role. His relations with both
women show him at his most vulnerable and involuntarily self-re-
vealing.

Actually, the trouble with his relation with Mona, his wife, is that
it is too thoroughly infected by his imposter's pretence. All Verdoux's domestic charades are like dreadful parodies of Charlie's
old dreams of domestic bliss. But his real domestic idyll is the

greatest irony of all. Verdoux, sincerely and deeply devoted to his true family, commits all his crimes in the service of this genuine love. Every danger is incurred in the interest of their protection and security. Yet he is to Mona what he is to all the others—a nomadic, irregularly resident imposter, forced to conceal the reasons for his absence and the real source of his income. At one point he even feels obliged to take his 'work' home with him—by pumping his pharmacist neighbour about the latest non-detectable poison. The love theme, in fact, provides him with his most insoluble contradiction: his true love is both threatened and corrupted by his false ones. And in the end he discovers that he cannot keep his true love uncontaminated by the sickness of the world: its malevolence destroys her before it overcomes him. In the light of this account, it is worth asking why Mona is disabled. It is not simply, as one may unthinkingly assume, to render her an object of pathos. The obvious function of her handicap is to emphasize her vulnerability (and hence Verdoux's protectiveness), and to confine her mobility (thus making Verdoux's impostures more plausible). But the most important function is to introduce the ideas of damage and constraint into the one relationship that matters to Verdoux. Mona represents both the corruption of this desperately protected portion of his life, and, by transference, his own tainted goodness: he is himself morally disabled. Not only does he fail to protect his domestic idyll, but he is condemned to see in it a reflection of his darker self.

Mona, far from being merely a sentimental touch, is one of the significant characters in the film. What her loss brings home to him is that the moral life is not divisible, and that one cannot without compunction behave as though it were. Modern material civilization, to whose tenets Verdoux subscribes, compartmentalizes the moral instinct, and regards it as in some way unreal in comparison with the practical, material and economic concerns of life. But experience teaches Verdoux that the moral instinct is not less real than the self-preservation instinct. He cannot keep the good in his life hermetically sealed against the evil. He sees his guilt reflected in his ruin and the loss of all he loves, and we see ours reflected in him. Both his bitter experience and our enforced complicity have the effect of personalizing the issues of the film, of making us feel them in terms of individuals—the choices of their lives, and the values by which they elect to live. *Monsieur Verdoux*, in fact, is as much a film about individual conscience and responsibility as it is about the social and economic system. It demonstrates that public and private sicknesses cannot in the last resort be distinguished, and that the first cannot exist without the second. This is another reason for not regarding it as a political polemic. It is hard to imagine any film that gives less comfort to the widespread instinct to blame others—classes or groups—for our misfortunes. It makes it impossible for us comfortably to disavow the responsibility for our actions. Like Verdoux, we can only look inward and blame ourselves.

It is perhaps misleading to talk of Verdoux blaming himself, or even learning from experience in the way I've described. He goes in more for urbane self-justification. Yet the need he feels to justify himself is itself perhaps an indication of the clarity with which the irony of his condition is revealed to him. And after his ruin and his family's death he is visibly a changed man: exchanging his dandyish outfits for a suit of sober black; bowed and shuffling in the streets where he once promenaded. It is the mask-like blankness of his face, rather than what he says or does, that betrays his consciousness of guilt and defeat. What he says is an expression of his only, and constant, mental defence against the contradictions of his nature and his chosen career: his cynicism.

Verdoux's cynicism is revealed, and tested, in his relationship with what might be called his second true wife: the girl he picks up in the street. She is a pivotal figure. In their brief meeting they conduct a kind of dialogue about the ends of life. She has suffered a spell of imprisonment for petty theft, but not allowed the experience to dull her zest for life. (We know that in the original treatment she was a prostitute, a history that would have stood in a nicer ironical relation to the high-class courtesan she eventually becomes. Chaplin was obliged by the censors to sanitize her role.) Her spirited optimism in degradation is intended to shame and disturb Verdoux's ingrained cynicism. In their conversation he doesn't show much sign of being persuaded, but he is clearly touched, both by her obstinate hopefulness and by the obviously evocative fact of her husband's having been disabled. He can't in the event carry through his plan of eliminating her in order to test the efficiency of his poison: the intention behind his taking her up in the first place. The poisoned bottle, prudently preserved, nonetheless comes in handy for the inconvenient police inspector: Verdoux's forbearance is not a sign of moral reformation but a tribute to human qualities in the girl that he recognizes as no longer possible for himself.

It is only, one is forced to conclude, in his soul that Verdoux recognizes the lessons his experience teaches him: outwardly he remains unmoved by the admonitory violence of events. The catastrophes that befall him—the destruction of his family and the evaporation of his fortune—have the effect of strengthening his profound cynical pessimism (which also seems to be vindicated by the girl's eventual defection to the ranks of the mercenary). So when he is called upon to justify his career to himself in his ruin, and to others at his arraignment, his glibly aphoristic excuses are the product of bitterness, not clear-sightedness. Verdoux in the dock, in fact, is strongly reminiscent of Oscar Wilde: one wonders whether Chaplin was consciously influenced by accounts of that cause célèbre. There is the same sense of intelligence deliberately and compulsively applied to the deflection of damaging truth. Like the society whose values he has adopted, Verdoux won't accept human responsibility for his crimes: their justification exists in a realm apart from that of ordinary moral choice. When the economic system defeats him a second time, and wipes out everything that he values, and that is the ostensible reason for his criminal career, he has no effective supports to fall back upon. He can only barricade himself behind his cynicism, and go to his death a victim of the moral contradiction his crimes were designed to expose.

Monsieur Verdoux is a very impressive achievement: a subtle, penetrating and richly comic dramatization of a serious theme. It is his most successful sound film, and one of the best films he ever made. Who would have supposed, when Chaplin set out to find a place for Charlie in the actual world, and to confront him with the problems of modern life, that it would end like this? Among other things, it finally resolves the difficulty of finding an appropriate shape for Charlie to assume. It learns the lessons in form from both of the other films in what I have called the trilogy. From *Modern Times* it takes the serious concern with modern civilization but rejects the inclusion of the unadapted traditional Charlie figure. From *The Great Dictator* it learns how the essential Charlie qualities, and hence his power to disturb, can be absorbed into a stylized dramatic character who is not Charlie. The result is a figure who combines Charlie's impact with greater plausibility than Charlie could any longer offer, and so a greater freedom to enter into new areas of experience. The creation of a character like Verdoux required more intelligence and courage than Chaplin is usually given credit for: intelligence to recognize that something new was needed, and courage to discard the familiar aspect of the old. Just as in its theme the film is the culmination of Chaplin's enquiry into the problems of modern life, so in its form it is the culmination of his attempt to use Charlie and his values to illuminate those problems. For once we are hardly aware of discrepancy or failure in his matching of theme and form, but rather of correspondence and success.

Plate 9. *Monsieur Verdoux*

Filmography

Detailed filmographies of Chaplin are available in the books, listed in the bibliography, by Theodore Huff (who first gave an accurate listing of Chaplin's early films), John McCabe (whose filmography is by Denis Gifford), Jean Mitry (*Tout Chaplin*), Uno Asplund and Timothy J. Lyons. Not all these authorities agree about every detail. I have drawn upon them all in compiling my own, and am grateful for their original researches.

Various information that is common to a chronological phase of Chaplin's career is brought together in the introductory note for that phase, and is not repeated in the individual entries. The date given for each film is that of the first American release. And Chaplin is not credited as a player unless he appears in a role other than that of the familiar tramp: in all other cases (the vast majority) it is understood that he is the leading player.

Keystone, 1914

The Keystone films were all made in Mack Sennett's Keystone Studios in Glendale, California. Unless otherwise described, they were all produced by Mack Sennett, written and directed by Charles Chaplin (with the occasional collaboration of Mabel Normand and Mack Sennett), and probably photographed by Frank D. Williams. Except where indicated, they were all approximately 1000 ft in length.

Making a Living

> 2 February 1914. Directed by Henry Lehrman. Written by Reed Heustis. *With* Henry Lehrman (reporter), Virginia Kirtley (his girl), Alice Davenport (her mother), Minta Durfee, Chester Canklin.

Chaplin plays a down at heel English aristocrat who tries to make a quick buck by scooping a news photograph from Henry

Lehrman (also the director of this and other early films): after first trying to ingratiate himself with his rival's fiancée. This improbable sequence of events is given interest first of all by Chaplin's costume, which, for the only time, is not his familiar garb but one derived from his music-hall act, comprising a frock coat, a top hat and a droopy moustache. This provides an instructive contrast to his usual appearance: it looks not just strange but *wrong*, and makes one reflect how all the constituent parts of his regular costume contribute to the total effect; the bowler hat and moustache suggesting the perpetual battle in clownish nature between raffish freedom and respectable constraint. This factor apart, the film contains a great deal of delightful, and fully characteristic, Charlie behaviour, including strutting walks, smirky expressions, cane-tossing and head-turning gags, and a moment when a gallant kiss upon the hand of a pretty girl is followed by some appreciative lip-smacking. It must have seemed a very auspicious debut indeed.

Kid Auto Races at Venice

> 7 February 1914. Written and directed by Henry Lehrman. *With* Henry Lehrman (director), Frank Williams (cameraman), Billy Jacobs, Charlotte Fitzpatrick, Thelma Salter, Gordon Griffiths (kids). 500 ft (split reel).

Charlie struts and parades, and generally makes a nuisance of himself, at an actual children's car race, to the particular annoyance of a camera crew filming the events. This film is discussed in Chapter 1.

Mabel's Strange Predicament

> 9 February 1914. Directed by Henry Lehrman. Written by Reed Heustis. *With* Mabel Normand, Chester Conklin (husband), Alice Davenport (wife), Harry McCoy, Hank Mann, Al St John.

A hotel comedy in which Charlie, sloshed but lecherous, pursues a pyjama-clad Mabel through corridors and rooms. There is a good scene in the foyer when Charlie, prevented by lack of coins from using the telephone (the first pay phone gag?), next gets entangled in Mabel's dog leash, thrusting his hand into a cuspidor as he falls—preserving throughout his air of exasperated dignity. But for the most part this story is repeated to better effect in *A Night Out*. It is the first of Mabel Normand's many appearances with

Chaplin. She was too strongly characterized to be his ideal partner, and too often plays in competition with him instead of being,
like Edna, perfectly complementary.

Between Showers

> 28 February 1914. Directed by Henry Lehrman. Written by Reed Heustis.
> *With* Ford Sterling, Chester Conklin (cop), Emma Clifton, Sadie
> Lampe.

The first of Chaplin's three appearances with Ford Sterling, the
Keystone lead whom he replaced. The contrast between their
comic styles is discussed in Chapter 2. The story involves their
rivalry to escort a pretty girl across a flooded street, and for the
possession of a stolen umbrella, while fending off the suspicious
attentions of a slow-witted cop.

A Film Johnnie

> 2 March 1914. Directed by George Nichols. Written by Craig Hutchin-
> son. *With* Roscoe Arbuckle, Mabel Normand, Ford Sterling, Mack
> Sennett (themselves), Virginia Kirtley, Minta Durfee.

Chaplin's first film studio comedy, and Charlie's earliest piece
of drama-confusions. We first encounter him in a cinema, weeping at a war film that looks like a dry run for *Birth of a Nation*,
applauding a Keystone girl, and causing a rumpus with a succession of leg-over-knee, hat-springing and coin-shooting gags. The
actress's charms entice him into the Keystone studio, where he
meets in their own persons Sennett, Sterling and Arbuckle (whose
paunch he pats in admiration). On the set, he obstructs the scene-
shifters, and—characteristically confusing art and life—interrupts
the drama to rescue the threatened heroine. The best gags are his
smacking himself out of a trance at the sight of a bosom-revealing
siren, and his clever and cocky revolver-toting: he picks his teeth
and lights his cigarette with it, and fires random shots with fancy
nonchalance. At the 'real-life' fire to which the unit is despatched,
Charlie warms his hands at the blaze (I have remarked upon the
faint shockingness of this), and, doused by the hose, engages in
the futile swimming strokes that the experience inevitably suggests. The first really attractive Keystone.

Tango Tangles

> 9 March 1914. Written and directed by Mack Sennett. *With* Ford Sterling (band leader), Roscoe Arbuckle (musician), Minta Durfee (hat check girl), Chester Conklin.

Like *Between Showers*, a location impromptu; and like that film, interesting for the contrast between Charlie's subtle clowning and Sterling's crude mimicry. The story concerns drunken shenanigans (motivated by love rivalry) at a night-club where Charlie is a guest and Sterling and Arbuckle musicians—all appearing without make-up. This film is discussed in Chapter 2.

His Favourite Pastime

> 16 March 1914. Directed by George Nichols. Written by Craig Hutchinson. *With* Roscoe Arbuckle, Peggy Pearce (wife).

As always, the pastimes are boozing and wenching, carried on here first at a bar where Charlie practices his usual forms of annoyance, and later at the home of a prospective conquest, whose assaulted virtue is saved by the appearance of her husband. The final melee is enlivened by a memorable moment, when Charlie, tumbling adroitly from a banister to a sofa below, contrives to retain both his lighted cigarette and the nonchalant air that goes with it.

Cruel, Cruel Love

> 26 March 1914. Directed by George Nichols. Written by Craig Hutchinson. *With* Minta Durfee (fiancée), Chester Conklin (butler), Alice Davenport (maid).

Charlie is Minta's rich suitor in the classier-than-usual milieu of this film. Spurned by her after being discovered in the act of embracing the maid, he decides to end it all. There follows a series of bungled suicide attempts, including poisoning, gassing and hanging, whose tragi-comic tension is part of a long humorous tradition that encompasses Clair's *A Nous la Liberté*, Marceau's *Bip Commits Suicide* and Ayckbourn's *Absurd Person Singular*.

The Star Boarder

> 4 April 1914. Directed by George Nichols. Written by Craig Hutchinson. *With* Minta Durfee (landlady), Edgar Kennedy (her husband), Gordon Griffith (son).

At a typical suburban boarding house (whose mahogany, chintzy interior forces itself upon the attention), Charlie's canoodling with the landlady wins him privileges, but is threatened by her precocious brat's compromising photographs. Her husband's wrath is deflected by the discovery that his own extra-marital exercises have also been captured on film. There are some good things in this comedy of intrigue, including Charlie's air of exaggerated abstraction as he purloins beer from the refrigerator (shuffling sideways to indicate his innocence of any intention); and the tennis match whose bouncing ball both (with its predictable suggestions of physical assault) bonks him on the nose, and provides the opportunity for a role-switching gag by needing to be searched for when the husband interrupts an amorous passage with the landlady.

Mabel at the Wheel

> 18 April 1914. Written and directed by Mack Sennett and Mabel Normand. *With* Mabel Normand, Harry McCoy (rival), Chester Conklin (father), Mack Sennett, Al St John. 2000 ft.

Charlie unaccountably sports a double-pronged beard and a top hat in this frenetic but lacklustre racetrack comedy, which doesn't deserve its extra reel. The story concerns Charlie's attempt to frustrate his rival in the big race (and for Mabel's attention) by locking him away, and causing Mabel to deputize for him. The best moment is when Charlie, trying to counter the attraction of Harry's hot rod by giving Mabel a ride on his insignificant motorbike, manages to deposit her in a puddle.

Twenty Minutes of Love

> 20 April 1914. Directed by Joseph Maddern. Written by Charles Chaplin. *With* Minta Durfee, Edgar Kennedy (lovers), Chester Conklin (thief), Gordon Griffith (boy), Joseph Swichard.

This rather tediously routine location impromptu set in the ubiquitous park, concerns Charlie's theft from Chester of an (already stolen) watch, and his attempt to sell it back to its original owner.

The park is populated by the usual assortment of courting couples, and Charlie predictably tries to muscle in. So the action is enlivened by a number of gags from his repertoire of seductive devices: including hand-on-knee; leg-over-knee; his half-mocking, half-envious embracement of a bush at the sight of an amorous pair; and a good moment when his reflective scratch at his ear indicates the fact that his inamorata's lips have been suddenly replaced by her boy-friend's bristly moustache.

Caught in a Cabaret

> 27 April 1914. Directed by Mabel Normand and Charles Chaplin. *With* Mabel Normand (rich girl), Harry McCoy (escort), Chester Conklin (waiter), Edgar Kennedy (manager), Alice Davenport (mother), Joseph Swichard (father), Gordon Griffith (boy), Minta Durfee, Phyllis Allen (dancers). 2000 ft.

An amusing imposture-drama with a better-than-average story in which Charlie, a waiter in a seedy café, rescues rich Mabel from the attentions of a rough who has frightened off her escorting fiancé. Invited to her garden party, he pretends to wealth and title himself, but his cover is blown when the vengeful fiancé conducts a party of nobs to Charlie's place of work. There is a well-known moment when he disguises the embarrassment of a hole in his shoe by hanging his hat on it, and some nice displays of his glass-collecting and other waiterly skills on the oddly cavernous café set.

Caught in the Rain

> 4 May 1914. *With* Alice Davenport (wife), Mack Swain (husband), Alice Howell.

Chaplin's solo directorial debut. A hotel comely of love intrigue, of the kind he was later to improve upon. Charlie pursues a married lady from the park to the hotel, is warned off by the husband, but installs himself in the next room. Providentially, the lady is a sleepwalker, and mistakes his room for hers at the dead of night. But the husband reintrudes, and Charlie is defenestrated on to a balcony in the rain. There is some good comedy involving Charlie's repeated difficulty in mounting the hotel stairs. What the hotel settings provide in these films, of course, is the insistent suggestion, though rarely the reality, of sexual misconduct.

A Busy Day

> 7 May 1914. *With* Mack Swain, Phyllis Allen. 500 ft (split reel).

Chaplin's first female impersonation, in which, kitted out like Old Mother Riley, he plays the vengeful wife in a marital misconduct comedy filmed on location in the harbour town of San Pedro, California. A surprising, and unrepeated, exception to the usually coy and flirtatious character of his female roles.

The Fatal Mallet

> 1 June 1914. *With* Mabel Normand, Mack Sennett, Mack Swain (rivals).

Although set in a charming sunlit garden, with adjacent barn, this is a weak and pointless triangular love intrigue comedy, with Mabel the object of the rival attentions of Charlie and the two Macks, and consisting of little but brick-throwing and mallet-bonking. That conventional missiles should be deemed insufficient, and Mack Swain brained with an oversize mallet that matches his own bulk, is at least a typical piece of Charlie-logic.

Her Friend the Bandit

> 4 June 1914. *With* Mabel Normand (rich girl), Charlie Murray (count).

A standard imposture drama in which Charlie, a bandit turned count, commits predictable solecisms and outrages at Mabel's posh party.

The Knockout

> 11 June 1914. Directed by Charles Avery. Written by Charles Chaplin. *With* Roscoe Arbuckle, Edgar Kennedy (contestants), Mack Swain, Alice Howell, Mack Sennett (spectators), Al St John, Hank Mann, Slim Summerville. 2000 ft.

An Arbuckle film in which Charlie appears briefly as the referee in a boxing match between Fatty and Edgar Kennedy. Its only source of interest is that Chaplin manages to work in, for the first time on the screen, material from his repertoire of boxing gags (misplaced wallops, rope strangulation, star counting, etc.), and so inaugurates a line of comedy that stretches to the richly suggestive fight scene in *City Lights*.

Mabel's Busy Day

> 13 June 1914. *With* Mabel Normand (vendor), Chester Conklin, Slim Summerville (cops), Harry McCoy, Billie Bennett (spectators).

Like *Mabel at the Wheel*, a racetrack comedy, but one in which Mabel is a hot-dog girl and Charlie an obnoxious spectator who flirts with her (and everyone else in skirts), purloins her wares, and disrupts her trade. Distributed among the largely unfunny walloping and chasing are some genuinely amusing passages. Charlie is unusually dandified, with a natty grey bowler, long tweed coat and a buttonhole. At one point he retrieves a cigar butt with exaggerated unobtrusiveness, stooping downwards by casual degrees; and, taking a puff, releases the smoke by stomach pressure. At another he engages in playful chaff with a trio of girl spectators: leaning languidly on one (earning a slap in the face, and, by way of retaliation, lifting his foot for a kick, studying it with interest when discovered, and readjusting it with his cane); and picking the purse of another (where he discovers a wig that he waves like a handkerchief, and whose fluff must be fastidiously picked from his mouth).

Mabel's Married Life

> 20 June 1914. *With* Mabel Normand (Charlie's wife), Mack Swain (her brother), Charlie Murray, Harry McCoy (bar clients), Alice Howell, Alice Davenport, Hank Mann, Al St John.

An unusual story in which Mabel, upset by Charlie's lack of manly ardour, first enlists her beefy brother Bill (Mack) to play the part of her lover (with the object of arousing Charlie's jealousy, but with the effect of getting Mack in trouble with his wife), and, when that fails, purchasing a boxer's dummy with eye to getting Charlie in better physical trim. The really amusing passage when Charlie, arrived home from propping up the local bar, treats the dummy first as an unwelcome intruder to be ordered from the house, and then as a long-lost friend: his reaction runs the gamut from aggression to nudging, confiding cordiality, and retains an undercurrent of perplexity at the dummy's disinclination to respond to any approach, and at its remarkable powers of recovery when walloped. It is eventually politely introduced to Mabel. (The episode reminds us of William. Willeford's description of the child's bouncing doll

as, in its automatism and resilience, a type of the clownish nature).
Mabel has some good comic moments of her own in this film, especially in an experimental sparring match with the dummy when
she first gets it home.

Laughing Gas

> 9 July 1914. *With* Fritz Schade (dentist), Alice Howell (his wife), Slim
> Summerville, Joseph Swichard (patients), Mack Swain.

Laughing Gas is undoubtedly one of the very best Keystones. Charlie plays a dentist's assistant who takes a variety of liberties with the
unfortunate patients in the intervals between flirting with the
boss's wife. The fairly routine intrigue involving the dentist and
his wife, and the quarrel with Mack Swain in the local saloon, turn
out to be subsidiary to the core of the film, which is Charlie's
versatile and creative display of dentistry. It is his first successful
professional-activity comedy, characterized by the poetic suggestiveness of his deployment of equipment and performance of
tasks. The keynote that is struck is erotic: it is anticipated by an ex-
traprofessional moment when, tripping on the wife's skirts as she
mounts the steps to her house, he manages to rip them off, revealing a voluminous pair of bloomers. So the sight of a pretty girl
in the dentist's chair rouses his inevitable ardour: tipping her back
for treatment seems a natural preliminary to love-play, and the
pincers are employed to pull her face round by the nose so that
he can kiss her. But the reclining chair also suggests a shoe-shine
establishment, and she gets her shoes polished as a bonus. In a
concession to the clinical atmosphere, Charlie tries to revive one
comatose male patient by listening to his foot and bonking him
with a mallet; and it is the energetic associations of tooth-tugging
that cause him determinedly to bestride another, flourishing an
oversize pair of pincers as if engaged on a heavy engineering job.
There are two interesting anticipations of later films. The difficulty he finds in keeping up with the revolving chair reminds us
of his similar trouble with a swivelling table in *One a.m.* More
striking is his being mistaken in the waiting room, by his purposeful professional air, and the manner in which he pulls off his
gloves and rubs his hands, for the dentist himself: which is
repeated in his 'executive' manner of opening the vault in *The*

Bank to retrieve his bucket and mop (a gag itself recycled in modified form for *The Pawnshop*).

The Property Man

> 1 August 1914. *With* Fritz Schade, Phyllis Allen, Alice Davenport, Charles Bennett (performers), Mack Sennett (in audience). 2000 ft.

Charlie plays a tipsy and lecherous property man in this back-stage comedy, involving a troupe of performers (two tragic thespians, a strong man and his wife, a duet of dancing sisters) and Charlie's pestering of their persons and disruption of their acts. The drama-confusion in this piece is minimal, confined to a final sequence in which audience and performers alike are doused with hose-water. Instead, interest is centred upon Charlie's relations with his aged assistant, and with the ladies of the troupe. The assistant is a bearded and decrepit old fogey, whom Charlie treats with a callousness remarkable even for him: pinioned to the floor by the strong man's trunk, his discomfort is aggravated by Charlie's attempting to stand on it and lift it at the same time, and he is the recipient of innumerable cuffs and wallops. Intermittently Charlie flirts with the strong man's wife (her frilly-skirted costume enabling him to work in a suggestive invitation to demonstrate some leg-flexing exercises), and he also shows an interest in the dancing sisters (whom he follows during rehearsal, apparently to inspect their bottoms, after blindfolding the fogey against temptation), The backstage setting licences a general state of undress, and so contributes to the pervasively erotic/indecent atmosphere (it is Charlie's filching of the strong man's tights that precipitates the crisis). A first Charlie film mainly, but the skylarking second Charlie surfaces in an old gag when Charlie tears his handkerchief as the strong man bends over.

The Face on the Bar Room Floor

> 10 August 1914. Based on the poem by Hugh Antoine D'Arcy. *With* Cecile Arnold (Madelaine), Fritz Schade (cad). Chester Conklin, Harry McCoy, Vivian Edwards.

There are some zany elements and characteristic touches in this dramatization of the lachrymose ballad about the degraded artist who recreates the image of his lost love for his fellow boozers.

There is plenty of scope for Charlie's inspired artist act, and the flashback is to an exotic studio furnished with drapery, statuary, a huge bear-skin rug with a gaping mouth, and a slinky, cigarette-puffing model. In Charlie's portrait, the curve of the model's bottom turns into a Grecian urn; his later rendering of the fat, moustachioed cad destined to blight his life is aided by adjustative pokes at the sitter with his cane, and by painful expressions of creative transport that result in tiny dabs the canvas. In the bar, he covers the floor with vacuous oval-headed images of the lost Madelaine.

Recreation

13 August 1914. *With* unidentified actors. 500 ft (split reel).

Another off-the-cuff (and off-the-peg) park/lake frolic, involving Charlie, a girl, the sailor from whom he tries to filch her and the inevitable complement of cops. Made up of chasing and brick-throwing, with a general cold plunge for finale.

The Masquerade

27 August 1914. *With* Roscoe Arbuckle, Chester Conklin (themselves), Charlie Murray (director), Fritz Schade (villain), Minta Durfee, Cecile Arnold, Vivian Edwards (actresses), Harry McCoy.

Both Chaplin's second film studio comedy and his second female impersonation. Charlie first appears without make-up in a changing room scene in which he attempts to snaffle Fatty's booze. He then clowns with a toy duck for the benefit of two delectable girls (primly hanging his hat over its rear end, and conjuring out of it a ping-pong ball 'egg') while waiting for his entry cue. On the set, he effects a very brisk piece of drama-confusion, variously foiling the fat, bowler-hatted villain in the melodrama by biffing him with the property 'baby', prodding his bottom with a dagger and tickling his armpit. Fired, he strikes a tragic pose and drops his suitcase on the director's foot. He smuggles himself back into the studio in female guise, and proceeds to give a beautifully judged performance, decked in thick white furs and a large feathered hat. The lecherous intentions of the director are foiled by playful clouts with his muff, and all-out seduction is prevented by a huge masculine scream. While the director is distracted, Charlie sneaks a quick puff at his cigarette, expelling the smoke sideways. He is at last discovered and re-ejected.

His New Profession

> 31 August 1914. *With* Fritz Schade (uncle), Minta Durfee (girl), Charlie Parrott (nephew), Harry McCoy (cop), Cecile Arnold.

A park/lake impromptu more memorable than most, by reason of its boardwalk setting and unusually coherent story. Charlie is hired to promenade the chair-bound uncle of a young man who prefers to canoodle with his girl-friend. On the sound Charlie principle that disabilities attract indignity, the uncle is dumped in the lake: but not before, decked with the purloined insignia of a bogus beggar, he has earned enough money to provide Charlie with a much-needed drink—a slightly shocking instance of comedy's traditional disregard for age and infirmity.

The Rounders

> 7 September 1914. *With* Roscoe Arbuckle (pal), Phyllis Allen (Charlie's wife), Minta Durfee (Fatty's wife), Fritz Schade, Al St John, Charles Parrott.

Charlie appears in cloaked and top-hatted splendour as Fatty's boozing companion in this comedy of dissipation of which *A Night Out* is a partial reprise (the gag in which he idly plucks flowers from the sidewalk while limply dragged on his companion's arm is common to both). At his hotel he regales us with a sample of his repertoire of inebriation gags: expelling cigarette smoke by twisting his ear, carefully treading the lines of the carpet (as in a sobriety test), greeting his dragonish wife with a cheerfully ingratiating smile. His fine impersonation of drunkenness includes a grave uncontrollability of action: held upright by his hectoring wife with his own cane, he finally collapses on to the bed in a state of up-ended rigidity. At the later scene in the café to which the companions escape, the emphasis is on his abstractedly insensitive dealings with people and objects: he strikes his match on a bald man's head (and then adjusts it for leaning on), gets his foot trapped under his chair, wipes his nose on his napkin, and finally decides to go to bed on the floor, dragging the table cloth over him. There is an unusual conclusion in which the ejected pair take to a boat and slowly and comfortably sink into the lake.

The New Janitor

> 24 September 1914. *With* Fritz Schade (boss), Minta Durfee (secretary), Jack Dillon (cashier), Al St John (elevator boy).

This excellent comedy ranks with *Laughing Gas* and *Dough and Dynamite* as one of the best of all Keystones. Its story (a clear anticipation of *The Bank*, without the fantasy ending) concerns Charlie's resourceful foiling of a robbery at the bank where he is an absent-minded janitor, and his consequent capture of the secretary's affections from the rascally cashier. Its comedy (which is discussed in Chapter 2) issues from his eccentric performance of his janitorial duties, and also includes, in his pathetically mimed indication of the number of his dependants, the first appearance of the third Charlie.

Those Love Pangs

> 10 October 1914. *With* Chester Conklin (rival), Norma Nichols (landlady), Edgar Kennedy (dude), Cecile Arnold, Vivian Edwards (girls), Harry McCoy (cop).

A boarding house/park/lake comedy, reminiscent of both *The Star Boarder* and *Twenty Minutes of Love*, in which Charlie competes with Chester for the favours of his landlady, and with Edgar for those of a younger and prettier prey. Charlie and Chester duel with forks (with Charlie at one point prudently stationing the landlady between them); Charlie's abortive pick-up of the young girl is embroidered by his trick of twirling his watch into his top pocket; in the park, he despondently picks his nails and teeth with his cane; he attempts to recover from his bemusement at Chester's success with women by thumping himself on the back; approaching Edgar with a murderous brick in his hand, he drops it on his foot. There is an amusing climax in a cinema, to which Charlie gains access by blowing the banknotes to the cashier from the palm of his hand: with an arm round each of two girls, he resorts to applauding with his feet; when the girls are silently replaced by Chester and Edgar, Charlie registers the change by a puzzled exploration of the different facial textures.

Dough And Dynamite

> 26 October 1914. *With* Chester Conklin (waiter), Fritz Schade (boss), Norma Nichols (his wife), Cecile Arnold, Vivian Edwards (waitresses), Edgar Kennedy, Charles Parrott, Slim Summerville (bakers), Phyllis Allan (customer). 2000 ft.

In this charming bake-house comedy, Charlie and Chester are waiters who are forced by a strike of kitchen hands to take on the baking tasks themselves. There is an unusual piece of verbal humour at the beginning, when Charlie pointedly associates the notice 'Assorted French Tarts' with the mincing gait of a dressy female customer. This saucy note is continued in Charlie's flirtatious relations with the girls in the shop. He clowns around with the dough for their benefit, getting the flour on his hand and transferring it to their bottoms under the guise of helping them reach the high shelves. The boss notices these dissolute insignia, and is even less pleased when he sees a similar floury impress (quite innocently acquired) on his own wife—an unusually calculated variation gag. As well as this emphasis on the erotic, there is a great deal of professional activity comedy. Some of this arises fairly obvious from the café and kitchen tasks: such as Charlie's tray-balancing act, or the washing-up gag (repeated in *Shanghaied*) in which clean plates handed to a preoccupied companion are allowed to crash upon the floor. But much of the humour is generated by the dough itself, the establishment's staple product, whose intractability and adhesiveness are emphasized throughout. I have often cited Charlie's difficulties with kneading the stuff into any kind of shape as a type of the clown's relations with intransigent matter: an instance of his success is his demonstrated method of making doughnuts by moulding them round his wrist (a gag repeated in mimicry—and elaborated—in *A Woman*). The climax is precipitated by the striking kitchen hands (who, like all strikers in Chaplin films, harbour homicidal resentments that give an alarming impression of American industrial relations): a bomb they place in a loaf causes a massive explosion, from the debris of which Charlie's protruding head provides the film's final image.

Gentlemen of Nerve

> 29 October 1914. *With* Mack Swain, Chester Conklin, Mabel Normand, Phyllis Allen, Edgar Kennedy (cop).

A standard racetrack impromptu, in which Charlie and Chester do battle over Mabel, and Mack is subject to incidental indignities. There is a well remembered food-filching moment when Charlie surreptitiously sucks at the straw of a girl spectator's soda, feigning innocence when she turns her head. But most attractive section is Charlie's and Mack's attempt to enter the racetrack unobserved, in a nice appeal to common experience suggested by the setting. The joke here is Mack's bulk. Charlie has trouble with this from the first, at one point walloping it with his cane to make it move aside: when Mack gets stuck in the fence hole, Charlie's remedies include the inevitable boot in the rear, and the inspired use of a siphon by way of lubrication. A moment when Charlie does battle with a bunch of urchins is strongly reminiscent of *Kid Auto Races.*

His Musical Career

> 7 November 1914. *With* Mack Swain (mate), Fritz Schade (Mr Rich),
> Alice Howell (his wife), Charles Parrott, Joe Bordeaux, Norma Nichols.

This excellent professional activity comedy (a precursor to *Work*, and, as has often been noted, to Laurel and Hardy's *The Music Box*) features Charlie and Mack as removal men, who, charged with delivering a piano to one address and retrieving one from another nearby, inevitably confuse the two. The second Charlie predominates throughout, heralded by his quixotic but poetically logical method of limbering up for the job by lubricating his joints with the oil-can. On the way to delivery (affording us a rare glimpse of the busy streets of actual Los Angeles), Mack is on the receiving end of a succession of physical-indignity gags, with the piano at one point resting on his head. Arrived at the fernily opulent mansion of Mr Rich, Charlie blithely sets about clearing the decks by pitching the expensive ornaments, baseball-fashion, to Mack; ogling Mrs Rich in between times. In the film's best-remembered gag, he staggers about the room with the piano an his back while Mrs Rich vacillates about where to put it: finding himself, once it is deposited, unable to straighten up, but having to waddle round dwarf-fashion until the strain wears off. After Mr Rich's return, and the inevitable furore, the piano ends up in the lake. As in *The New Janitor*, the comedy of this film is refreshingly relaxed unemphatic, with no frenetic action or pointless knockabout.

His Trysting Place

> 9 November 1914. *With* Mabel Normand (Charlie's wife), Mack Swain, Phyllis Allen (Mack's wife). 2000 ft.

Charlie is a harassed husband and father who seeks relief from his domestic duties at the local lunch counter, where he gets involved in a punch-up with Mack and inadvertently leaves with his coat. Mabel, his wife, discovers in the pocket a billet-doux intended for Mack, and vengefully pursues Charlie to the park, where Mack is taking refuge from *his* wife: after much violence and complication, the muddle is resolved. *His Trysting Place*, which sounds like a conventional love-intrigue comedy, has some very distinctive features, and is further proof that the Keystones get better as they go on. Its plot, although complex, is easily followed, and is even productive of genuine dramatic suspense. The early part is enlivened by some unfamiliar glimpses of Charlie *en famille*, when the comedy issues from the detail of domestic life: he absently wipes his nose on the doormat on entering, and, charged with minding the baby, distracted plonks it on a pile of dough, carries it around by the scruff, gives it what looks like a gun to play with, and, after carefully plumping the cushions of its cot, settles upon them himself. The central section at the lunch counter builds up to a fine crescendo of mayhem, which is preceded by a series of eating gags, in which Charlie wipes his hands on a customer's beard, mimes Mack's soup-drinking and furtively gnaws his meat bone like a scavenging dog, and gets a free mouth-wipe on Mack's sleeve as it is stretched across for the condiments. Only in the feuding climax in the park does the film revert to stereotype: but even here there is a surprising moment when the quarrelling group freezes into a tableau of amiability on the approach of a cop—a gag that indicates that the old material is being treated with a new degree of sophistication.

Tillie's Punctured Romance

> 14 November 1914. Directed by Mack Sennett. Written by Hampton Del Ruth (adapted from the musical play *Tillie's Nightmare* by Edgar Smith). *With* Marie Dressler (Tillie), Mabel Normand, Mack Swain, Charles Bennett, Charlie Murray, Chester Conklin, Charles Parrott, Edgar Kennedy, Harry McCoy, Minta Durfee, Phyllis Allen, Alice Davenport, Slim Summerville, Al St John, Gordon Griffith, Billie Bennett. 6000 ft.

Charlie, a wastrel with an eye for the main chance, tempts Marie, a lumpish farm girl with good financial prospects, away from her rural seclusion to the gay life of the big city. Here he re-encounters Mabel, an old flame, who conspires with him to decamp with Marie's money. Their guilty relations are interrupted by Charlie's discovery that Marie's uncle has died and left her a fortune: he promptly reinsinuates himself into her favour and installs them both in the uncle's grand mansion, pursued by Mabel in the guise of a housemaid. When Marie discovers Charlie and Mabel canoodling, it sends her beserk. Simultaneously the uncle returns, very much alive, and summons the police to evict the intruders. There is a mad chase to he edge of a pier, a reconciliation of the girls, and Charlie is consigned to jail.

I have not seen the full version of this, Chaplin's first full-length film. Its resume reads like a farcical version of *A Woman of Paris*, and his character that of a sort of fledgling Verdoux. It was clearly a vehicle as much for Marie's and Mabel's talents as for Charlie's, and, while an important venture of his early career, it cannot prevent me thinking of *The Kid* as the first true Chaplin feature. The extract that is often shown is the climax, with Marie firing her gun at random at her discovery of Charlie and Mabel in an embrace, which is probably the weakest part of the film. The mansion set has a draped and gilded ferny opulence that is extreme even by Charlie's standards. It is likely that Charlie takes predictable advantage of his imposture both to enjoy and ridicule the life of luxury, as the well-known still of him leaning idly against a uniformed flunkey indicates.

Getting Acquainted

> 5 December 1914. *With* Mack Swain, Mabel Normand (his wife), Phyllis Allen (Charlie's wife), Harry McCoy, Edgar Kennedy, Cecile Arnold.

A park comedy in which Charlie attempts to evade the dragonish Phyllis and attach himself to the pretty Mabel, whose husband is trying to attend to their stalled car. A Turk in full oriental gear, and his girl companion, are also improbably involved in the proceedings. It sounds like, and to a large extent is a reversion to a familiar type, but it has some interesting features that allow it to be dated as a late Keystone. There is the pervasive eroticism, more bold and pointed than in earlier films: when the Turk's girl bends over, Charlie covers his eyes in mock alarm, and, at his first meeting with Mabel, his cane inadvertently taps her on the behind. Later, it hitches up her skirt. And the increasing sophistication of the comic business (cf. *His Trysting Place*) shows itself in a running gag in which a series of guilty partners are, at various crises in the story, formally introduced to each other.

His Prehistoric Past

> 7 December 1914. *With* Hank Swain (King), Fritz Schade, Gene Marsh, Cecile Arnold, Al St John.

Chaplin's last Keystone is one of the most surprising of all: a cave-man film whose comic anachronisms prefigure those of Keaton's *Seven Ages*. The story, such as it is, concerns a rivalry with Mack that turns into outright battle and culminates in Charlie's elevation to the headship of the tribe. The prehistoric setting generates a brilliant series of poetically suggestive gags. The animal skins that everyone sports (with the addition, in Charlie's case, of his standard hat) suggests both hairs (which Charlie plucks out and uses as a tobacco substitute) and vermin (a flea extracted from Mack's skin is placed delicately on a rock and walloped with a huge club). The straggly hair that is part of the cave-woman stereotype is characteristically put to advantage by Charlie when he pulls a girl round by the locks in order to kiss her. And Charlie's obstinate quixotry demands that he shoot his bow and arrow (the only available weapon) an inch away from Mack's belly. It is of course of great interest anthropologically that Charlie should kill the king of the tribe and then take his place, in the best tradition of heroes. And our vague disquiet at Charlie's total immersion in an alien culture is eased by his final bemused awakening, on a palm beach, from what turns out to have been dream.

Essanay, 1915–1916

The name of the Essanay Company derives from the initials of its founders, George K. Spoor and G.M. 'Broncho Billy' Anderson. The Essanay films were all produced by Jesse J. Robbins, written and directed by Charles Chaplin and photographed by Rollie Totheroh (usually with the collaboration of either Harry Ensign or William C. Foster). Except where indicated, they were all approximately 2000 ft in length.

His New Job

> 1 February 1915. *With* Ben Turpin, Leo White (actor), Charlotte Mineau (actress), Charles Insley (director), Frank J. Coleman (manager), Gloria Swanson, Agnes Ayars (secretaries).

Charlie gets a job as a carpenter in a film studio, upstaging Ben Turpin who joins him as his assistant. He graduates to acting, and enjoys a brief moment of glory as the hero of a costume drama before his incompetence dissolves the proceedings into riot.

His New Job is a confusion-drama comedy in a line that stretches from *A Film Johnnie* and *The Masquerader* to *Behind the Screen*, *The Circus* and *Limelight*. Charlie and Ben make only a moderately successful double act, since their characters are too similar for their relationship to generate much business. Ben seems to bring out all that is callous and vindictive in Charlie. Their scenes contain a lot of routine knockabout involving swinging doors and a carried plank, but there is one good moment when Charlie appears to begin to saw through Ben's rump. (They interact best when each behaves as though unaware of the presence of the other)

The best moments are Charlie's alone. His grand acting debut is particularly fine. He is kitted out with a Ruritanian officer's costume, including a bear-skin helmet in which, inevitably, he searches for fleas, and a floppy rubber sword that wallops him whenever he salutes and that he employs to lop the ash off his cigarette. The humour of the occasion arises from the contrast between his swaggeringly confident manner and his various acts of incompetence. These include knocking the lens off the camera as he leans against it, and detaching a large portion of his leading lady's skirt as she sweeps upstairs (capping this gag by kissing it in homage, and wiping his eyes and blowing his nose on it). At such moments, the drama-confusion is largely inadvertent, and ministers, not to our sense of destructiveness, but to our fear of making fools of ourself in public.

A Night Out

> 15 February 1915. *With* Ben Turpin, Les White (dude), Bud Jamison (waiter), Edna Purviance (his wife), Fred Goodwins.

Charlie and Ben go on a prolonged binge, starting in a restaurant, from which Ben is ejected. They move to a hotel, where Charlie, whose behaviour shows that he hardly knows where he is, encounters Edna in compromising circumstances and is forced to make a hurried departure.

The talents of Charlie and Ben mesh together rather better in this film than their previous one. The opening section is amusing, with a succession of gags involving randomly swung objects—cane, bag, hand—that strikes innocent bystanders. Charlie's casually insensitive treatment of Ben seems less gratuitous in this context, and it is in keeping with his traditional immunity that he looks on with equanimity while Ben is ejected for what Charlie has done. Their most deservedly remembered moment together is when Charlie, dragged limply along the sidewalk by the obliging Ben, improves the occasion by plucking vergeside flowers.

Yet again it is what Charlie does that stays in the mind. He sustains throughout a fine impersonation of teetering, paralytic drunkenness complete with carefully pondered falls upstairs. His condition gives licence to his metaphorical invasions of reality, which do not need an excuse, but, given one, can be bolder. Here the comedy of misapprehension takes place at the hotel, whose desk he mistakes for a bar: feeling for the foot rail, sipping the ink, and wiping the pen on the clerk's beard. Upstairs, reality seems no nearer; he puts his cane to bed, hangs his coat out of the window, tries to get a drink out of the phone, and cleans his boots with his toothbrush. A gag in the restaurant scene, when Charlie interprets a lady's inadvertently roving hand as an invitation to dalliance, and imprisons her handbag between his legs, strikes an erotic note that is continued in the climax of the hotel scene: Edna, in her nightdress, follows her little dog into Charlie's room, and hides under his bed when he enters; his expression of pleasure when he discovers her is one to savour. Edna makes her first appearance in *A Night Out.*

The Champion

11 March 1915. *With* Edna Purviance (assistant), Bud Jamison (boxer) Leo White (crook), Lloyd Bacon (manager), Ben Turpin (salesman), G.M. Anderson (spectator), Billy Armstrong, Paddy McGuire, Carl Stockdale (sparring partners).

Charlie's chronic hunger and poverty lure him into employment as a sparring partner in a gymnasium, where he ensures his
success by secreting a horseshoe in his glove. He resists the blan-
dishments of a villain who attempt to bribe him to take a fall,
shows off to Edna while exercising in the gym, and, with a little
help from his faithful bulldog, wins the big bout to which he is
promoted.

The plot interest in *The Champion* is negligible, as are the relationships, and most of the interest centres upon Charlie's imaginative comic use of the materials of the gymnasium and the act of
boxing. As always, it is the intrinsic properties of the equipment
that he manages to emphasize: bonking himself with the Indian
clubs and the punch-bag, and mowing down bystanders with the
dumb-bells in a series of long horizontal object gags. Periodically
he refreshes himself by anointing his brow and his feet with beer,
and then pouring some down his ear—an eccentric procedure that
anticipates Hynkel's self-fortifying rigmarole with a glass of water
in *The Great Dictator*. His characteristic approach to the whole enterprise is indicated by the satisfied smile that accompanies the
fitting of the horseshoe into his glove and the prudence that
causes him to instruct the stretcher-bearers to follow him to the
ringside: Charlie's reaction to danger always involves devising a
variety of precautionary stratagems. Edna, fetchingly kitted out as
the general help, is a mute looker-on at this, existing only to be
chatted up by Charlie (rubbing one foot against the other, in a
nicely observed expression of embarrassed familiarity), and eyed
lasciviously by the villainous Leo White (whose attention is distracted by a jerk on his standard-issue villain's moustache). Leo's
attempt to nobble Charlie is rendered in terms that neatly express
the association, in Charlie's pantheons of satisfactions, of money
and food: a bill is waved under his nose like a tasty tidbit, and he
latches on to it with his teeth before it can be withdrawn.

The climax of the film is Charlie's bout with Bud Jamison (Eric
Campbell's predecessor as the heavy in many of the Essanay films).
This sequence is over long and disorganized, but it contains some
good moments. Preceded by Charlie's emotional farewell to his
bulldog, it begins with his behind jutting fighter's stance and goes
on to include examples of tightrope walking and waltzing, and a
moment when a bemused Charlie starts searching for his oppo-

nent on the floor. Retrospectively, its chief merit is to serve as a foil to Chaplin's more sophisticated and disciplined transformation of the act of boxing in *City Lights*.

In the Park

> 18 March 1915. *With* Edna Purviance (nursemaid), Leo White (lover), Lloyd Bacon (tramp), Bud Jamison (beau), Ernest Van Pelt (cop) Billy Armstrong, Margie Reiner. 1000 ft.

As Theodore Huff says, this film is virtually a remake of *Twenty Minutes of Love*, with a stolen string of sausages improbably substituted for a stolen watch and chain. It is a superior example of the location impromptu, but its succession of incidents—include Charlie's canoodling with Edna, stealing and losing the sausages, retrieving a stolen handbag, clashing with a heavy and helping a love-sick dude to drown himself—can hardly be dignified with the name of plot. Charlie makes the most of his opportunities, doffing his hat to the tree branches, falling off the park bench, and executing a particularly neat backward tumble into a pram. He makes good play with his cane, which wallops him repeatedly, and manages to retrieve the stolen handbag all by itself. His behaviour remains fairly firmly at the aggressive end of its spectrum, represented by the manner in which he flips his cigarette ash into the sleeping heavy's mouth, a circumstance that together with its plotlessness, establishes this film in the Keystone tradition. Its best moment is probably when, seated on the bench, Charlie registers his gradual realization of the proximity of a noxious smell (emanating from a hot-dog vendor): his search for its source includes examining the sole of his boot for adhesive matter—a gag whose casual repetition at the beginning of *Limelight* contributes much to establishing *that* as a Charlie film.

The Jitney Elopement

> 1 April 1915. *With* Edna Purviance (heiress), Leo White (Count), Fred Goodwins (father), Lloyd Bacon (butler), Paddy McGuire (retainer), Bud Jamison, Ernest Van Pelt (cops).

Charlie impersonates a count to rescue Edna from the unwelcome attention of the original. His behaviour at her parents' house, especially at mealtimes, casts doubts upon his authenticity that are confirmed when the real Count turns up, and the action is transferred first to a park, then to a car chase. Charlie's car finally butts its rival off a pier.

The *Jitney Elopement* is chiefly a charming imposture drama, in which attention is centred upon Charlie's eccentricities and solecisms. In this, as in its general story, it prefigures *The Count.* Charlie's Count-behaviour is erotic (he covertly scrutinizes a naked statuette on the banister, and, to cover both his interest and embarrassment, blows smoke at it), and insulting (he leans on and examines the butler, and monkey-mimes his simian appearance). Above all, he is governed by his own codes of habit and association: the politely bowing father is yanked up by Charlie's cane, the whisky-and-soda gargled with, the purloined cigars stuffed in his hat (to re-emerge when he shows his customary politeness to Edna by doffing it). His most alarming transgressions are reserved for the dinner table, where he stuffs his napkin in his top pocket, theatrically cools his hot coffee, cuts the bread cleverly concertina-wise, and broadcasts the pepper to the company's discomfiture. It all adds up to a very lively series of transformations and an excellent example of Charlie's benignly disruptive social role.

The car chase is dramatically a disappointment, being poorly paced, but it derives a historical value from taking place on the bumpy and puddly roads of actual California—an unusual excursion from the studio. The chintz and potted plants of Edna's house have a similar sociological interest, as do many of the interiors of this period.

The Tramp

> 11 April 1915. *With* Edna Purviance (daughter), Fred Goodwins (father), Leo White, Bud Jamison (tramps), Paddy McGuire (farmhand), Lloyd Bacon (suitor), Billy Amstrong (poet).

Charlie, in the country, saves Edna from a pair of desperadoes, and is rewarded with a job on her father's farm. Here he practises his own brand of husbandry while making up to Edna. The thugs return, and he first connives at their plan to rob the farm, then helps to rout them. He is rewarded again by a period of luxurious invalidism, but his romance with Edna is dashed by the arrival of a more presentable suitor, and he makes a philosophical exit.

I used to be prejudiced against *The Tramp* because of its exaggerated reputation as the first expression of the 'pathetic' Chaplin —an element that is given undue prominence in accounts of this film, as of Chaplin generally. Here Charlie's lovelornness is really just of way of ending the story and isn't brought to the forefront as it is to be later. It is true that both in its love interest and in its sunny rural setting it looks forward to *The Vagabond* and *Sunnyside.* And not the least of its qualities is its anticipations, in incident and theme, of these and other later successes Charlie's importation into the country, for instance, of polite urban habits—such as his production of a brush to dust himself off after being spattered by a car, or his fastidious post-prandial manicure act—remind us of the way he knocks on the fence before climbing it in *The Vagabond.* And his strange relationship with the thugs, whom he twice helps to eject but at one stage appears to collaborate with, is a reminder that he inhabits the borderland between virtue and vice. His switch of allegiance, decided by his colonization by the world of virtue (represented by Edna), is reminiscent of his similar conversion in *Police,* but in *The Tramp* it doesn't so pointedly emphasize as in the later film his moral ambiguity, and so never starts to become a theme.

Yet the excellent comedy that justifies one's thinking of *The Tramp* as, after all, a very fine film, is independent of these anticipations. Rather it is professional activity comedy: a matter of Charlie's eccentric accomodations to rural life and his chosen profession of farmhand. His random employment of the jabbing properties of the pitchfork, or of the carting properties of the wheelbarrow (into which Leo White is unceremoniously scooped) are predictable perhaps, but less so is his method of testing an egg for badness: he taps it on the barn door and listens to it—the gag is capped by the egg's being dropped, in a paroxysm of surprise, onto the open book of the visiting preacher. The best-known moments are the spectacle of Charlie watering the trees (working in a nice backhand wrist action), and his perplexity in face of the task of milking the cow—he eventually decides that its tail is a pumphandle. There is also a memorable example of Charlie's idiosyncratic improvisations: his bedroom companion's offensively smelly socks are ejected from the window by the use of a set of concertina-like clothes pegs which, dismounted from the wall, are trans-

formed into a pair of conveniently extendable pincers. Only
Charlie would notice the grasping properties of this furniture, or
turn it to such advantage.

By the Sea

> 19 April 1915. *With* Edna Purviance, Bud Jamison (husband), Billy Arm-
> strong (man with hat), Margie Reiger (his girl), Carl Stockdale (cop).
> 1000 ft.

Like *In the Park*, this film is basically a Keystone park/lake location impromptu, but it gains freshness from its unusual seaside
setting, and from the stylization of comic business that was already
evident in the later Keystone versions of the type. Like the others
it consists of passages of flirting, interspersed with passages of fighting, with Charlie this time feuding with Billy in the intervals of
trying to get off with Edna. The flirting includes a battle with ice-
cream cones (with the innocent Bud, unusually dandified as a top-
hatted husband, coming in for his share); much play with a life-
belt, employed as a projectile hoopla fashion (into which Billy is at
one point pinioned like a sandwich); and an interlude when the
strings of Charlie's and Billy's hats become entwined in the wind,
bringing them both to the ground. There is also a good banana
skin gag when Charlie, by miscalculating his back-kick, creates the
conditions for his own pratfall. The finale has all the characters
lined up on a bench, immobilized by the approach of a cop (cf.
His Trysting Place), with Charlie making his escape by tipping the
whole ensemble backwards on to the sand.

Work

> 21 June 1915. *With* Edna Purviance (maid), Charles Insley (boss), Billy
> Armstrong (husband), Marta Golden (wife), Leo White (lover), Paddy
> McGuire.

A decorator's assistant, exploited by his idle and bullying boss,
Charlie doubles as workhorse by dragging both boss and equip-
ment to their place of work. Arrived, his incompetent decorating
is diversified by some canoodling with Edna, and complicated by
the lover of the household-wife, whose husband is obsessed by a
malfunctioning gas stove. Mayhem and explosions conclude the
action.

Work is extremely lively and full of inventive business. Its open-ing sequence, with Charlie seen in silhouette lugging the cart up an exaggeratedly steep hill, is an unusual example of Chaplin's use of a composed frame, and the journey is complicated by the necessity of crossing a busy street-car line, from whose heedlessly careering traffic the cart and its contents are rescued in the nick of time. Arrived at the inevitably plush mansion, our heroes de-vote themselves to comic activity that resolves itself into three kinds: domestic, professional and erotic. The weakest of these is the domestic, with which they are only marginally involved. This starts off promisingly, with Billy Armstrong doing a creditable irate husband act, and Edna more strongly characterized than usual as a petulant and disrespectful maid. It degenerates with the arrival Leo White's top-hatted vaudeville lover. But there is a good mo-ment when, in response to the haughty wife's locking up of her valuables, Charlie and his mate pointedly amalgamate and wrap up the contents of their pockets.

Paperhanging is a tailor-made professional activity for Charlie, and the havoc he wreaks with paper, paste, buckets, brushes, ladders and planks is predictable but nonetheless diverting. The absurdities of his behaviour include: dusting the boss's coat with the distemper brush, and dropping his hat in the pail; tightrope walking the bear-skin rug; wiping his hands on a doily, and neatly folding it back; attaching the paper to the wall by its dry side, so that his hands stick to the paste; shifting the safe with ease once it has been relieved of the weight of his coat; and finally dousing the boss with plaster by abandoning his end of the plank at a sudden summons from Edna. Perhaps 'predictable' is not the right word for this after all.

It is the erotic element that is really interesting. This partly re-volves around a nude statuette (again) that arouses Charlie's fasci-nated attention, and which at one moment he 'clothes' with a lampshade so that he can saucily peep under its skirt. But chiefly it concerns Edna, with whom Charlie's relations take on an in-creasingly intimate character. The keynote is struck at their first meeting, when she inadvertently feather dusts his backside, and he offers to retaliate with the paste brush. It is the sight of *her* bend-ing rump, in the bedroom to which he has been despatched to work, that makes him hesitate reflectively in the act of dipping his brush. Soon they are seated on the bed, and he is recounting the sad story of his life. We don't need a title to tell us this, since his play of expression conveys the nature of their colloquy, as does the extraordinary manicure act with which he idly and shyly occupies himself: trowel, file and sandpaper are pressed into service to recondition his nails as his mournfully confiding tale proceeds. Edna registers an appropriate mixture of sympathy and alarm. It is brilliantly original comedy, and to my mind more of a milestone in the evolution of comic feeling than the conclusions of *The Tramp.*

A Woman

> 12 July 1915. *With* Edna Purviance (daughter), Charles Insley (father), Marta Golden (mother), Billy Armstrong (lover), Margie Reiger, Leo White.

Paying suit to Edna, Charlie is ejected by her father, with whom he had previously clashed. He insinuates himself back into the house and dons some of Edna's clothes. As a woman, he is the object of admiring attention from both the father and the mother's lover, which lasts until his disguise is penetrated and he is once again booted out.

In a park/lake preamble, the boring and repressive character of Edna's family life is revealed in a series of telling shots of the principals. Then much comic use is made of Charlie's cane, which is dipped into the water to sound the depths for Charles's ducking, coyly hooked round the neck of a cop, and finally employed to tug Edna closer for an intimate perusal. In the house, the second Charlie is in evidence, as he takes possession with a lordly air (managing with difficulty to avoid sitting on lethal hat-pins), secures the doughnuts by sliding them down his knife (as well as miming their manufacture around his wrist, and playfully slipping an imaginary doughnut 'ring' on Edna's finger), and gargles with the tea.

But the best section is inaugurated by his looking around for a disguise in which to re-enter the fray. Charlie's third female impersonation is also his most enjoyable, and his performance is very skilful. A lot of time is devoted to the leisurely preliminaries, when the act of donning the clothes is emphasized. Charlie's bashful undressing of the dummy on which Edna's garments are hung is made to seem an act of seduction in itself, and there is a nice moment when he laboriously secures his voluminous skirts with a pin, whose gingerly progress through the material is conveyed by his stooping posture and the nervous expression of his face. A pleasant addition to the business is the willing and delighted complicity of Edna herself, who sinks to the floor in a helpless display of hilarity as he parades before her, wriggling his rump and trying to salvage his collapsing bosom. The comedy of this scene is emphasized by an unusual number of close-ups of Edna and Charlie. The scene in the drawing room, when Charles and Billy compete for Charlie's favours while Edna and her mother eavesdrop, is more predictable, and culminates with Charlie artfully contriving that the two philanderers inadvertently kiss each other, and with his cover being blown when the wrenching down of his skirts reveals his manly underwear.

The Bank

> 16 August 1915. *With* Edna Purviance (stenographer), Carl Stockdale (cashier), Billy Armstrong (janitor), Charles Insley (manager), John Rand (salesman), Fred Goodwins, Frank J. Coleman, Wesley Ruggles (crooks), Leo White, Paddy McGuire, Lloyd Bacon.

Charlie is the janitor at a bank. Besotted with the manager's secretary he woos her with flowers, but sees them rejected. As he goes about his work a gang of robbers gather in the bank. They start by abducting Edna, but Charlie, galvanized into action, rescues her, foils the robbers' attempt, and discredits his cowardly rival in love. Edna, clasped in his arms, turns into a mop as he awakes from his dream.

The Bank raises in an acute form the problem of the relation between fantasy and reality in Chaplin. In *Shoulder Arms* we accept that his extravagant heroics are a dream, since their culmination —the capture of the Kaiser—offends both likelihood and historical fact. But here the consignment of his energetic rescue act to the realm of fantasy has the effect of focusing our attention too squarely upon Charlie's feelings of inadequacy and loss. Both the famous shots—of Charlie watching Edna discard his gift and his rude awakening—are sentimental in effect. We have our cake and eat it, of course, because we enjoy the heroics while they last. Chaplin's whole career could be regarded as an attempt to bring fantasy and reality into a satisfactory relation.

This film is considered briefly in Chapter 2. It contains a great deal of enjoyable business, including the 'false appearances' joke at the beginning (when Charlie opens the vault with the self-important efficiency of a high official, to extract his mop and bucket), much professional activity comedy involving a prolonged series of long horizontal object gags, and a neat metaphorical gag when, after sampling the cleaner's plainly disgusting tipple he wipes his mouth with blotting paper. Charlie's heroics are exuberant too, and characterized by a sense of rather anguished effort, as he is forced to do about six things at once. Supporting the comatose Edna with one hand, he locks the crooks into the vault with the other; then heaves her on to his shoulder, somewhat ungallantly mopping his brow. These vintage activities help to qualify our sense of Charlie's pathetic vulnerability.

Shanghaied

> 4 October 1915. *With* Edna Purviance (daughter), Wesley Ruggles (father/owner), John Rand (captain), Bud Jamison (mate), Billy Armstrong, Paddy McGuire, Fred Goodwins, Leo White (hands).

In love with Edna, but spurned by her father, Charlie is duped into press-ganging crew members for a ship doomed to be exploded for its insurance value, and becomes the last victim himself. On board, he sets about his usual task of turning work into non-functional display. Edna smuggles herself aboard, and is discovered at the same time as the explosive mixture, which Charlie manages to dump on to the boat of the retreating villains. He is reunited with Edna after overcoming her father's objections in his distinctive fashion.

Shanghaied is one of the most attractive Essanays, with a strong, if somewhat ridiculous, story-line that still leaves room for one of Charlie's most winning displays of gratuitous high spirits. The eccentricities begin at the garden gate, where he uses the hooking properties of his cane to pull Edna towards him for a kiss. Once aboard the lugger, he is impressed by the promise of physical injury implied by the chief mate's demeanour, and lapses into his most abject manner of ingratiating appeasement: nodding frantically at the demand for hard work when he sees what happens to those who resist it, and briskly trundling an empty barrow, and uselessly shovelling grain, as a token of his willingness to comply.

As well as demonstrating his imperfect conception of the nature of work, this behaviour betrays his awareness of unpredictability and threat: a strong sense of danger, that essential ingredient of a Chaplin drama (missing from many of the Essanays), is what *Shanghaied* supplies.

I refer more than once above to the beautiful central section in which Charlie, consigned to the galley, is able to relax and to indulge in some of his most impudent transformations. These include: scrubbing the plates and dumping them on the floor; serving the captain dishwater-soup and oiling his salad from the lamp; role-switching into a series of innocent culinary activities when the captain interrupts his homicidal assault upon the cook; carting unspilt plates along the rolling deck through a series of tumbles and back-flips; and, above all, juggling and dancing the hornpipe with the ham bone. There is also a nice line in seasickness jokes (prefiguring *The Immigrant*): at one point, to rid himself of the sight of his companion's disgusting forkful of food Charlie hangs his hat on it (on the established Charlie principle that what the eye doesn't see, the stomach, or the conscience, doesn't grieve over). The film has an especially satisfying trick ending, when, rejected again by Edna's intransigent dad, whose life he has saved, he mimes his intention of suicide and leaps overboard only to re-emerge on the other side of the boat and back-kick the ungrateful parent into the drink.

A Night at the Show

> 20 November 1915. *With* Edna Purviance, Dee Lampton (fat boy), Leo White, May White, Bud Jamison (performers), James T. Kelly, John Rand, Paddy McGuire.

At a variety show, two drunken spectators—fastidious and aggressive Mr Pest in the stalls, and vulgar Mr Rowdy in the gallery (both played by Chaplin)—continually disrupt the acts and insult the performers.

About the only interest *A Night at the Show* now has is that of providing a glimpse of 'A Night in an English Music Hall', the Karno sketch that made Chaplin famous in his tours of America. One hopes, and can imagine, that the original was much better. Perhaps the unhappy result is an example of how badly live theatrical material can transfer to the screen when deprived of the immedi-

acy and the stylization of its original context. For this film is surely
the weakest of this period, and probably my least favourite Chaplin of all: full of grotesque figures and obnoxiously childish behaviour. Indeed, the whole proceedings have a nightmarish quality.

All else one can say is that the film is an anthology of first-
Charlie experience at its most primitive: including a nude statue
in the foyer to which he gravely doffs his hat; a variety of match-
striking, arm-resting and leg-dangling gags; and a preoccupation
with physical indignity. It is true that the characters of Pest and
Rowdy axe nicely distinguished—the one insolent and vindictive,
the other tipsily genial and fun-loving—and their mischief-making
is of different kinds. And there is a pointed instance of class distinction comedy when the posh spectators who laugh at the discomfiture of the performers are themselves doused with Mr Rowdy's hose (turned, in innocent alarm, upon the fire-eating act).

Carmen

> 22 April 1916. *With* Edna Purviance (Carmen), John Rand (Escamillo),
> Leo White, Bud Jamison (soldiers), Mary White (Frasquita), Ben Tur-
> pin, Jack Henderson, Wesley Ruggles.

This film renders in abbreviated form the story of Bizet's opera,
Chaplin has testified that it was intended as a spoof of De Mille's
film version rather than of the original. It was released without his
permission in an enlarged version in which a lot of irrelevant material featuring Ben Turpin was intercut with Chaplin's footage.

Shorn of its excrescences, *Carmen* has a rather disjointed look,
but it contains some of the most imaginative and high-spirited comedy of any Essanay film. Its centre-piece is a prolonged battle with
Leo White, first with dagger and sword, then hand-to-hand, which
is notable for its extraordinarily fast and inventive series of metaphorical gags, together with other Charlie attributes such as an
eye for advantage and a compulsion to eccentric display. The tool-
like properties of Leo's sword prompt Charlie to sharpen his
dagger upon it; possessed of a sword of his own, he recognizes the
pool room possibilities in the onions that decorate the tavern
setting, and his sword becomes a cue, a string of onions a marking
chalk, and a solitary onion on the table a ball; later, when they have
turned to wrestling, the activity suggests a species of physiother-
apy, and the battle turns into a massage session—in the course of

which Charlie stumbles on the whereabouts of Leo's wallet and pockets it himself. Perhaps the best-remembered moment is in the duelling section, when Charlie, bored by the repetitively rhythmic sword-clashing, starts tidying his hair and brushing his clothes. At the end, deserted by Carmen, what looks like an emotional shoulder-shrug against the wall of the barracks turns out to be a piece of back-scratching: the burlesque mode gives Charlie ample scope for effects of anti-romantic surprise.

Bizet plays no part in Chaplin's *Carmen*, of course, but despite our knowledge that he was satirizing another film, we may fairly infer that he was familiar with the original, and the film is a useful focus of speculation about Chaplin's own music. This abundantly shows the influence of the rich store of popular romantic melody to which Bizet is one of the most important contributors. And the opera's music has many of the attributes of Chaplin's film music: its swift transitions of mood, for example, and its matching of rhythm to physical movement, as in the Children's March and the Habanera. One of the few revealing disclosures Chaplin has ever made about his working methods is his account of how the mood and rhythm of his silent films were often mentally guided by musical themes.

Police

> 27 March 1916. *With* Edna Purviance (daughter), Wesley Ruggles (crook), Leo White (landlord/vendor/cop), James T. Kelly (drunk/tramp), Fred Goodwins (minister/cop), John Rand, Bud Jamison, Frank J. Coleman (cops).

Charlie, released from prison, is accosted by a bogus preacher who purloins both Charlie's money and the watch of a lounging inebriate that Charlie himself had longingly fingered. The clergyman he proceeds to assault turns out to be a genuine one. He repairs to a doss-house, unsuccessfully feigning consumption in an attempt to get in free, and more stealing goes on, this time by an inmate apparently asleep. The next day he joins an old cell-mate in burgling Edna's house, but takes her part when his friend gets rough she rewards him with her protection when the cops arrive, and he briefly lords it in high style until his cover is blown.

I give reasons in Chapter 2 for finding *Police* to be the best of all Essanays. It is a professional activity comedy, exhibiting Charlie's eccentric methods of burglarizing. It also, by dramatizing Charlie's moral ambiguity, inaugurates a line that runs through *Easy Street* and *The Pilgrim* to *Monsieur Verdoux*. This last element is chiefly demonstrated at the start in the mix-up over the preachers, but it is also wittily expressed in the single image of Charlie, held up at gunpoint by his cell-mate, niftily rifling his attacker's pockets—so neatly combining the roles of victim and miscreant.

Triple Trouble

> 11 August 1918. Partly directed by Leo White. *With* Edna Purviance (drudge), Leo White (anarchist), Billy Armstrong (cook), James T. Kelly (drunk), Bud Jamison, Wesley Ruggles.

Charlie is the assistant cook in a house where a scientist is concocting a powerful explosive, and where Edna is also a drudge. He spends his nights in a doss-house, where he is occupied with a drunken client and his quantity of purloined loot. A group of plotting anarchists thwarted in their attempt to obtain the explosive, hire a thug who enters the house and terrorizes the scientist and his daughter. The meleé ends with an explosion.

Triple Trouble is an unauthorized compilation, but differs from others of its kind in offering something like a coherent story, and in containing pieces of film that don't seem to have appeared in any other form. It is made up of bits of *Police* (some of the doss-house scene and most of the finale), *Work* (the final explosion) and fleshed out with linking footage shot by Leo White in 1918 (presumably all the parts that feature himself as the leading anarchist). The central doss-house section is quite the most interesting, containing as it does what seem to be off-cuts from the same scene in *Police*: including a moment when Charlie lies with his hands in his boots to lull the suspicion of the loot-collecting drunk, in a gag that uniquely prefigures his similar deception of Mack in *The Gold Rush*.

Mutual, 1916–1917

The Mutual films were made at the Lone Star Studio in Hollywood. They were all written, produced and directed by Charles Chaplin, photographed by William C. Foster and Rollie Totheroh and approximately 2000 ft in length.

The Floorwalker

> 15 May 1916. *With* Edna Purviance (secretary), Eric Campbell (manager), Lloyd Bacon (assistant manager), Albert Austin (floorwalker), Charlotte Mineau and Tom Nelson (detectives), Leo White (customer).

Charlie becomes a participant (at first unwitting, then enthusiastic) in a conspiracy between the floorwalker and the manager of a posh city store to expropriate the day's takings. The floorwalker (who, when suitably dressed, bears a remarkable resemblance to Charlie) double-crosses the manager and makes off in Charlie's guise. The attempts of all three to nobble the loot and to escape each other's clutches are complicated by the presence of a pair of house detectives (one of whom, an imposingly glamorous lady, behaves more like a theatrical spy). The inevitable chase concludes with the hapless manager's being crushed by the elevator.

Theodore Huff says that this film was inspired by the sight of the escalator in a New York store. This contrivance was hardly a novelty at the time the film was made, though no earlier comedian seems to have exploited its comic potential. It cannot be said that much is made of it here, for it does not produce the best moments of comedy. These rather arise from other types of store furniture and behaviour. *The Floorwalker* does not hang together very well: there is a discontinuity between the plot and the comic business, and between the behaviour at different times of Charlie, who seems uncertain which of his selves should predominate.

It is true that the plot itself gives rise to a certain amount of comedy. The vigilance of the suspicious store detectives produces a couple of familiar role-switching gags, for instance: when, under their gaze, Charlie's purpose of booting Albert Austin's rear is converted into a piece of innocent foot-dusting; and when Eric Campbell's attempt to throttle Charlie is periodically changed to an appearance of hearty fraternizing (this last a process that Charlie visibly enjoys, and turns into a sort of game). There is also the famous encounter between Charlie and his 'double', when the coordinated gestures of each produce the illusion of a mirror image (a gag later elaborated by Max Linder). And at the climax, Charlie's discovery of the loot is marked by a whimsical display of exhilaration, as he unbelievingly kicks a banknote under the table, like litter, and then scrambles for it; and is followed by a final assault on the part of Eric, whom he eludes with a series of grace-ful pirouettes.

It will be clear from this that Charlie's talent for non-functional display is to the fore in this film. A lot of comedy has little or noth-ing to do with the plot, but is inspired by the setting. Charlie first appears in one of his unaccommodating and disruptive manifesta-tions, displaying a typically insensitive use of others and their pos-sessions that is here played *against* the deference-inducing atmo-sphere of the luxury store and its acolytes. His cane, gestured in response to a request for directions from a fellow customer, con-trives wholly to demolish an artful arrangement of goods; later, at the toiletries counter, he lathers and shaves himself and wipes his face on a nearby model's gown. My favourite episode of all is the shoe department scene, whose relation to the rest of the story is obscure. Here, Charlie, apparently taking refuge in the guise of an assistant, responds delightfully to the athletic suggestion of the sliding ladder by mobilizing it, skate fashion, with his leg; to the metaphorical suggestion of a display of floral hats by watering them; and to the erotic suggestion of the task of shoe-fitting by tickling the soles of the girls' feet. In this last gag in particular, his instinct for larky display is combined with one his strongest interests.

The Fireman

> 12 June 1916. *With* Edna Purviance, Eric Campbell (fire chief), Lloyd Bacon (Edna's father), Leo White (house owner), Charlotte Mineau (mother), Albert Austin, John Rand, James T. Kelley and Frank J. Cole-man (firemen).

Charlie is a harried but cheerful menial at a fire station, presid-ed over by the redoubtable Eric, where more ingenuity is devoted to avoiding fires than to dousing them. The plot involves a con-spiracy between Eric and a local notable (for whose daughter Eric and Charlie are rival suitors) to let a mansion burn and collect the insurance. In the resulting blaze the daughter (Edna, naturally) is trapped, while Charlie is occupied at a distant (genuine) fire. But Charlie is summoned to the scene and, in an act of energetic gal-lantry, rescues Edna and wins her band.

The Fireman is not especially subtle, and contains a lot of routine knockabout. Its story is perfunctory, which switches the burden of interest on to the comic business. Fortunately, this is often very inventive. A lot of it arises from the professional activity of fire-manship. A running gag established early on is Charlie's Pavlovian reaction to the fire bell. It is dinned into him that he mustn't ignore its summons, and with characteristic literal-mindedness, he reacts with the required alacrity to anything that sounds remotely like it: dumping a pie on the floor at the sound of the lunch bell, and clobbering Eric with the soup tureen on hearing the milk-man's signal. There are also, as one might expect many examples of Charlie's whimsically imaginative treatment of the tools of the trade in hand: he concludes the task of preparing the station's lunch by extracting coffee from the boiler of the fire engine (its watery, spiggotty associations are emphasized here); recovering from one of Eric's brutal assaults, he applies the oil-can to the bruised muscles of his neck; his contribution to cleaning the equip-ment is to dab at the hoses with a duster (for Charlie, any cleaning exercise invariably assumes a domestic or private character).

An unusual direction taken by the comedy of this film is the char-acterization of the whole station as chronically inefficient, helpless and hidebound (unusual because the absurdities of Charlie's pro-fessional role-playing are more often his alone). The effect is an anticipation the films of Will Hay, in which laziness, self-advantage and defensive prevarication regularly do battle with professional ethics and service (both comedians having in this, of course, a common music hall source). The first thing that Eric's crew must do upon arriving at a blazing house is to spend ten minutes on fruitless and ridiculous drill. Earlier, they render themselves oblivi-ous to Leo White's telephoned summons to the same fire by muf-fling the bell so as to enjoy their game of draughts undisturbed (a gag repeated in Hay's *Where's that Fire?*); when Leo arrives in per-son to attract their attention he is given a book to look at to calm him down, and—a nice touch—actually starts to get absorbed in it while they dash to the rescue.

Another centre of interest, as always, is Charlie's relations with Eric, the station captain. It is the ever-present threat of Eric's brutal discipline that induces Charlie's panic reaction to bell noises of all kinds. Eric is his reliably boorish self, but their relation is complicated by their rivalry for the affections of Edna, whose presence imposes upon Eric the periodic necessity for compunction and restraint. This is an advantage Charlie is quick to exploit: Eric, forced by Edna's concern to revive Charlie after throttling him, is allowed his moment of redress and then booted into the water butt for his pains. Later, Charlie solicits Eric's attention as he is engrossed in an embrace with Edna by knocking door-fashion on his rump (Charlie's habitual concession to polite usage), and then parodies his attitude by himself embracing a nearby bush. Their love rivalry gives their relationship as much the aspect of a doubleact as that of a contest.

The Vagabond

> 10 July 1916. *With* Edna Purviance (gipsy/heiress), Eric Campbell (gipsy chief), Leo White (Jew/gipsy hag), Lloyd Bacon (artist), Charlotte Mineau (mother), Albert Austin, John Rand, James T. Kelley and Frank J. Coleman (German bandsmen), Phyllis Allen.

Charlie is an itinerant violinist, first seen busking outside a city bar; Edna is an heiress, stolen at birth and brought up as a gipsy drudge. He rescues her from Eric, Leo and their gipsy crew, and establishes a domestic haven in their hijacked caravan. But her affections are seduced by a passing artist, stricken by her beauty, whose portrait of her is the means by which she is reunited with her wealthy, disconsolate mother. Charlie, momentarily overlooked in the excitement of discovery, is retrieved and carted off to, presumably, a life of luxury and ease. (See Chapter 3.)

One a.m.

> 7 August 1916. *With* Albert Austin (cabbie).

Charlie arrives home sozzled at his fashionable mansion after a night on the tiles and attempts to go to bed. He is defeated by the collaborative obstinacy of his household goods, which take on a viciously frustrating life of their own and, abetted by his befuddlement, contrive to delay his hour of retirement for two whole reels. He eventually takes refuge in the bathtub.

  This film is considered briefly in Chapter 2. *One a.m.* is a piece of virtuoso clowning in which, except for the brief appearance at the beginning of Albert Austin as a cabbie (into whose outstretched hand Charlie, characteristically, drops his cigarette), Chaplin performs alone. Most of its comedy is an imaginative elaboration of the distinctive qualities of the various bits of furniture that Charlie encounters on his way to bed: the revolving properties of the revolving table, for instance, which coyly deprives him of the siphon and decanter and, when he is standing on it to light his cigarette at the gas jet, makes him run on the spot as on a fairground machine (and which, in a rare moment of revenge, he utilizes for striking his match); the sliding properties of the mats; the enfolding properties of the staircase carpet; the mountaineering associations of the staircase itself, which he tackles with suitably athletic energy; and the bonking properties of the pendulum on the landing, invested with a power of terrible automatic violence. The film culminates in a prolonged tussle with a fold-away bed, the sort that disappears into the wall. At first Charlie clearly can't imagine where it is and starts looking under the carpet; but when he discovers the release button he is not much better off. From the idea of a bed that moves in an orderly diagonal it is a short step to the idea of a bed like this one, which jumps, wrestles, and performs belly flops: a fitting emblem of the constant possibility in Charlie's world of the triumph of matter over mind.

The Count

> 4 September 1916. *With* Edna Purviance (Miss Moneybags), Eric Campbell (tailor), Charlotte Mineau (Mrs Moneybags), Leo White (Count Broko), Albert Austin, John Rand (guests), James T. Kelley (butler), Frank J. Coleman (cop).

Eric is a tailor and Charlie is his assistant. (We first see Charlie creasing his trousers with his fingers, an action either inspired by his profession or in defiance of it). In a client's pocket, Eric discovers a note from Count Broko to Mrs Moneybags, regretting his absence from her forthcoming party. He decides to attend the shindig in the Count's place. But his designs are thwarted by Charlie, who, visiting the same house on a separate pretext, contrives to insinuate himself among the guests, upstaging Eric, causing him continual discomfiture and reducing the proceedings to a riot by his calmly outrageous behaviour. The arrival of the real count inaugurates a grand free-for-all and chase.

No synopsis can reproduce the flavour of *The Count*. Although it is an imposture-drama—a multiple one, since Eric is an imposter as well—the tension of concealment plays very little part in the proceedings. What are to the fore instead are those traditional clown characteristics, oddity and display. *The Count* is a masterful demonstration of Charlie' benignly disruptive foreignness. The note is struck at the start when Charlie is introduced to a group of bowing and bearded guests: he thrusts a bowed head out of the way, as constituting an obvious threat, and shakes hands with one of the beards. This comedy of incomprehension gives way to Charlie's evident pleasure in his own creative flights of fancy, and the film builds up a fine momentum. The battleground is the familiar one of festivity: food, drink, women and dance provide both the occasion and the ammunition for the comic business. Charlie's way with food is again a matter of extracting its essential qualities: consumption of the water melon necessitates a rinsing of ears and a mopping of neck; at the buffet table, the punch bowl naturally suggests the need for a medicinal gargle, and the gooey, cherry-topped desserts, in combination with Charlie's cane and the proximity of a pretty girl, prompt a showy display of golfing strokes.

Much of the fun involves the embarrassment of Eric, who in this film is in an awkward position. Only Charlie knows that Eric is an imposter too, and this reason for tempering his vindictiveness is added to those provided by the occasion itself. Eric is at a chronic disadvantage, so Charlie is free to mock his eating habits (stopping him in mid-guzzle to catch what Edna is saying, and playfully 'conjuring' away his strands of spaghetti); to blame him for the purloined silverware that at one point cascades from Charlie's person; and to boot his backside with impunity during the fancy high-stepping dance number. Edna, as Miss Moneybags, plays a minor role in these proceedings, competing for Charlie's attention with the matronly cook he initially comes to visit and the slinky, bosom-revealing siren whom he ogles at the buffet table (swinging his cane suggestively as she bends to tie her shoe).

The Pawnshop

2 October 1916. *With* Edna Purviance (daughter), Henry Bergman (pawnbroker), John Rand (assistant), Eric Campbell (thief), Frank J. Coleman (cop), Albert Austin (customer with clock), James T. Kelley (customer).

Charlie works in a pawnbroker's shop, where he spends his time feuding with John, his fellow-employee, and carrying on with

Edna, the daughter. We see him 'helping' with the professional and domestic activities of the shop, including tendering advice of doubtful value to customers. His high-spirited larking about nearly gets him the sack, but he is reprieved after a theatrically pathetic plea. One client, a thinly disguised Eric Campbell, turns out to be a jewel thief, whose evil designs Charlie manages to thwart in the nick of time, earning his boss's gratitude and Edna's hand.

Everyone remembers the clock dissection sequence in this film, in which Albert Austin's timepiece is reduced to its constituent parts by Charlie's calmly destructive tinkering. I have described it above in an account of the increasing complexity of Chaplin's metaphorical gags. It is certainly one of the most memorable of these, and interesting also in being surely one of the longest bits of business in the films of this period. But perhaps it has received too much attention. It is a little spoiled for me by one part—the moment when the coils and springs, isolated on the bench, are activated by the winding mechanism in a process of sympathetic 'magic' that is surely over-fanciful. (Squirting oil at them to 'kill' them is a good touch, though.) The clock sequence should be put into the larger context of the eccentricities—so familiar yet surprising—of Charlie's pawnbroking. *The Pawnshop* is, among other things, a professional activity comedy. Charlie's understanding of his pawnbrokerly role includes the necessity for: keeping his lunch in the safe; in accordance with his cleaning ritual, feather-dusting a random selection of objects, including his hat and cane, a violin, a canary cage and the canary, and an active electric fan; and polishing the golden balls. As well as Albert Austin and his clock, his clients include an aged thespian, who, when his sob story has wrung the desired hand-out from Charlie, proffers him change from a huge wadful of notes—a rather conventional gag, this, in which Charlie plays an unusually passive part.

My own favourite parts of this film are those depicting his relations with John Rand and with Edna. The larky spirit of camaraderie that informs his dealings with each is extremely attractive. Both relationships interfere with work, so both have to be disguised from the curmudgeonly proprietor: thus giving rise to a number of role-switching gags, when, on the boss's entrance, a pugilistic work-out with John is converted in a furious fit of floor-scrubbing, or a canoodle with Edna into a busy pretence of washing the dishes. John is the butt and victim of Charlie's creative audacities and Edna the object of his humorously amorous attentions. What is so striking about these passages is their spirit of witty and dextrous playfulness, the sense of fooling about for the sake of it Nowhere is this more evident than in the scene in which Charlie affords Edna his version of assistance in the kitchen: his notion of his duties includes putting the crockery through the wringer (then wringing his hands to dry them), satirically testing the weight of her doughnuts, and, in a fit of lightning inspiration, converting himself into a Hawaiian serenader with the help of a pastry collar and a ladle-ukelele.

Eric has only a minor part in this film. Perhaps his absence contributes to the freedom and self-sufficiency of Charlie's clowning, relieving the action of its customary burden of antagonism? One wouldn't, however, want him to be absent from all the films. Here his late intrusion gives Charlie the opportunity for a theatrical gesture that precisely suits the tone of a piece largely devoted to his talent for display—the cheery pirouette with which he invites the audience's applause for his foiling of the robbery.

Behind the Screen

> 13 November 1916. *With* Edna Purviance (starstruck girl), Eric Campbell (property man), Henry Bergman, Lloyd Bacon (directors), Charlotte Mineau (actress), Albert Austin, John Rand (stagehands), Frank J. Coleman (assistant director), James T. Kelley (cameraman).

Charlie is an assistant property man at a film studio. The property man is Eric, who is content to sleep all day and collect the credit while Charlie does his work as well. Charlie's set-dressing causes predictable havoc to the three films in production—a costume piece, a melodrama and a comedy. Edna is an aspirant to stardom who disguises herself as a property boy to infiltrate the studio. Charlie penetrates her disguise, but Eric doesn't and draws wrong conclusions when catching them kissing. Asking Charlie to operate the trap door is an act of folly that the performers live to regret when Charlie, stung by their impatience, turns the studio into a custard pie battleground. A bomb planted by disaffected strikers brings the proceedings to a kind of conclusion.

Behind the Screen is a very attractive film, full of fast and inventive business. It mixes professional activity comedy and confusion-drama comedy in about equal proportions. They are really the same thing, since it is Charlie's professional activities that confound the drama. There is a particularly nice running gag involving a trolley (employed to hump a single cushion) and a tripod, in which our expectations are repeatedly teased and surprised: for all Charlie's care to avoid it (at one point he lifts its leg and ducks underneath), the tripod ends up on the floor—a good example of Chaplin's refinement of the basic hazardous stationary object gag. Another major threat to the drama is posed by the huge pillar that Charlie is asked to erect for the costume piece. This is a sort of obese long horizontal object, and the business it generates includes its continually imminent collapse upon the set, its bonking of director Henry Bergman (who is then stood upon as an aid to its re-erection), and Charlie's attempt to sit on it and lift it at the same time. The ultimate havoc is caused by the custard pie routine that Charlie is so unwisely called in to help with. This confuses the drama in an especially suggestive sense—by confusing its categories, so that pies chucked from the comedy set end up plastered over the king, queen and archbishop in the costume piece: a neat encapsulation, when one thinks of it, of the clown's traditional power to muddy the distinction between high rank and low, and an assertion of his privileged relations with the highest rank of all.

I have described above the 'porcupine chairs' and 'coiffeured rug' gags that occur early in this film. As well as being examples of professional activity, they are examples of Charlie's gratuitous creative improvisations, and so associate themselves with the remarkable central section, the lunch break, with its sudden eruption of delightful food gags. Eric's belly must be measured against the huge heap of pies he proposes to consume; Albert's onion-munching suggests the need for fumigation with the bellows; and the embarrassment of Charlie's discovery in the act of filching from Albert's ham bone is covered by his ingratiating impersonation of a dog. As in much of *The Pawnshop*, this is pure second Charlie stuff, clowning inspired by good-natured devilment: later instances are Charlie's tearing his handkerchief as Henry Bergman bends over and his tight rope act along a rolled-up carpet.

As always, Charlie's relations with Eric and Edna play their part
As a boss, Eric is both tyrannical (the fear of his violence causes an
exaggerated increase in Charlie's productivity) and slothful (he
does nothing but takes all the credit). They unite in an uneasy alliance against the threat of the strikers (Eric's propitiatory hand
clasp has to be loosened with a blow of the hammer), but when
hostilities break out on the set they are inevitably in opposite
camps, and Eric is the victim of Charlie's stratagems and the
object of his ammunition. Edna has a minor role, but a most interesting one. The comedy she generates has all to with her
masculine disguise. Charlie discovers her powdering her nose,
and his interest is naturally aroused. In the course of his investigation Edna faints at the sight of a hole in Henry Bergman's
trousers (indicating her sex by a humorously exaggerated display
of susceptibility to shock) and in reviving her Charlie loosens her
hair. It is a short step to giving her a kiss: they are discovered in
the act by Eric, who puts on a remarkable display of teasing remonstrance. It is hardly paradoxical that all this should strike us as
wholly innocent. *We* know what has really happened, and the
misunderstandings are simply a device for enabling us to enjoy
the suggestion of misconduct without being disturbed by the fact
of it. Comedy abounds in such compromising false appearances: a
good later example is the film in which Laurel and Hardy are
repeatedly discovered by third parties, in corners and alleyways, in
the act of divesting themselves of their trousers.

The Rink

> 4 December 1916. *With* Edna Purviance, Eric Campbell (Mr Stout),
> Henry Bergman (Mrs Stout), Frank J. Coleman (Edna's father), Albert
> Austin, James T. Kelley (cooks), John Rand, Lloyd Bacon, Charlotte
> Mineau.

Charlie is a waiter in a restaurant who seeks lunchtime recreation
at the local roller-skating rink. As a waiter, he is slapdash and
eccentric in his serving of guests, and aggressive in his dealings
with kitchen hands. At the rink, posing as Sir Cecil Selzer, he rescues Edna from the attentions of Mr Stout, whom he proceeds, by
accident and design, to aggravate. At a skating party to which
Edna has invited him he finds Mr Stout (still hankering after
Edna), Mrs Stout and Edna's father (who is also Mrs Stout's secret

admirer). Charlie manages to cause the maximum havoc and embarrassment, escaping the eventual melee clinging to a car with his cane.

The Rink is a love intrigue comedy and an imposture comedy, but these plot elements do not contribute very much at all. The story and its relationships are not really very interesting, and are something of an anachronism in spirit: *The Rink* is a bit like an unusually stylish and inventive Keystone. Only in the amusing line-up towards the end, when all the intriguers, aware of each other, form a theatrical tableau of guilt, do we sense a new self-consciousness in the handling of plot. The film's centres of interest are elsewhere: in the eccentricity of Charlie's performance as a waiter, and in the dexterity of his performance as a skater.

Without a plausible story, Charlie's restaurant skills inhabit some thing of a vacuum: they could be part of any film. They give much pleasure and surprise, all the same. They range from such clever improvisations as compiling Mr Stout's bill from an inventory of the food debris on his shirt front, or breaking off the arms of a chair to accommodate Mrs Stout's ample bottom, to such random expressions of independence as the sniff of distaste he confers upon his own cocktail, or the exaggerated shimmy-like dance that accompanies its mixing—taking in on the way much material from his standard repertoire of aggression, like the chicken stuffing he contrives to discharge upon Edna's dad. Restaurants were an unfailing source of inspiration to Chaplin, and he was never to exhaust their possibilities.

As a skater, Charlie performs with style and panache: we are forcibly reminded that he was a genuinely accomplished athlete and acrobat. His coordination and poise are remarkable. His entry to the party as Sir Cecil, sweeping in an elegant curve and tapping cigar ash into his hat, is among the film's memorable moments. He doesn't neglect the erotic suggestions of the activity, particularly when escorting Edna, or when he contrives to get his behind in the way of a foot-waggling girl. One would have liked more of this. A lot of the skating sections are devoted to the physical discomfiture of Eric, and here the necessary fighting and falling, one would imagine, involve even greater skills. A nice touch that everyone remembers is his decorous replacement of Mrs Stout's skirt after he has pinned her to the floor.

Easy Street

> 27 January 1917. *With* Edna Purviance (missionary), Eric Campbell
> (thug), James T. Kelley (missionary/cop), John Rand (tramp/cop),
> Albert Austin (minister/cop), Frank J. Coleman, Leo White (cops),
> Charlotte Mineau (wife), Lloyd Bacon (addict).

Charlie is born again at the Hope Mission, under Edna's kindly
tutelage. As a token of the change, though after understandable
hesitation, he joins the hard-pressed police force and is despatched
to Easy Street, where Eric is giving an impersonation of Attila the
Hun. They have a long and involved battle, in the course of which
Eric is temporarily anaesthetized, and finally immobilized by a
huge missile (a stove). In an interval, Charlie helps Edna dispense
alms to the needy. He succeeds in pacifying the street, in the process rescuing Edna from a bunch of desperadoes. (See Chapter 3.)

The Cure

> 16 April 1917. *With* Edna Purviance, Eric Campbell (patients), Henry
> Bergman (masseur), Frank J. Coleman (proprietor), Albert Austin,
> John Rand, James T. Kelley, Lesta Bryan (attendants).

Charlie is being dried out at a health resort, but has brought a
huge trunk of booze with him for emergencies. His first taste of
the waters is not reassuring. He contrives, with his usual mixture
of deliberation and inadvertence, to frustrate Eric's leering attempts to ingratiate himself with Edna. While he is undergoing
the massage and cold plunge, his stock of booze is discovered and
chucked into the medicinal spring by a befuddled attendant, where
its benefits are spread among all the inmates. A puzzled Charlie
rescues Edna from a revelling crew before himself encountering
the source of the infection. Hangover and remorse ensue.

I used not to like *The Cure* very much, though its virtues grow
upon me. A film in which Charlie is sloshed for much of the time
can only be a first Charlie film, and the resulting contraction of attitude can have a monotonous effect. There is a certain amount of
conventional knockabout concerning the revolving door and Eric's
gouty foot (grotesquely swaddled in the regulation comic book
manner), and their equally routine feuding over Edna is enlivened by a moment when Charlie imagines that Eric's salacious
invitations are being directed at him, and reacts with a mixture of

embarrassment and pleasure. The denizens of the resort are types of frumpish respectability, and the attendants, with their improbable straggly beards, are grotesque.

Yet *The Cure* does have a single-minded and traditional aim: the celebration of drunkenness and the defeat of decorum. It is this aspect of 'demonic self-assertion' that makes John Fraser call the film, surprisingly, 'that greatest of all comic shorts' (*Violence in the Arts*, 1974). I cannot go as far as that: but the moment when Charlie realizes that the tasteless spring water is actually hard liquor, and exchanges his small can for a large jug, is very funny in a liberating way. (Marcel Marceau attempts the same gag in one of his Bip mimes, but cannot manage Charlie's gradual transition of expression from resignation to alacrity.) A passage I like even better, equally expressive of Charlie's irreverent attitude to the health resort ideal, comes earlier in the film. Charlie has been greeted by an attractive girl attendant, who sits beside him on the bench with a child's abandoned toy dog. Their talk is of Charlie's health, and he tests his biceps as a token of his determination to improve. It then occurs to him to test hers, and then for good measure to test the muscles of his thigh: shyness prevents him carrying the game any further, and he wallops a passing attendant to cover his embarrassment. It is a beautiful example of Charlie's ability to turn an innocent gesture to erotic advantage at the slightest suggestion of anything physical. The embarrassment of this episode spills over into the next, when the dribble of medicinal water that Charlie is trying to dispose of into his hat is blamed upon the dog, before the whole moment collapses into saucy amusement.

I have described above the massage and *tableau vivant* section, which is one of the best parts of the film, a welcome intrusion of Charlie's high-spirited second self into a comedy otherwise notable for its uncompromising aggression.

The Immigrant

> 17 June 1917. *With* Edna Purviance (immigrant), Kitty Bradbury (her mother), Eric Campbell (waiter), Albert Austin (immigrant/diner), James T. Kelley (immigrant/tramp), Henry Bergman (fat lady/artist), Frank J. Coleman (proprietor).

On the boat to America, Charlie befriends Edna and her mother. He out-manoeuvres villainous Mack Swain in a dice game, and,

when Mack steals the women's money, repairs the loss at the risk
of his own safety. On shore, he enters a restaurant presided over
by the redoubtable Eric, and there again meets Edna, now be-
reaved. He expends much ingenuity in attempting to conceal from
both Edna and Eric that he cannot pay the bill. A friendly artist
takes an interest in the pair and unwittingly proves their salvation
from embarrassment. (See Chapter 3.)

The Adventurer

> 22 October 1917. *With* Edna Purviance (rich girl), Eric Campbell (her
> admirer), Henry Bergman (her father), Marta Golden (her mother),
> Albert Austin (butler), Toraichi Kono (chauffeur), Frank J. Coleman
> James T. Kelley, John Rand.

An escaped convict, Charlie is pursued on a heathy cliff-top by
incompetent policemen and makes off into the sea. He steals a
bathing costume from a handy boat and, making for the shore,
comes across Edna's mother in difficulties in the water. He under-
takes a complicated rescue exercise, in the course of which Eric,
Edna's cowardly admirer, is soundly dunked. They all end up at
Edna's house, where Charlie continues to chat up Edna and thwart
Eric's designs, despite his discovery that Edna's father is the judge
who sent him down. Eric gets suspicious and calls the police, whom
Charlie, after a chase about the house, again manages to elude.

The Adventurer must be classed with *Behind the Screen* and *The
Pawnshop* as one of the best of the second-rank Mutuals. It is an
imposture drama in a line that includes *The Jitney Elopement* and *The
Count* and leads to *The Pilgrim*. It resembles the later film in that
the imposter's fear of discovery contributes strongly to the dramatic tension. In this it is an improvement on the earlier ones, as also
in its variety of mood and setting (there are three distinct locales)
and its abundance of business. These qualities make for a very attractive film.

The cliff-top preamble is a very original chase, making full use
of the hilly terrain, and at times apparently taking place underground. Our first view of Charlie is of a head emerging from the
sand, which quickly covers itself up again at the sight of an inat-
tentive policeman's rifle: the suspicion of an ostrich habit is reinforced by a later moment when Charlie propitiates his uncomfortable awareness of a pursuer's suddenly appearing foot by brushing

sand over it, as if *that* will dispose of the threat. Another good gag is the alarmingly authentic death throes act that turns out to be a prelude to booting an incautious policeman over the cliff.

From the excitement of pursuit and Charlie's stratagems for survival we move to a landing stage and the rescue of Edna's mother. Here Charlie's helpfulness and gallantry are played off against Eric's cowardice and malice. Charlie's ministrations, as usual, have their decidedly eccentric aspect; to comfort Edna's mother, he tenderly places a cushion underneath her stretcher; later, having rescued Eric as well, he himself quaffs the brandy intended for the victim and wipes his mouth on Eric's beard; lifting his end of Eric's stretcher without ensuring that anyone else is holding the other, he lands him back in the drink—and searches hopefully under the stretcher when noticing the omission. Charlie's heroism finds him a place in Edna's good books.

The second half of the film takes place at Edna's house. Charlie's awakening in his bed is accompanied by a sizeable misgiving as he registers his striped pyjamas and the bars of the bed-head—a witty instance of guilty associations. (Later, a popping cork is to make him raise his hands in surrender.) The comedy of this long and enjoyable section arises from the discrepancy between Charlie's suave and confident impersonation of a gentleman house guest and his occasional lapses into jail-bird shrewdness and aggression, and from Eric's tetchy and frustrated attempt to undermine Charlie's bogus authority. In the intervals of being polite, Charlie is quick to augment his own drink with the dregs from abandoned glasses, or to purloin somebody else's by a piece of legerdemain; in a nicely underplayed moment, his expression reveals that he contemplates sticking a pin into the distracting bottom of a shimmying matron; he varies his affable attentions to Edna at the piano with kicks aimed at Eric's backside on the terrace outside. Eric's and Charlie's feuding continues up to, and during, the chase that results from the re-entry of the cops. Its most memorable episode I have already described—the extended gag involving a dollop of ice-cream that travels down Charlie's leg and eventually earns Eric an indignant wallop as he tries to retrieve it from a lady's person. At this nemesis, Charlie is a smug looker-on. At last, as from so many of his impostures, he exits running.

First National, 1918–1923

Chaplin's famous contract with the First National distribution company accorded him one million dollars for making 8 films in 18 months (a timetable he was not able to adhere to). They were made in a specially constructed studio on La Brea Avenue and Sunset Boulevard, Hollywood. They, were all written, produced and directed by Charles Chaplin, usually with the assistance of Charles Reisner, and were photographed by Rollie Totheroh. They were of various lengths.

A Dog's Life

> 14 April 1918. *With* Scraps (herself), Edna Purviance (singer) Sydney Chaplin (stall owner), Tom Wilson (cop), Albert Austin, James T. Kelley (thugs), Henry Bergman (tramp/fat lady), Billy White (proprietor), Charles Reisner (clerk), Janet Sully (singer), Bud Jamison, Loyal Underwood (customers), Park Jones (waiter). 2600 ft.

Shoulder Arms

> 20 October 1918. *With* Edna Purviance (French girl), Sydney Chaplin (Kaiser/sergeant), Jack Wilson (Crown Prince), Henry Bergman, Albert Austin (German officers/other parts), Tom Wilson, John Rand, Loyal Underwood, Park Jones (soldiers). 3200 ft.

Sunnyside

> 15 June 1919. *With* Edna Purviance (farm girl), Henry Bergman (her father), Tom Wilson (employer), Albert Austin (city slicker), Loyal Underwood, Park Jones, Tom Ward, Tom Terriss. 2700 ft.

A Day's Pleasure

> 7 December 1919. *With* Edna Purviance (Charlie's wife), Tom Wilson (cop), Sydney Chaplin (father), Henry Bergman (captain), Babe London (fat girl), Albert Austin, Loyal Underwood (musicians), Raymond Lee, Jackie Coogan (kids). 1700 ft.

The Kid

> 6 February 1921. *With* Jackie Coogan (kid), Edna Purviance (mother), Carl Miller (father), Tom Wilson (cop), Charles Reisner (bully), Henry Bergman (doss-house proprietor), Albeit Austin (crook), Phyllis Allen

(angry woman), Nellie Bly Baker (neighbour), Lita Grey (angel), Raymond Lee (brat), Jack Coogan, Monta Bell. 5300 ft.

The Idle Class

25 September 1921. *With* Edna Purviance (wife), Mack Swain (father), Henry Bergman, John Rand (tramps), Rex Storey (thief), Allan Garcia (golfer), Loyal Underwood (guest), Lillian McMurray, Lita Grey (maids). 1900 ft.

Pay Day

2 April 1922. *With* Edna Purviance (foreman's daughter), Mack Swain (foreman), Phyllis Allen (Charlie's wife), Sydney Chaplin, Henry Bergman, Allan Garcia, Albert Austin, John Rand, Loyal Underwood (mates). 1800 ft.

The Pilgrim

25 February 1923. *With* Edna Purviance (daughter), Kitty Bradbury (her mother), Mack Swain (deacon), Sydney Chaplin (visiting father), Mai Wells (his wife), Dinky Dean Reisner (their brat), Tom Murray, (sheriff), Charles Reisner (thug). Monta Bell (cop), Henry Bergman, Edith Bostwick, Florence Latimer, Phyllis Allen, Raymond Lee, Loyal Underwocd. 4300 ft.

A Dog's Life, Shoulder Arms and *The Pilgrim* were reissued as *The Chaplin Revue* on 25 September 1959 with a musical soundtrack by Chaplin (including a song, 'Bound for Texas' written and composed by Chaplin and sung by Matt Munro). In subsequent television screenings *A Dog's Life* has usually been omitted.

United Artists, 1923–1952

Chaplin formed the United Artists Company with Mary Pickford, Douglas Fairbanks and D.W. Griffith in April 1919, and, after the completion of his First National contract, all his films except the last two were made under its aegis. They were made in the studio on La Brea Avenue, and were all written, produced and directed by Charles Chaplin (who also composed the music for the sound films), and photographed by Rollie Totheroh. The lengths are given in feet for the silent films and in minutes for the sound films.

A Woman of Paris

> 1 October 1923. *Assistant director*: Edward Sutherland. *Art director*: Arthur Stibolt. *With* Edna Purviance (Marie St Clair), Adolphe Menjou (Pierre Revel), Carl Miller (Jean Millet), Lydia Knott (Mme Millet), Charles French (M. Millet), Clarence Geldert (M. St Clair), Betty Morrissey (Fifi), Malvina Polo (Paulette), Karl Guttman (conductor), Henry Bergman (head waiter), Harry Northrup (valet), Nellie Bly Baker (masseuse), Charles Chaplin (porter). 7500 ft.

Reissued December 1977 with a musical soundtrack composed by Chaplin (the last film enterprise before his death).

The Gold Rush

> 16 August 1925. *Associate directors*: Charles Reisner, Henri d'Abbadie d'Arrast. *With* Georgia Hale (Georgia), Mack Swain (Big Jim Mackay), Tom Murray (Black Larson), Malcolm White (Jack Cameron), Henry Bergman (Hank Curtis), Betty Morrissey (Betty), John Rand, Albert Austin, Heinie Canklin, Allan Garcia, Tom Ward (prospectors). 8500 ft.

Reissued 18 April 1942 with a musical soundtrack composed, and narration spoken, by Chaplin.

The Circus

> 7 January 1928. *Assistant director*: Harry Crocker. *Art director*: Charles D. Hall. *With* Merna Kennedy (equestrienne), Betty Morrissey (vanishing lady), Harry Crocker (Rex), Allan Garcia (ringmaster), Henry Bergman (clown), George Davis (magician), Stanley J. Sanford, John Rand (property men), Steve Murphy (thief), Doe Stone, Albert Austin, Heinie Conklin. 6700 ft.

Reissued December 1970 with a musical soundtrack composed by Chaplin (including a song which he also sings).

Modern Times

> 5 February 1936. *Assistant directors*: Carter De Haven, Henry Bergman. *Art directors*: Charles D. Hall, J. Russell Spencer. *Music director*: Alfred Newman. *With* Paulette Goddard ('gamine'), Henry Bergman (café owner), Chester Conklin, Heinie Conklin (workmen), Stanley Sanford, Hank Mann. Louis Natheaux (cell-mates), Stanley Blystone (sheriff), Allan Garcia (factory president), Cecil Reynolds (chaplain), Myra McKinney (his wife), Lloyd Ingraham (governor), Dick Alexander,

Frank Moran (convicts), Wilfred Lucas, Edward Kimball, John Rand. 85 mins.

City Lights

6 February 1931. *Assistant directors*: Harry Crocker, Henry Bergman, Albert Austin. *Art director*: Charles D. Hall. *Music director*: Alfred Newman. *With* Virginia Cherrill (blind girl), Florence Lee (her grandmother), Harry Myers (millionaire), Allan Garcia (butler), Hank Mann (boxer), Henry Bergman (mayor/neighbour), Albert Austin (street cleaner/thug), John Rand (tramp), James Donnelly (foreman), Stanhope Wheatcroft (diner), Jean Harlow (party guest), Robert Parrish (newsboy). 87 mins.

The Great Dictator

15 October 1940. *Assistant directors*: Daniel James, Wheeler Dryden, Robert Meltzer. *Art director*: J. Russell Spencer. *Music director*: Meredith Wilson. *With* Charles Chaplin (Hynkel/barber), Paulette Goddard (Hannah), Jack Oakie (Napaloni), Henry Daniell (Garbitsch), Reginald Gardiner (Schultz), Billy Gilbert (Herring), Maurice Moskovich (Mr Jaeckel), Emma Dunn (Mrs Jaeckel), Bernard Gorcey (Mr Mann), Paul Weigel (Mr Agar), Grace Hale (Madam Napaloni), Carter De Haven (ambassador), Chester Conklin (barber-shop customer), Les White (Hynkel's barber), Eddie Gribbon, Hank Mann. Richard Alexander (storm troopers), Lucien Prival (officer). 126 mins.

Monsieur Verdoux

11 April 1947. From an idea by Orson Welles. *Associate directors*: Robert Florey, Wheeler Dryden. *Art director*: John Beckman. *Music director*: Rudolph Schrager. *With* Charles Chaplin (Verdoux), Martha Raye (Annabella Bonheur), Isobel Elsom (Marie Grosnay), Marilyn Nash (the Girl), Mady Correll (Mona Verdoux), Allison Rodell (Peter Verdoux), Robert Lewis (Maurice Bottello), Audrey Betz (Martha Bottello), Margaret Hoffman (Lydia Floray), Ada-May (Annette), Marjorie Bennett (maid), Helen Haigh (Yvonne), Edwin Mills (Jean Couvais), Virginia Brissac (Carlotta Couvais), Eula Morgan (Phoebe Couvais), Bernard J. Nedell (Prefect), Charles Evans (detective), Arthur Hohl (estate agent), John Harmon (Joe Darwin), Vera Marshe (Mrs Darwin), William Frawley (Jean La Salle), Barbara Slater (florist), Fritz Lieter (priest), Wheeler Dryden (bond salesman), Christine Ell, Pierre Watkin, Lois Conklin, Barry Norton, Tom Wilson, Edna Purviance (extra at wedding). 122 mins.

Limelight

23 October 1952. *Associate director*: Robert Aldrich. *Art director*: Eugene
Lourie. *With* Charles Chaplin (Calvero), Claire Bloom (Terry), Sydney
Chaplin (Neville), Nigel Bruce (Postant), Buster Keaton (pianist),
Norman Lloyd (Bodalink), Andre Eglevsky (Harlequin), Melissa
Hayden (Columbine), Marjorie Bennett (Mrs Alsop), Wheeler Dryden
(doctor/clown), Barrie Bernard (John Redfern), Leonard Mudie
(doctor), Snub Pollard (musician), Charles Chaplin Jr (clown), Geral-
dine Chaplin, Michael Chaplin, Josephine Chaplin (kids), Edna Pur-
viance, Loyal Underwood, Stapleton Kent, Mollie Blessing, Julian
Ludwig. 143 mins.

Final Films, 1957–1966

Chaplin sold his shares in United Artists in 1955. His last two films
were made, for different production companies, in London—the
first at Shepperton, the second at Pinewood—Chaplin having by
this time left the United States and settled in Switzerland. Both
films were written, produced, and directed, and featured musical
scores by, Chaplin. *A Countess from Hong Kong* was his only film to
be made in colour.

A King in New York

12 September 1957. Attica–Archway. *Photographer*: Georges Perinal.
Art director: Allan Harris. *With* Charles Chaplin (King Shahdov), Dawn
Addams (Ann Kay), Oliver Johnston (Jaume), Maxine Audley (Queen
Irene), Jerry Desmonde (Prime Minister), Michael Chaplin (Rupert
McAbu), Harry Green (lawyer), Phil Brown (headmaster), John Mc-
Laren (Mr McAbu), Alan Gifford (school superintendent), Shani Wal-
lis, Joy Nichols (singers), Joan Ingram (Mona Cromwell), Sidney
James (Johnson), Robert Arden (elevator boy), Nicholas Tannar (but-
ler), Lauri Lupino Lane, George Truzzi (comedians), George Wood-
bridge, Macdonald Parke. 109 mins.

A Countess from Hong Kong

November 1966. Universal. *Assistant director*: Jack Causey. *Photographer*:
Arthur Ibbetson. *Art director*: Robert Cartwright. *Music director*: Lambert
Williamson. *With* Marlon Brando (Ogden Mears), Sophia Loren
(Countess), Sydney Chaplin (Harvey Crothers), Tippi Hedren (Martha
Mears), Patrick Cargill (Hudson), Margaret Rutherford. (Miss Gaul-

swallow), Michael Medwin (John Felix), Oliver Johnston (clerk), John
Paul (captain), Angela Scoular (society woman), Peter Bartlett (stew-
ard), Bill Nagy (Crawford), Dilys Lake (saleswoman), Angela Pringle
(Baroness), Jenny Bridges (Countess), Arthur Gross (immigration
officer), Balbina (maid), Anthony Chin, Jose Sukhus Boonlvel (Hawai-
ians), Geraldine Chaplin, Janine Hill (women at dance), Burnell Tuck-
er (receptionist), Leanord Trolley (purser), Len Lowe (electrician),
Francis Dux (head waiter), Cecil Cheng (taxi driver), Ronald Rubin,
Michael Spice, Ray Marlowe (sailors), Geraldine Chaplin, Victoria
Chaplin (young women), Kevin Manser (photographer), Marianne
Stone, Len Lenton, Larry Cross, Bill Edwards, Drew Russell, John
Sterland. Paul Carson, Paul Tamarin (reporters), Carol Cleveland
(nurse), Charles Chaplin (steward). 120 mins.

Select Bibliography

Bibliographies are formal and rather indiscriminate adjuncts to a book. Even a very selective listing cannot adequately indicate the relative merits John annot by itself reveal, for instance, the importance to me personally of Robert Payne's *The Great Charlie* the book which, for all its critical extravagance, kindled my own youthful enthusiasm. Nor can it suggest the critical superiority, in the huge corpus of Chaplin literature, of such items as the article by Michael Roemer and the book by Raoul Sobel and David Francis. And there is conventionally no room at all for books that, although nothing to do with film comedy, have told decisively upon my own attempts to think about the subject, such as James Smith's *Shakespearean And Other Essays* (1974), whose constituent studies are models of how to approach comedy as a serious art form, or Marion Milner's *On Not Being Able to Paint* whose painstaking discovery of the contrary forces that feed creativity seems to me to correspond to my account of Charlie's emotional/social dilemma.

What follows is a list of those items I have consulted and can recommend, for various purposes, to others. All the books cited are either wholly about Chaplin or have important sections on him; or else, as their titles indicate, are notable books about comedy in general.

Adeler, Edwin, and Con West, *Remember Fred Karno? The Life of a Great Showman* (London: Long, 1939).

Agee, James, 'Comedy's Greatest Era', *Life*, 5 September 1949, pp. 48-59. Included in *Agee on Film*, VI (New York: McDowell–Oblensky, 1958).

Amengual, Barthelemy, *Charles Chaplin* (Lyon: Premier Plan, 1963).

Asplund, Uno, *Chaplin's Films* (trans. P.B. Austin; Newton Abbot: David & Charles, 1973).

Bazin, André, *What Is Cinema?*, I (Berkeley: University of California Press, 1967).

Bazin, André, Eric Rohmer, *Charlie Chaplin* (Paris: Cerf, 1972).

Bentley, Eric, *Monsieur Verdoux* as 'Theatre', *Kenyon Review* 10 (1948), pp. 705-16.

Bessy, Maurice, and Robert Florey, *Monsieur Chaplin, ou le rire la nuit* (Paris: Jaques Damase, 1952).

Bessy, Maurice, and Robin Livio, *Charles Chaplin* (Paris: Denoël, 1972).

Blistein, Elmer M., *Comedy in Action* (Durham, NC: Duke University Press, 1964).

Bowman, William Dodgson, *Charlie Chaplin: His Life and Art* (London: Routledge, 1931).

Brownlow, Kevin, 'The Early Days of Charles Chaplin', *Film* 40 (1964), pp. 12-15.

Brunius, Jacques, '*Monsieur Verdoux*', *Horizon* 17 (1948), pp. 166-78.

Caputi, Anthony F., *Buffo: The Genius of Vulgar Comedy* (Detroit, MI: Wayne State University Press, 1978).

Chaplin, Charles, 'Does the Public Know What It Wants?', *Adelphi* 1 (1924), pp. 702-10.

—*My Autobiography* (London: Bodley Head, 1964).

—*My Life in Pictures* (London: Bodley Head, 1974).

—*My Wonderful Visit* (London: Hurst & Blackett, 1922).

Chaplin, Charles, Jr, *My Father, Charlie Chaplin* (New York: Random House; London, Longmans, 1960).

Ciné-Club 4 (January-February 1948). (Special issue.)

Clair, René, *Cinéma d'hier, cinéma d'aujourd'hui*, (Paris: Gallimard, 1970). ET *Cinema Yesterday and Today* (New York: Dover, 1972).

—*Reflection faite* (Paris: Gallimard, 1951). ET *Reflections on the Cinema* (London: Kimber, 1952).

Cooke, Alistair, 'Charlie Chaplin', *Atlantic Monthly* 164 (1939), pp. 176-85.

Cooke, Alistair (ed.), *Garbo and the Night Watchman* (London: Cape, 1937).

Cotes, Peter, and Thelma Niklaus, *The Little Fellow* (London: Elek, 1951).

Cott, Jeremy, 'The Limits of Silent Film', *Literature/Film Quarterly* 3 (1975), pp. 99-107.

Delluc, Louis, *Charlie Chaplin* (trans. Hamish Miles; London: Bodley Head, 1922).

Disher, Maurice Wilson, *Clowns and Pantomimes* (London: Constable, 1925).

Duchartre, Pierre Louis, *The Italian Comedy* (London: Harrap, 1929).

Durgnat, Ray, *The Crazy Mirror: Hollywood Comedy and the American Image* (London: Faber & Faber, 1969).

Eisenstein, Sergei M., 'Charlie the Kid', *Sight and Sound* 15 (1946), pp. 12-14; (1946), pp. 53-55.

Eriksson, Lennart, *Books on/by Chaplin* (Vasteras: Lennart Eriksson, 1980).

Feibleman, James Kern, *In Praise of Comedy: A Study in its Theory and Practice* (London: George Allen & Unwin, 1939).

Film Comment 8 'Charlie Chaplin, Faces and Facets' (September–October 1972). (Special issue.)

Florey, Robert, *Charlie Chaplin* (Paris: Jean Pascal, 1927).

—*Hollywood d'hier et d'aujourd'hui* (Paris: Prisma, 1946).

Fowler, Gene, *Father Goose: The Story of Mack Sennett* (New York: Covici Friede, 1934).

Frank, Walso, 'Charles Chaplin: A Portrait', *Scribner's* 86 (1929), pp. 237-44.

Gallagher, Joseph Peter, *Fred Karno: Master of Mirth and Tears* (London: Hale, 1971).

Gifford, Denis, *Chaplin* (London: Macmillan; Garden City, NY: Doubleday, 1974).

Grace, Harry, 'Charlie Chaplin's Films and American Culture Patterns', *Journal of Aesthetics and Art Criticism* 10 (1952), pp. 353-63.

Hoyt, Edwin Palmer, *Sir Charlie* (London: Hale, 1977).

Huff, Theodore, *Charlie Chaplin* (New York: Abelard–Schman; London: Cassell, 1952).

—*The Early Work of Charles Chaplin* (Index Series; London: British Film Institute, 2nd edn, 1961) (originally published as 'An Index to the Films of Charles Chaplin', *Sight and Sound*, Supplement 3 [1945]).

Hunter, William, *Scrutiny of Cinema* (London: Wishart, 1932).

Hurley, Neil, 'The Social Philosophy of Charlie Chaplin', *Studies* 49 (1960), pp. 312-20.

Jacobs, David, *Chaplin, the Movies and Charlie* (New York: Harper & Row, 1975).

Kerr, Walter, *The Silent Clowns* (New York: Knopf, 1975).

Knights, Lionel Charles, 'Notes on Comedy', *Scrutiny* 1 (1933), pp. 356-67.

Kracauer, Siegfried, 'Silent Film Comedy', *Sight and Sound* 21 (1951), pp. 31-32.

Lahue, Kaltan C., *World of Laughter: The Motion Picture Comedy Short, 1910–1930* (Norman: Oklahoma University Press, 1966).

Lahue, Kaltan C., and T. Brewer, *Kops and Custards: The Legend of Keystone Films* (Norman: Oklahoma University Press, 1967).

Lambert, Gavin, 'The Elegant Melancholy of Twilight: Impressions of *Limelight*', *Sight and Sound* 22 (1953), pp. 123-27.

Lauter, Paul (ed.), *Theories of Comedy* (New York: Doubleday, 1964).

'Hommage à Charles Chaplin', *L'Avant Scène* 219–22 (January 1979). (Special issue.)

Le disque vert 4–5 (1924). (Special issue.)

Leech, Clifford, 'The Comedy of Charles Chaplin', *Cambridge Journal* 7 (1953), pp. 51-64.

Leprohon, Pierre, *Charles Chaplin* (Paris: Nouvelles Editions Debresse, 1957).

—*Charles Chaplin* (Paris: Corymbe, 1970). (A different book from the above.)

—*Charlot, ou la naissance d'un myth* (Paris: Corymbe, 1935).

Les chroniques du jour (15–31 December 1926). (Special issue.)

Lloyd, Harold, *An American Comedy* (London: Longmans, 1928).

Lyons, Timothy J., *Charles Chaplin: A Guide to References and Resources* (Boston, MA: G.K. Hall, 1979).

—'The Gold Rush, Compiled from the Film', *Cinema* 4 (1968), pp. 17-44.

—'Roland H. Totheroh Interviewed: Chaplin Films', *Film Culture* 53–55 (1972), pp. 230-85.

MacDonald, Dwight, *Dwight MacDonald on Movies* (Englewood Cliffs, NJ: Prentice–Hall, 1969).

McCabe, John, *Charlie Chaplin* (New York: Doubleday; London: Robson, 1978).

McCaffrey, Donald W., *Four Great Comedians: Chaplin, Lloyd, Keaton, Langdon* (London: Zwemmer; New York: Barnes, 1968).

—*Focus on Chaplin* (Englewood Cliffs, NJ: Prentice–Hall, 1971).

McDonald, Gerald D., Michael Conway and Mark Ricci, *The Films of Charlie Chaplin* (New York: Citadel, 1965).

McVay, Douglas, 'A Proper Charlie', *Films and Filming* 11 (1964), pp. 10-15.

Madden, David, *Harlequin's Stick, Charlie's Cane* (Bowling Green, OH: Popular Press, 1975).

Manvell, Roger, *Chaplin* (London: Hutchinson; Boston, MA: Little, 1974).

—'Monsieur Verdoux', *Penguin Film Review* 7 (1948), pp. 77-82.

Martin, Marcel, *Charlie Chaplin* (Paris: Seghors, 1966).

Mast, Gerald, *The Comic Mind: Comedy and the Movies* (Chicago, IL: University of Chicago Press, 1979).

Mellor, G.J., 'The Making of Charlie Chaplin', *Cinema Studies* 2 (1966), pp. 19-25.

Meryman, Richard, 'Chaplin: Ageless Master's Anatomy of Comedy', *Life*, 10 March 1967, pp. 80-94. (Interview.)

Meyerhold, Vsevolod, 'Chaplin and Chaplinism' (trans. Margerie L. Hoover) *Tulane Drama Review* 11 (1966), pp. 188-95.

Minney, Rubeigh James, *Chaplin, the Immortal Tramp* (London: Newnes, 1954).

Mitry, Jean, *Charlot et la 'fabulation' Chaplinesque* (Paris: Editions Universitaires, 1957).

—*Tout Chaplin: tous les films, par le text, par le gag, et par l'image* (Paris: Seghers, 1972). (Originally published as a special number of *Image et son*, April 1957.)

Moss, Robert F., *Charlie Chaplin* (New York: Pyramid, 1975).

Nicoll, Allardyce, *The World of Harlequin* (Cambridge: Cambridge University Press, 1963).

Payne, Robert, *The Great God Pan* (New York: Hermitage House, 1952).

—*The Great Charlie* (London: Deutsch, 1952).

Positif 152–53 (1973). (Special issue.)

Quigley, Isobel, *Charlie Chaplin: Early Comedies* (London: Studio Vista, 1968).

Roemer, Michael, 'Chaplin: Charles and Charlie', *Yale Review* 64 (1974), pp. 158-84.

Raynor, Henry, 'Chaplin as Pierrot', *Sequence* 7 (1949), pp. 30-33.

Rotha, Paul, *Celluloid: The Film Today* (London: Longmans, 1931).

Sadoul, Georges, *Vie de Charlot* (Paris: Editeurs Français Réunis, 1952).

Schuster, Mel, *Motion Picture Directors: A Bibliography of Magazine and Periodical Articles, 1900–1972* (Metuchen, NJ: Scarecrow, 1973).

Sennett, Mack, as told to Cameron Shipp, *King of Comedy* (London: Peter Davies, 1955).

Sobel, Raoul, and David Francis, *Chaplin: Genesis of a Clown* (London: Quartet, 1977).

Spiegel, Alan, 'Chaplin's Austerity', *Salmagundi* 43 (1979), pp. 163-72.

Stewart, Garrett, 'Modern Hard Times: Chaplin and the Cinema of Self-Reflection, *Critical Inquiry* 3 (1976), pp. 295-314.

Tyler, Parker, *Chaplin, Last of the Clowns* (New York: Vanguard Press, 1947).

—'Chaplin: The Myth of the Immigrant', *Western Review* 18 (1953), pp. 74-80.

—'Kafka's and Chaplin's America', *Sewanee Review* 58 (1950), pp. 299-311.

Vardac, A. Nicholas, *Stage to Screen: Theatrical Method from Garrick to Griffith* (Cambridge, MA: Harvard University Press, 1949).

Viazzi, Glauco, *Chaplin e la critica* (Bari: Lettera, 1955).

Von Ulm, Gerith, *Charlie Chaplin, King of Tradegy* (Caldwell, ID: Caxton Printers, 1940).

Warshow, Robert, 'A Feeling of Sad Dignity', *Partisan Review* 21 (1954), pp. 664-75.

—'*Monsieur Verdoux*', *Partisan Review* 14 (1947), pp. 380-89.

Welsford, Enid, *The Fool: His Social and Literary History* (London: Faber & Faber, 1935).

Willeford, William, *The Fool and his Sceptre: A Study in Clowns and Jesters and their Audience* (Evanston, IL: Northwestern University Press; London: Arnold, 1969).